TRANS-METRO-POLITAN:

SPIDER'S THRASH

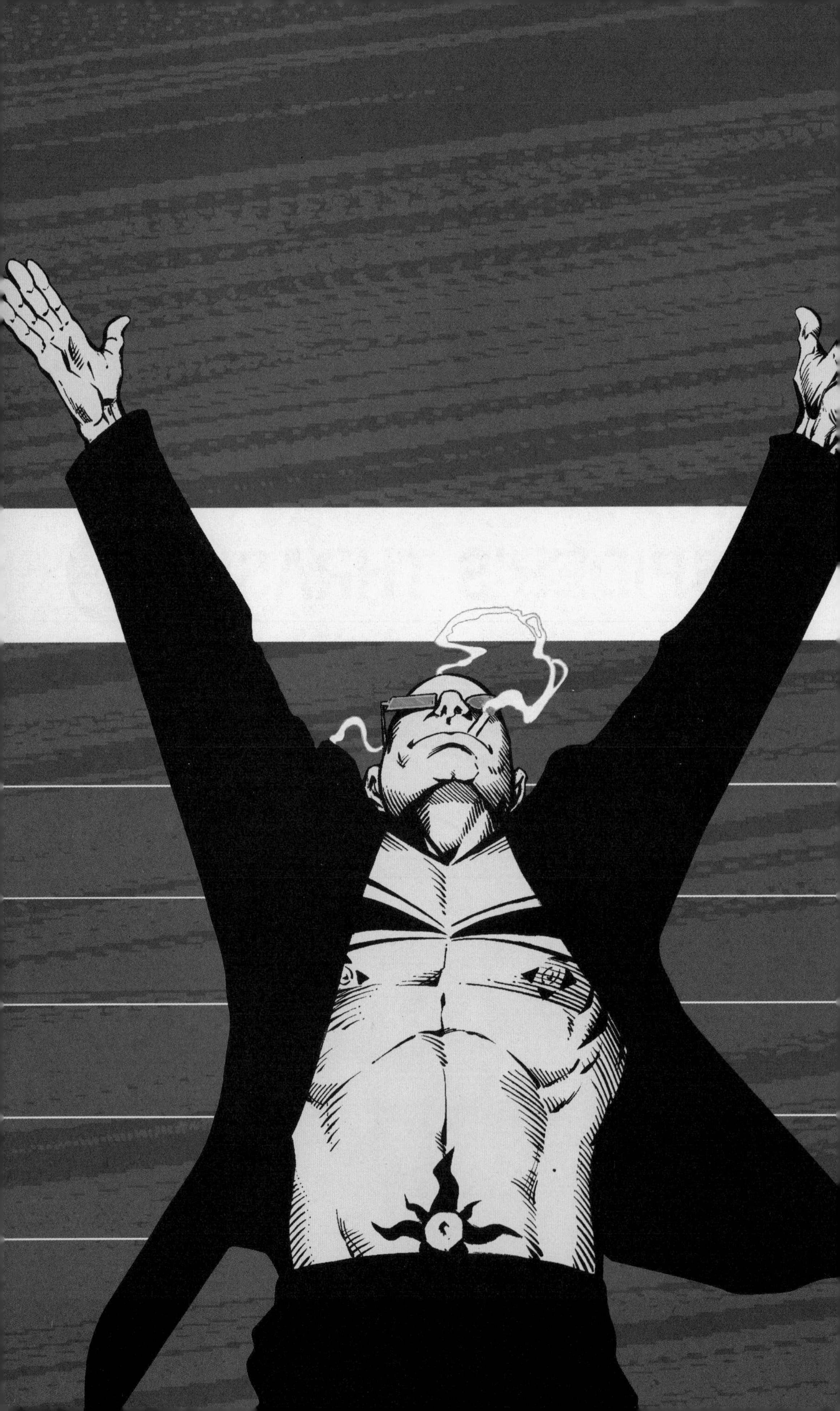

TRANS-METRO-POLITAN:

SPIDER'S THRASH

Warren_Ellis

Writer

Darick_Robertson

Penciller

Rodney_Ramos
Inker

Nathan_Eyring
Colorist

Clem_Robins
Letterer

Tim Bradstreet (#37-39)
Matt Wagner (#40-42)
Original Series Covers

TRANSMETROPOLITAN created by
Warren_Ellis and Darick_Robertson

Karen Berger SVP – Executive Editor Axel Alonzo Tony Bedard Editors – Original Series Jennifer Lee Assistant Editor – Original S
Georg Brewer VP – Design & DC Direct Creative Bob Harras Group Editor – Collected Editions Scott Nybakken Editor
Robbin Brosterman Design Director – Books

DC COMICS

Paul Levitz President & Publisher Richard Bruning SVP – Creative Director Patrick Caldon EVP – Finance & Operations
Amy Genkins SVP – Business & Legal Affairs Jim Lee Editorial Director – WildStorm Gregory Noveck SVP – Creative Affairs
Steve Rotterdam SVP – Sales & Marketing Cheryl Rubin SVP – Brand Management

Cover illustration by Tim Bradstreet.
Publication design by Ternard Solomon.

TRANSMETROPOLITAN: SPIDER'S THRASH

DC Comics, 1700 Broadway, New York, NY 10019. A Warner Bros. Entertainment Company. Printed in Canada. First Printing.
ISBN: 978-1-4012-2815-6

SUSTAINABLE
FORESTRY
INITIATIVE

Certified Fiber
Sourcing

www.sfiprogram.org

INTRODUCTION

I wasn't a comic book kid.

I didn't grow up on super-heroes. I bought the occasional *King Conan*, but that was about it.

For me, it began in high school when someone told me the comic came before the band.

"What!?" Me shocked.

"Yeah, it was a comic first." My goth friend.

"Love and Rockets?" I checked.

"Yeah."

"With super-heroes?" Incredulous.

"Never read it." She ended the conversation, turned up her Walkman.

So I tracked down a copy. Had never been in a comic book store till then. I saw the great spirit of Marquez hanging over those pages. I was hooked. Great characters, great tone, great spirit.

Who said comics need super-heroes?

Enter *Watchmen*.

A punk friend lent me his worn copy. He said the only rule is that you can read only one chapter a night. Lord knows it was hard not to read the whole thing in one sitting. But I followed the rules and took twelve nights.

Famished now, I needed more. *Batman: The Dark Knight Returns, Ronin, Elektra, Swamp Thing*, I dined for awhile. Lotsa dessert!

But soon, this heyday of the late '80s, just like early hip-hop, started to dry up.

The Hernandez Brothers stopped printing. Miller produced his gems but took his damn good time. Moore was a mystery. He seemed to disappear into one of his conspiracies.

Every few months I'd wander the aisles of St. Mark's Comics or Forbidden Planet (in its original, more grand location) searching for something. Something new, something breathtaking.

Wandering. Up and down.

But there was nothing much.

For years. Nothing much.

I started to lose interest. My trips to the comic book store became more and more rare.

Then, after a bite in Koreatown, I stumbled on Jim Hanley's Universe, a new comic emporium in the shadow of the Empire State Building. I entered, not expecting much. But hoping.

And then I was eye to eye with some bald freak wearing a pair of 3-D glasses and an Abe Lincoln hat and beard. The artwork was superb — clever and sharp. The maniacal grin on the character — interesting.

Picked it up, flipped it open.

From word one, I got it. Profanity + anger + revolution + cynicism + drugs + cigarettes + truth + justice – fair = Spider Jerusalem. Attitude perfect, tattoos perfect, sidekicks perfect. His name perfect.

He enters the gallery of classics. A true original. I await his new issue with little patience.

But rumor has it — this is the end?

THE END?!?!?

It can't be. Our world needs Spider. Please Warren. Please Darick. Keep him coming. Have him kick Batman's ass. Have him knock up Wonder Woman. Break him into our world. Have him educate Bush on truth. Let him bring peace to the Middle East.

Otherwise, I'll be forced to return to the aisles. Famished. Wandering up and down. Hoping inspiration strikes this planet again.

— Darren Aronofsky
June 6, 2002

Darren Aronofsky was born and raised in Brooklyn, NY. He wrote and directed the films π (1997), Requiem for a Dream (2000) and The Fountain (2006), and directed the Academy Award-nominated The Wrestler (2008).

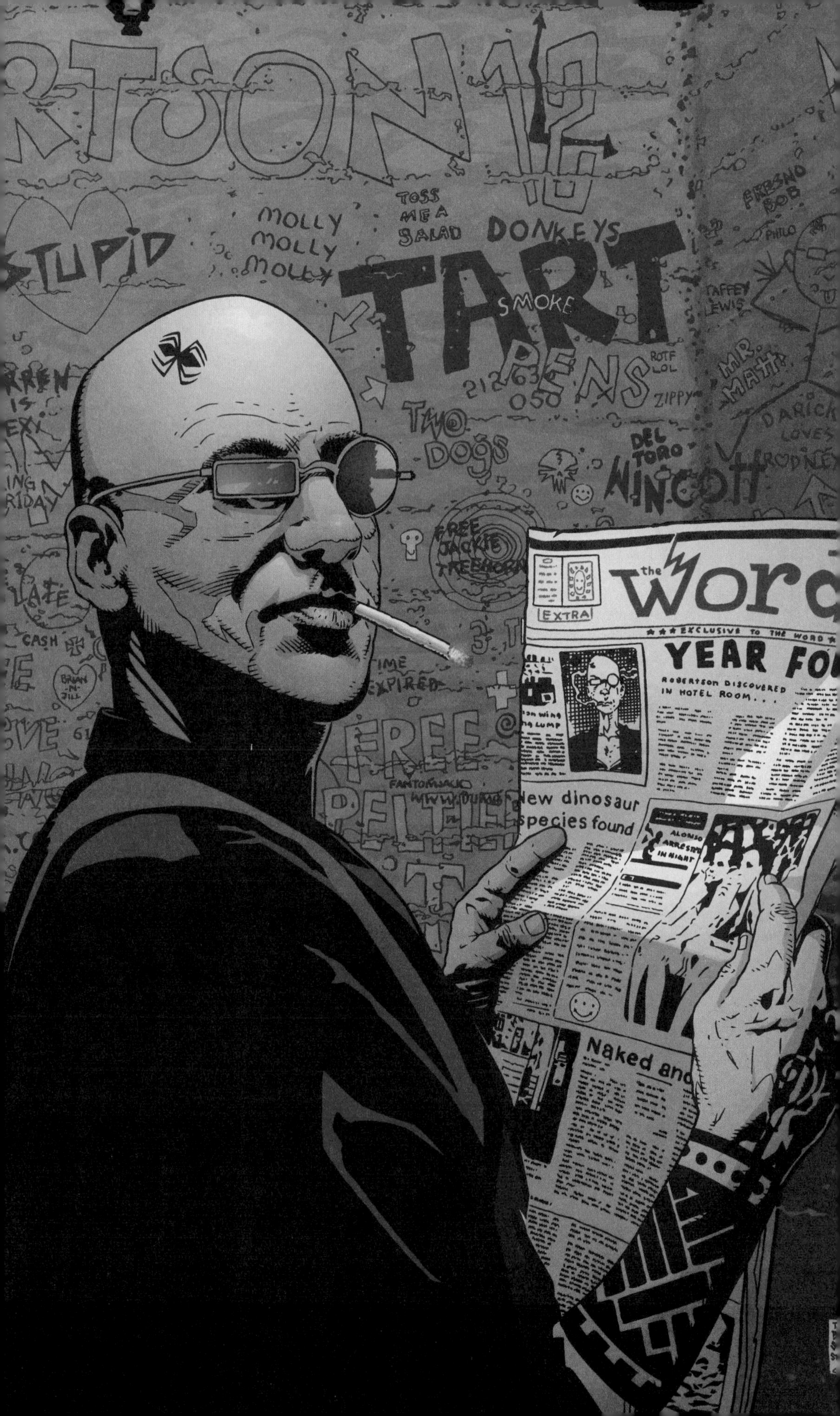

STUPID
MOLLY MOLLY MOLLY
TOSS ME A SALAD
DONKEYS
TART
SMOKE
PENS
ROTF LOL
ZIPPY
FRESNO BOB
PHILO
TAFFEY LEWIS
MR. MATT
DARICK LOVES RODNEY
TWO DOGS
DEL TORO
WINCOTT
FREE JACKIE TREEHORN
CASH
BRIAN -N- JILL
TIME EXPIRED
FREE
the word
EXTRA
EXCLUSIVE TO THE WORD
ROBERTSON DISCOVERED IN HOTEL ROOM...
New dinosaur species found

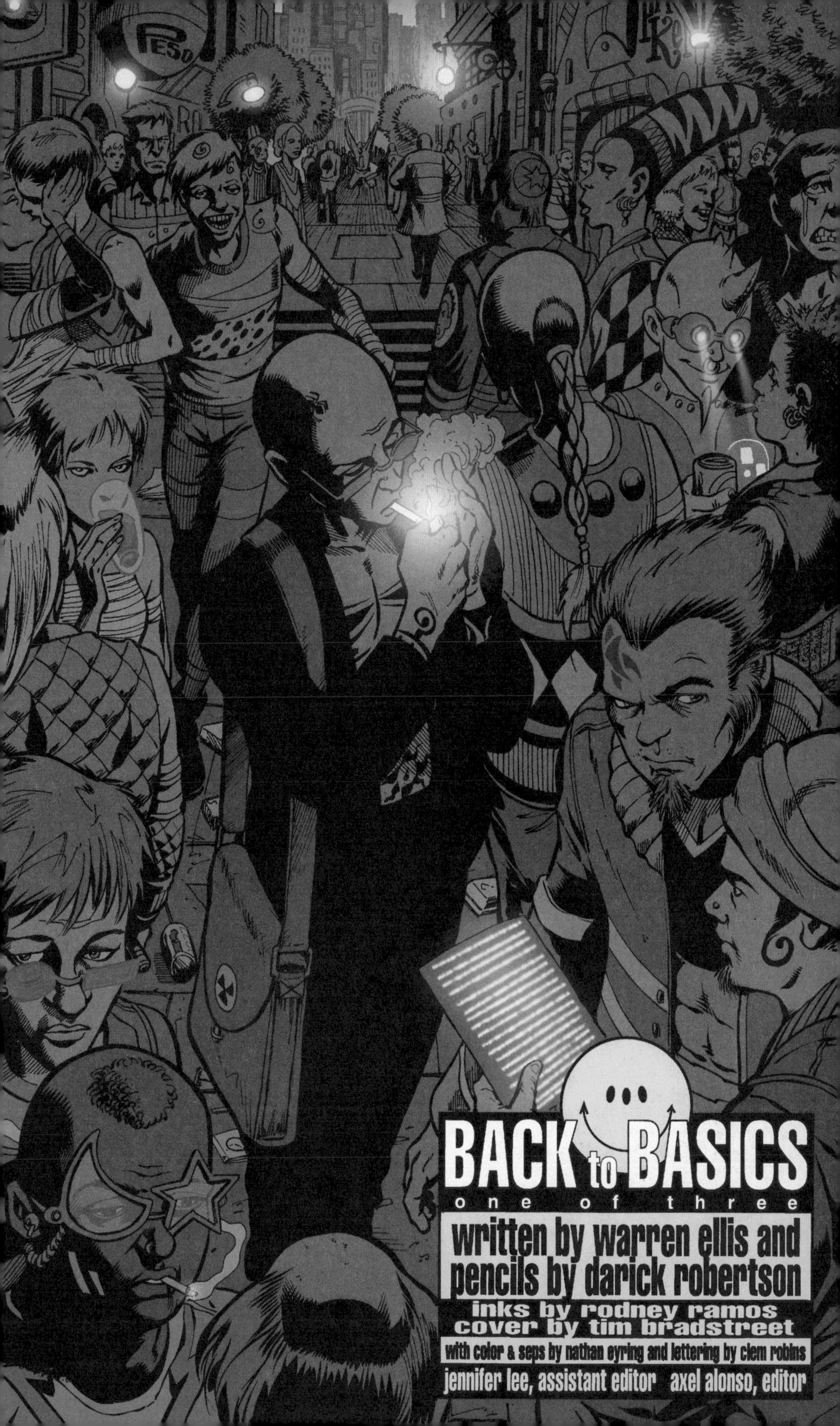
BACK to BASICS
one of three
written by warren ellis and
pencils by darick robertson
inks by rodney ramos
cover by tim bradstreet
with color & seps by nathan eyring and lettering by clem robins
jennifer lee, assistant editor axel alonso, editor

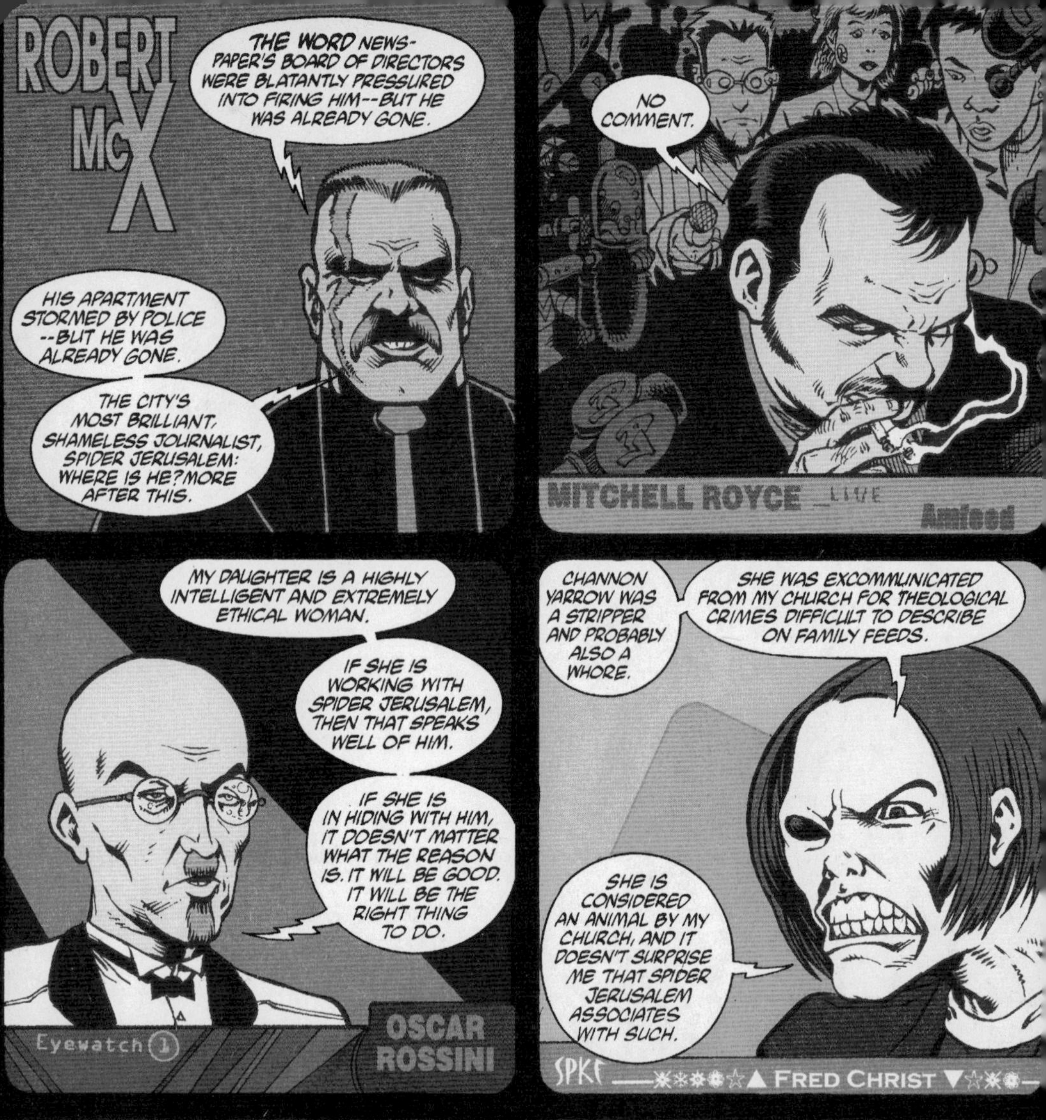
ROBERT McX
THE WORD NEWSPAPER'S BOARD OF DIRECTORS WERE BLATANTLY PRESSURED INTO FIRING HIM--BUT HE WAS ALREADY GONE.
HIS APARTMENT STORMED BY POLICE --BUT HE WAS ALREADY GONE.
THE CITY'S MOST BRILLIANT, SHAMELESS JOURNALIST, SPIDER JERUSALEM: WHERE IS HE? MORE AFTER THIS.
NO COMMENT.
MITCHELL ROYCE _LIVE
Amfeed
MY DAUGHTER IS A HIGHLY INTELLIGENT AND EXTREMELY ETHICAL WOMAN.
IF SHE IS WORKING WITH SPIDER JERUSALEM, THEN THAT SPEAKS WELL OF HIM.
IF SHE IS IN HIDING WITH HIM, IT DOESN'T MATTER WHAT THE REASON IS. IT WILL BE GOOD. IT WILL BE THE RIGHT THING TO DO.
Eyewatch 1
OSCAR ROSSINI
CHANNON YARROW WAS A STRIPPER AND PROBABLY ALSO A WHORE.
SHE WAS EXCOMMUNICATED FROM MY CHURCH FOR THEOLOGICAL CRIMES DIFFICULT TO DESCRIBE ON FAMILY FEEDS.
SHE IS CONSIDERED AN ANIMAL BY MY CHURCH, AND IT DOESN'T SURPRISE ME THAT SPIDER JERUSALEM ASSOCIATES WITH SUCH.
SPKF
FRED CHRIST
I SUPPORT FREE SPEECH, OBVIOUSLY.
BUT EQUALLY OBVIOUSLY, ALL THINGS MUST BE TAKEN IN MODERATION.
THIS IS SOMETHING WE NEED TO STRONGLY COMMUNICATE TO THE MEDIA.
LARGE MOUNDS OF HUMAN BODILY WASTE FOUND PILED ON ALAN SCHACT'S GRAVE--LEAKED REPORT CLAIMS DNA TESTING LINKS TURDS TO MISSING WRITER--
ALAN SCHACT
Brisk Rockwell
InfoSparQ

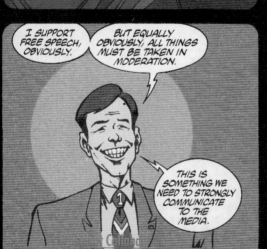

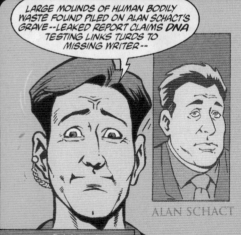

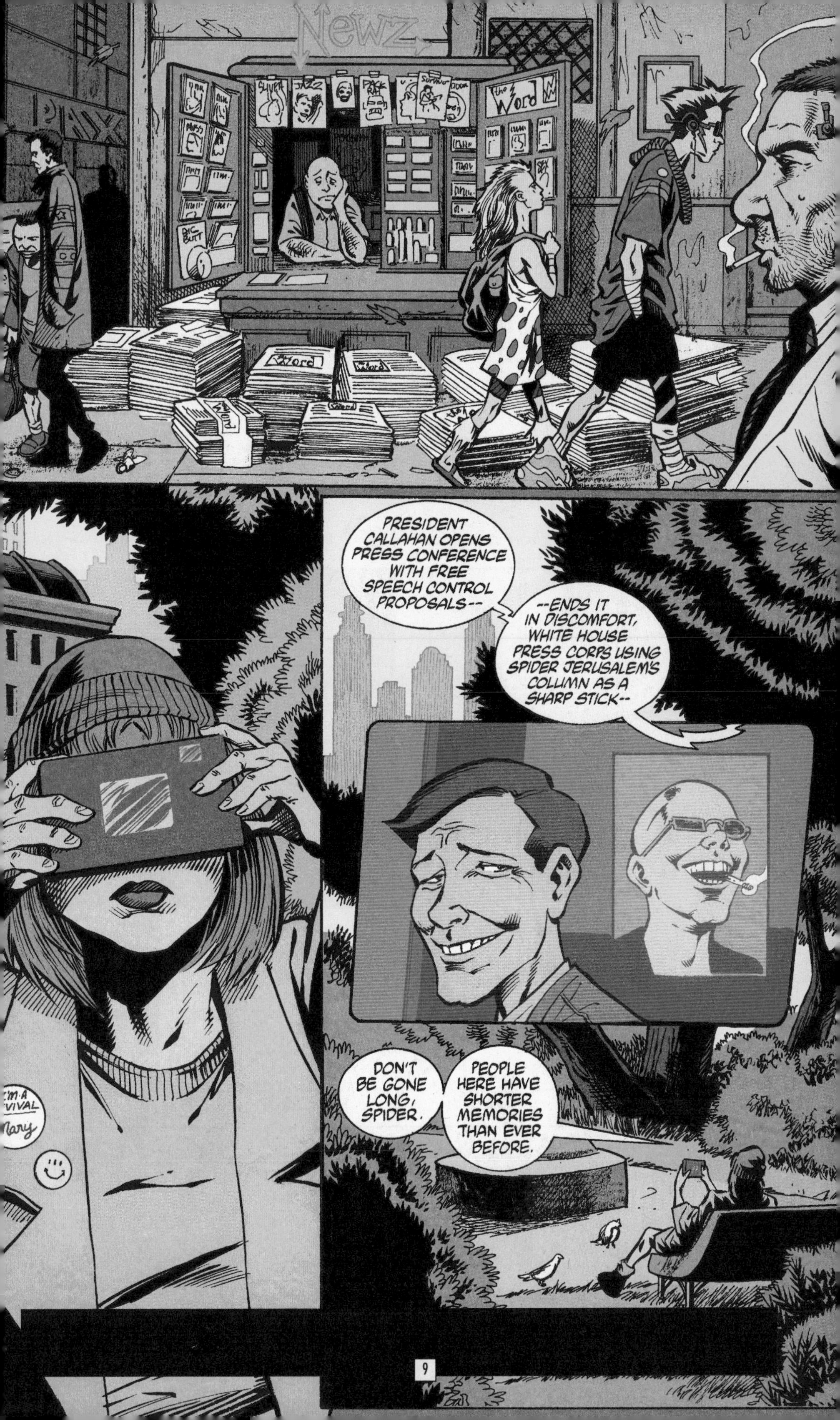
Newz
PRESIDENT CALLAHAN OPENS PRESS CONFERENCE WITH FREE SPEECH CONTROL PROPOSALS--
--ENDS IT IN DISCOMFORT, WHITE HOUSE PRESS CORPS USING SPIDER JERUSALEM'S COLUMN AS A SHARP STICK--
DON'T BE GONE LONG, SPIDER.
PEOPLE HERE HAVE SHORTER MEMORIES THAN EVER BEFORE.

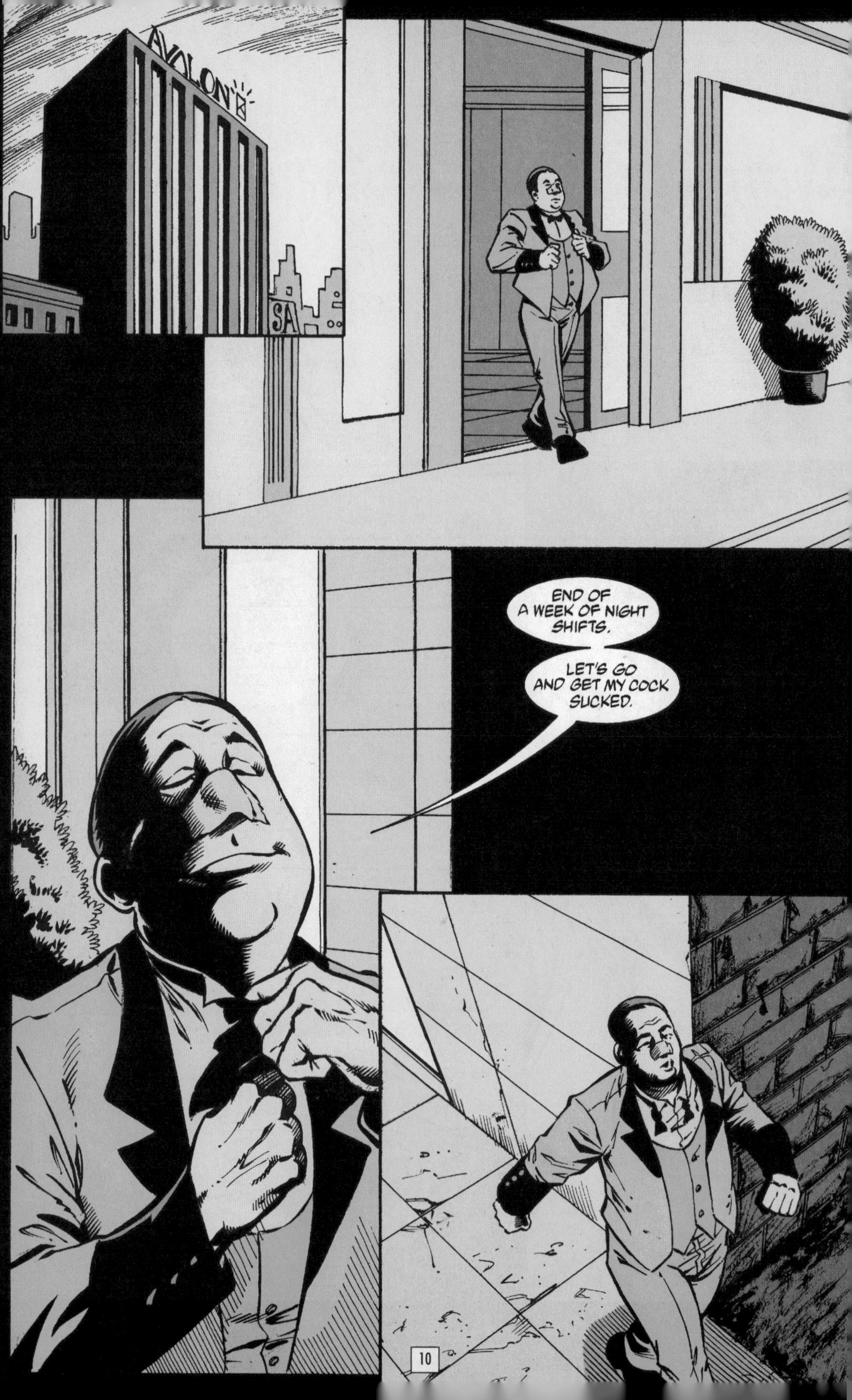

AVALON
SA
END OF A WEEK OF NIGHT SHIFTS.
LET'S GO AND GET MY COCK SUCKED.

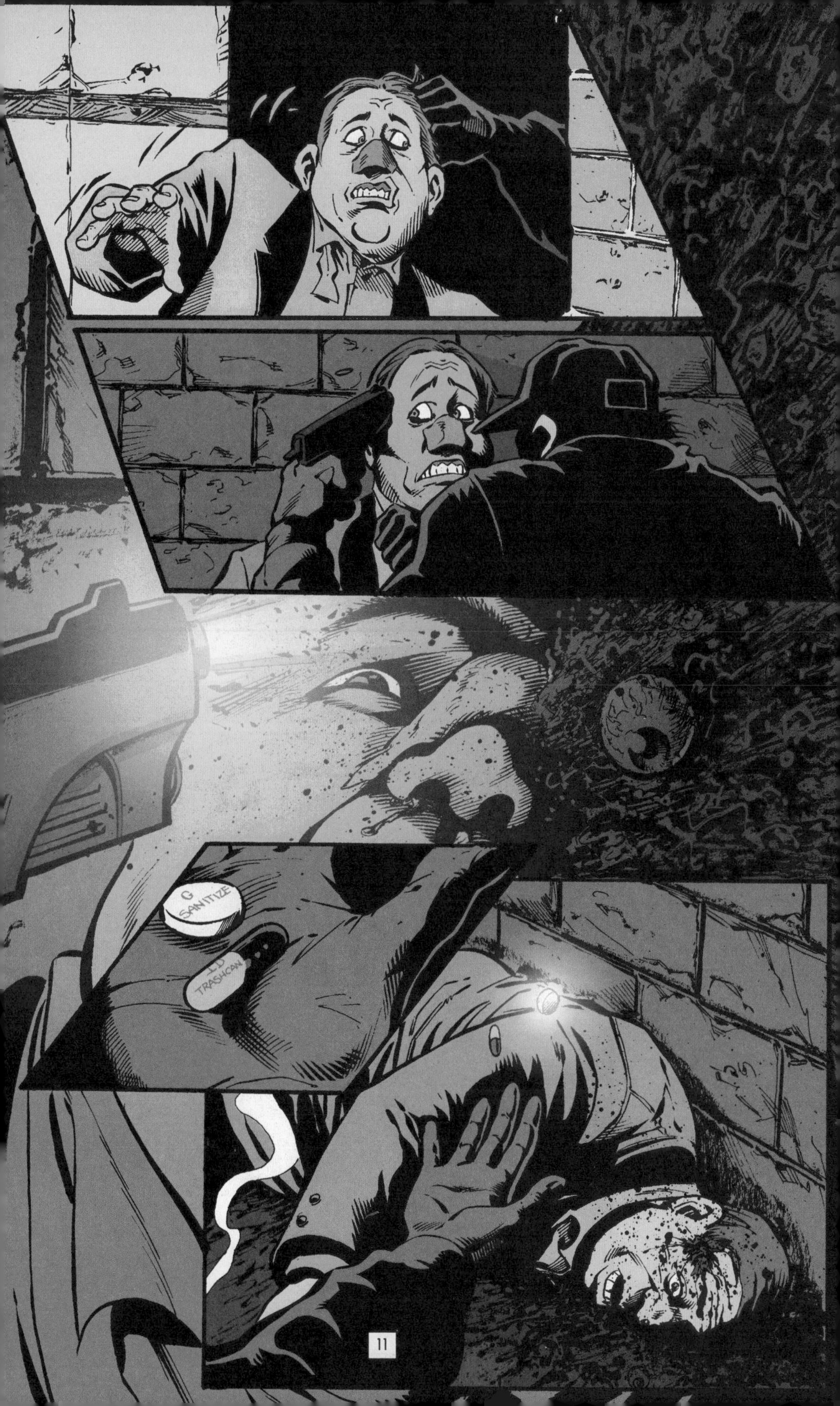
G
SANITIZE
1D
TRASHCAN

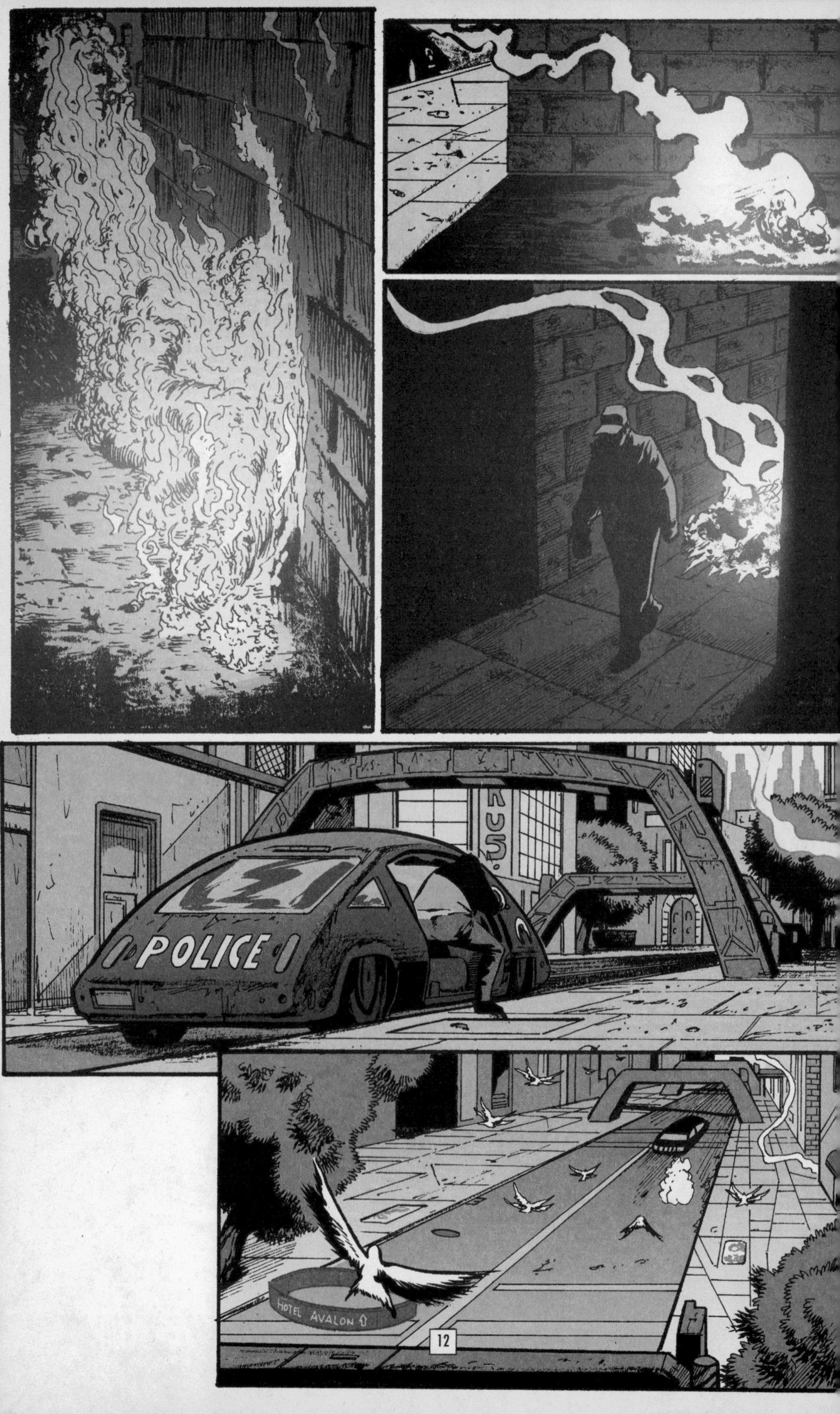
POLICE
HOTEL AVALON

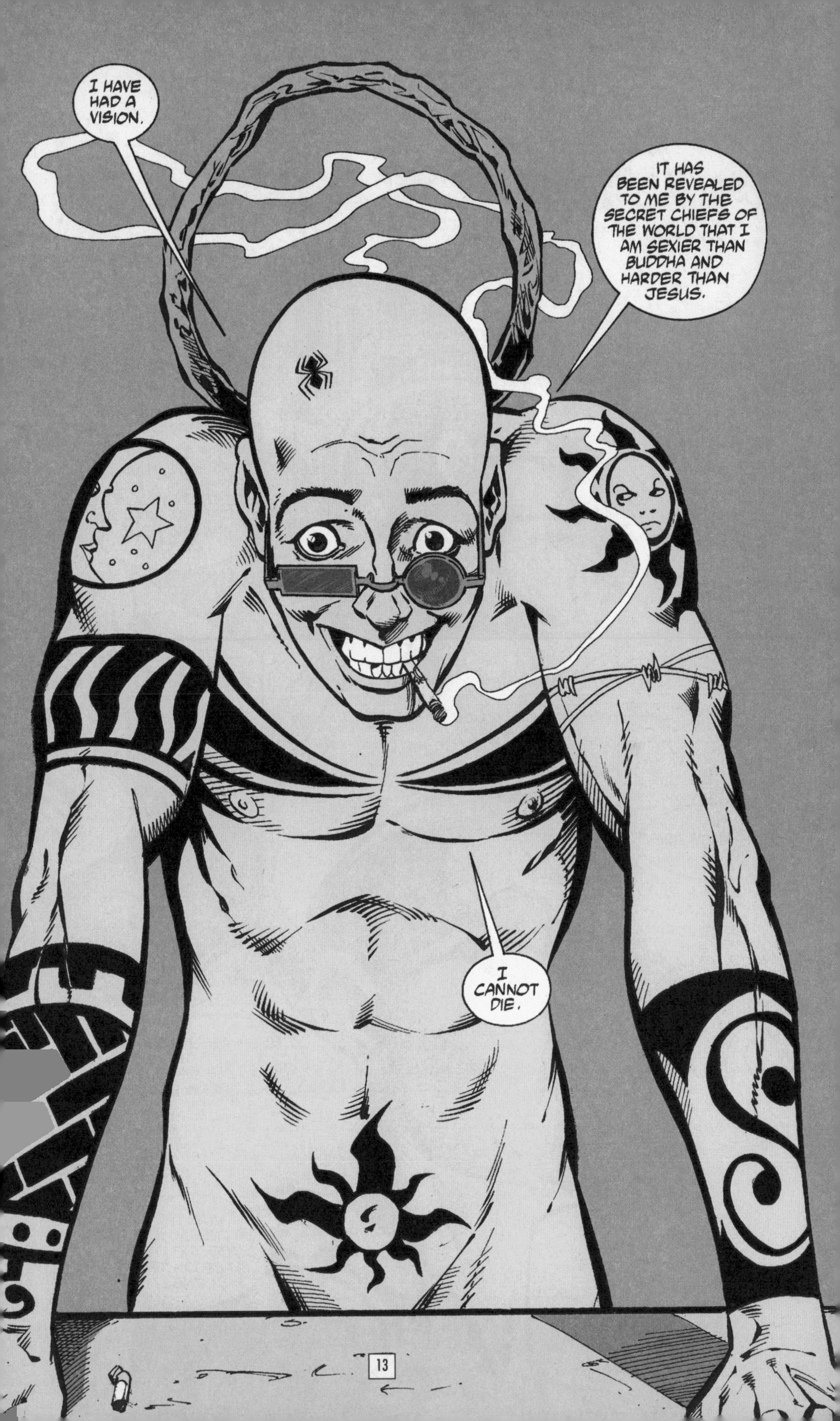
I HAVE HAD A VISION.
IT HAS BEEN REVEALED TO ME BY THE SECRET CHIEFS OF THE WORLD THAT I AM SEXIER THAN BUDDHA AND HARDER THAN JESUS.
I CANNOT DIE.

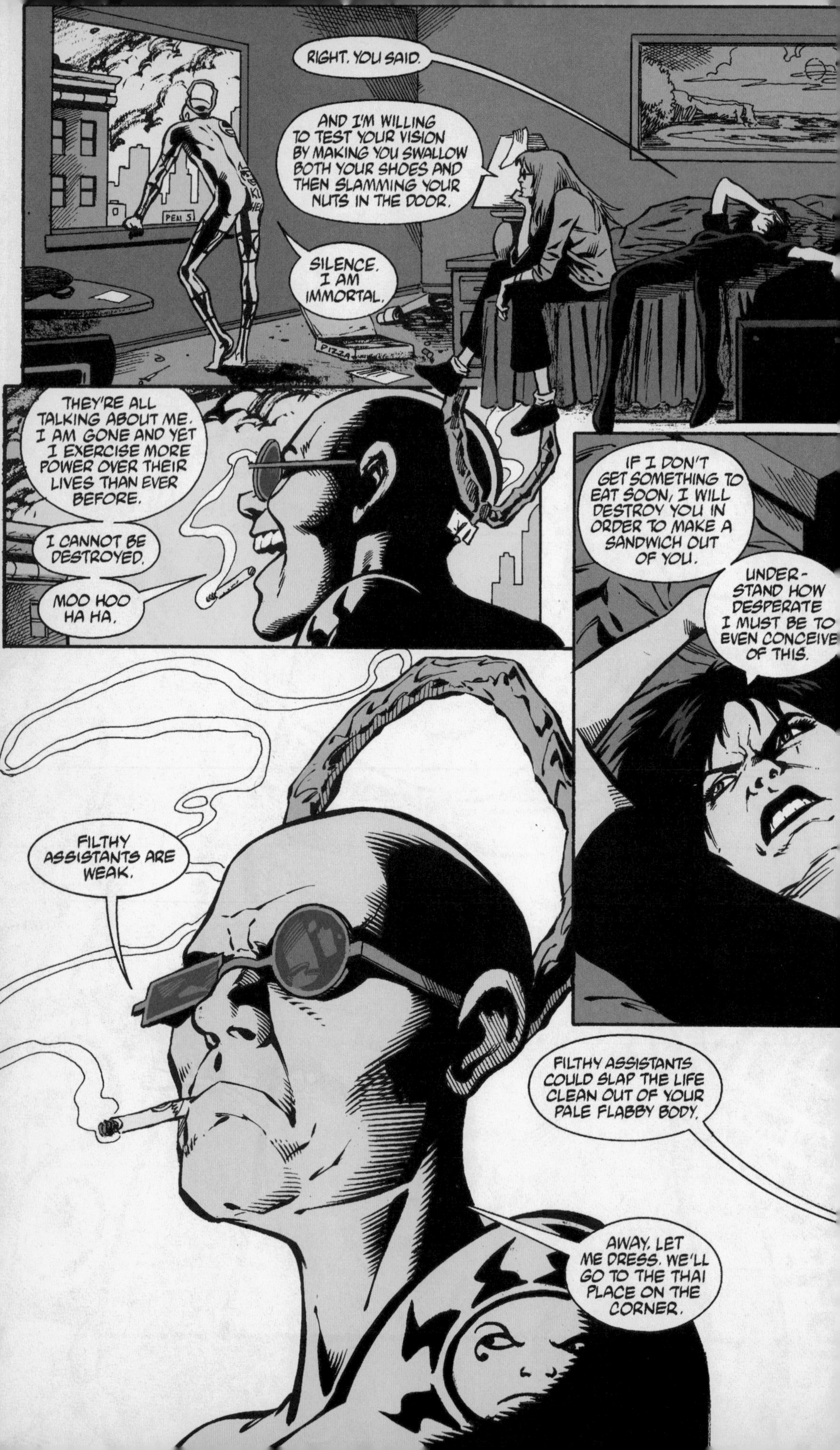
RIGHT. YOU SAID.
AND I'M WILLING TO TEST YOUR VISION BY MAKING YOU SWALLOW BOTH YOUR SHOES AND THEN SLAMMING YOUR NUTS IN THE DOOR.
SILENCE. I AM IMMORTAL.
PIZZA
THEY'RE ALL TALKING ABOUT ME. I AM GONE AND YET I EXERCISE MORE POWER OVER THEIR LIVES THAN EVER BEFORE.
I CANNOT BE DESTROYED.
MOO HOO HA HA.
IF I DON'T GET SOMETHING TO EAT SOON, I WILL DESTROY YOU IN ORDER TO MAKE A SANDWICH OUT OF YOU.
UNDER-STAND HOW DESPERATE I MUST BE TO EVEN CONCEIVE OF THIS.
FILTHY ASSISTANTS ARE WEAK.
FILTHY ASSISTANTS COULD SLAP THE LIFE CLEAN OUT OF YOUR PALE FLABBY BODY.
AWAY. LET ME DRESS. WE'LL GO TO THE THAI PLACE ON THE CORNER.

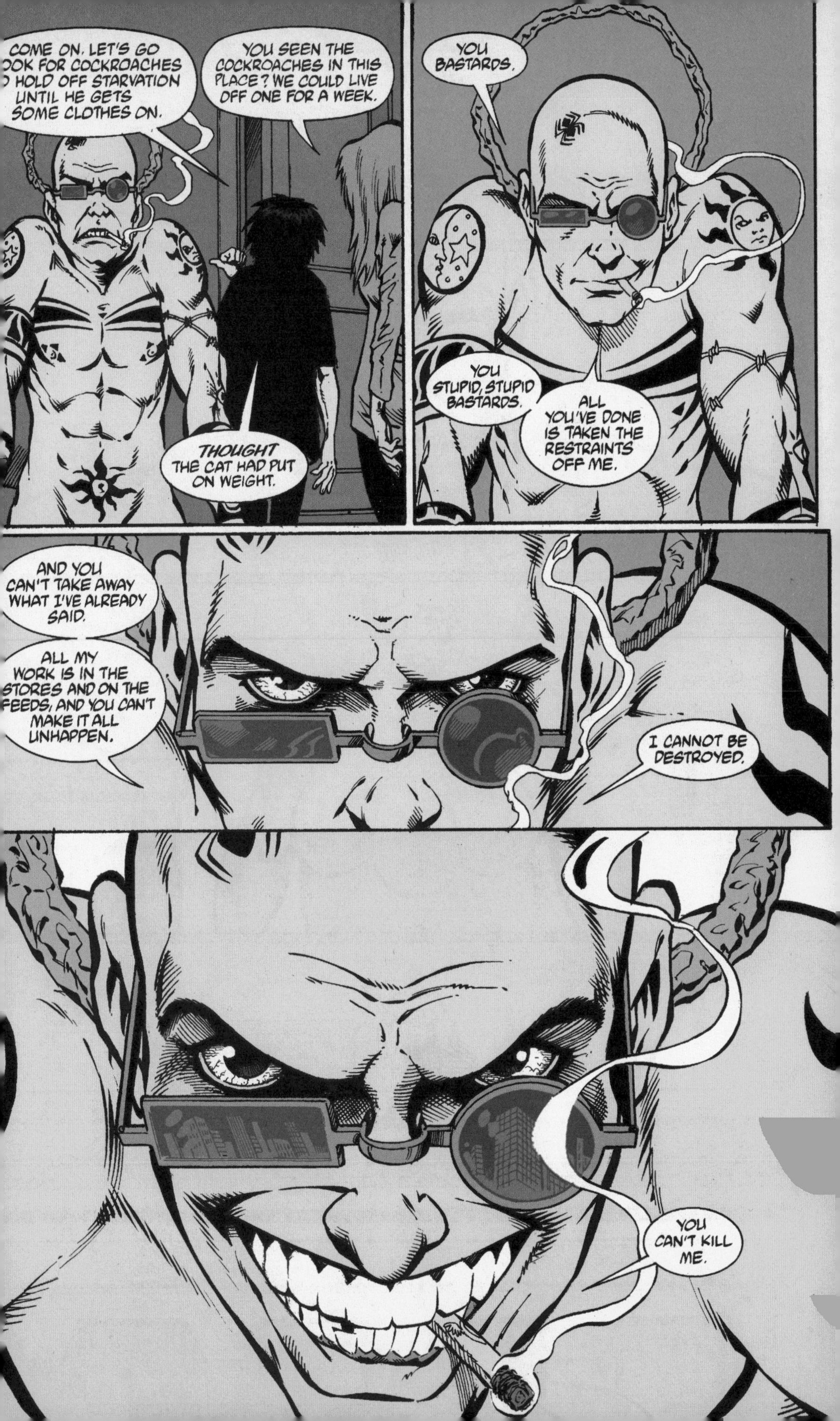
COME ON. LET'S GO LOOK FOR COCKROACHES TO HOLD OFF STARVATION UNTIL HE GETS SOME CLOTHES ON.
YOU SEEN THE COCKROACHES IN THIS PLACE? WE COULD LIVE OFF ONE FOR A WEEK.
THOUGHT THE CAT HAD PUT ON WEIGHT.
YOU BASTARDS.
YOU STUPID, STUPID BASTARDS.
ALL YOU'VE DONE IS TAKEN THE RESTRAINTS OFF ME.
AND YOU CAN'T TAKE AWAY WHAT I'VE ALREADY SAID.
ALL MY WORK IS IN THE STORES AND ON THE FEEDS, AND YOU CAN'T MAKE IT ALL UNHAPPEN.
I CANNOT BE DESTROYED.
YOU CAN'T KILL ME.

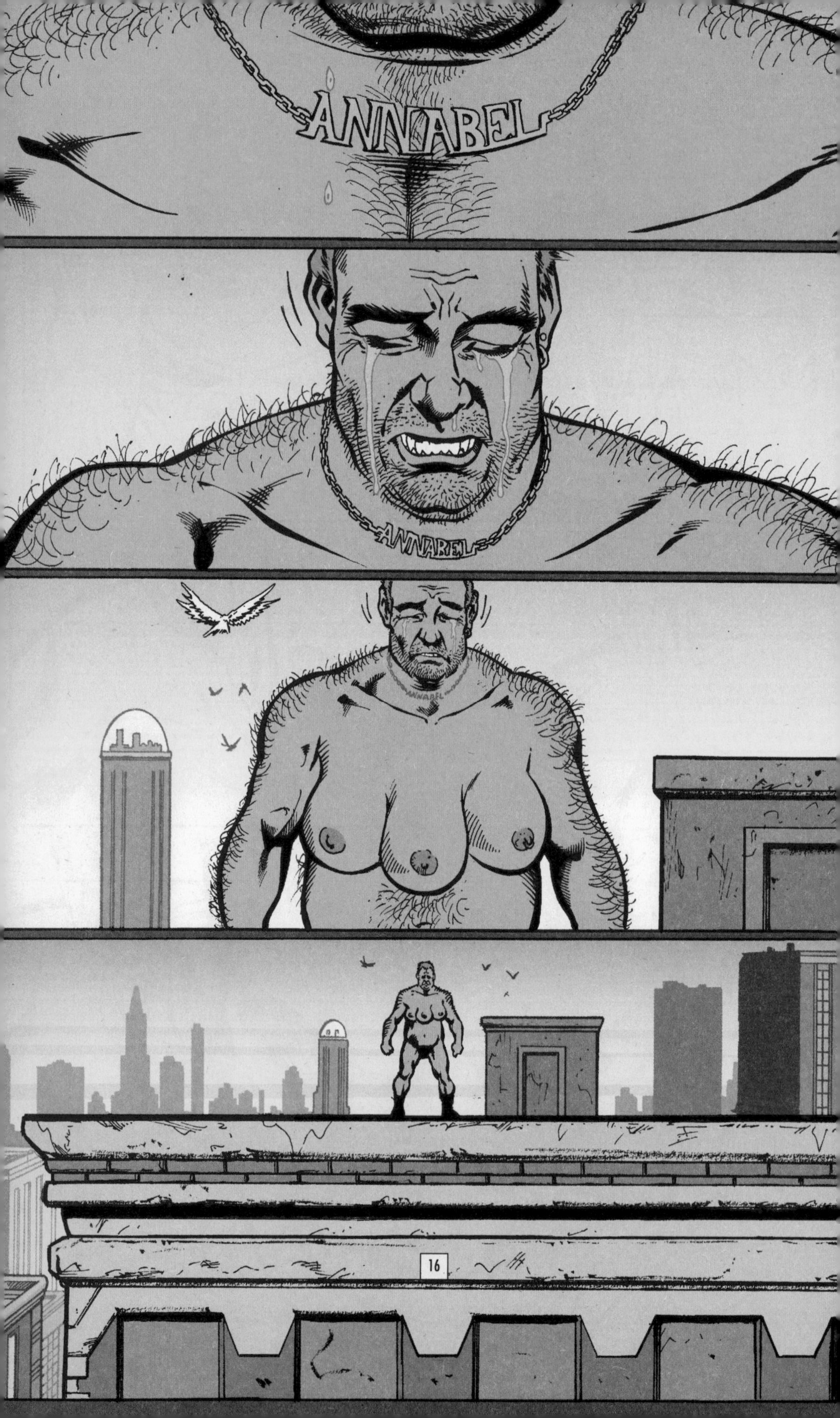
ANNABEL
ANNABEL
ANNABEL

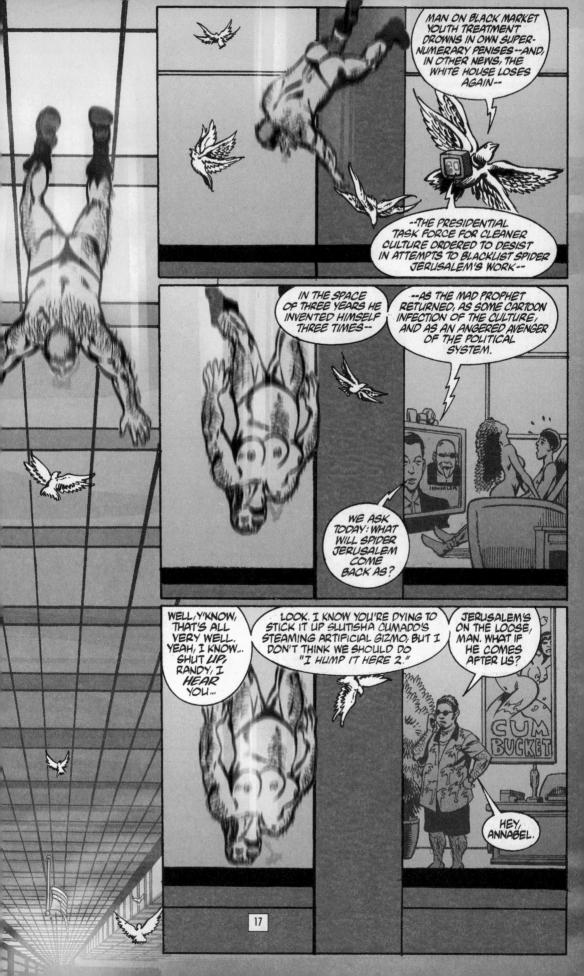

MAN ON BLACK MARKET YOUTH TREATMENT DROWNS IN OWN SUPER-NUMERARY PENISES--AND, IN OTHER NEWS, THE WHITE HOUSE LOSES AGAIN--

--THE PRESIDENTIAL TASK FORCE FOR CLEANER CULTURE ORDERED TO DESIST IN ATTEMPTS TO BLACKLIST SPIDER JERUSALEM'S WORK--

IN THE SPACE OF THREE YEARS HE INVENTED HIMSELF THREE TIMES--

--AS THE MAD PROPHET RETURNED, AS SOME CARTOON INFECTION OF THE CULTURE, AND AS AN ANGERED AVENGER OF THE POLITICAL SYSTEM.

WE ASK TODAY: WHAT WILL SPIDER JERUSALEM COME BACK AS?

WELL, Y'KNOW, THAT'S ALL VERY WELL. YEAH, I KNOW... SHUT UP, RANDY, I HEAR YOU...

LOOK, I KNOW YOU'RE DYING TO STICK IT UP SLUTISHA CUMADO'S STEAMING ARTIFICIAL GIZMO, BUT I DON'T THINK WE SHOULD DO "I HUMP IT HERE 2."

JERUSALEM'S ON THE LOOSE, MAN. WHAT IF HE COMES AFTER US?

CUM BUCKET

HEY, ANNABEL.

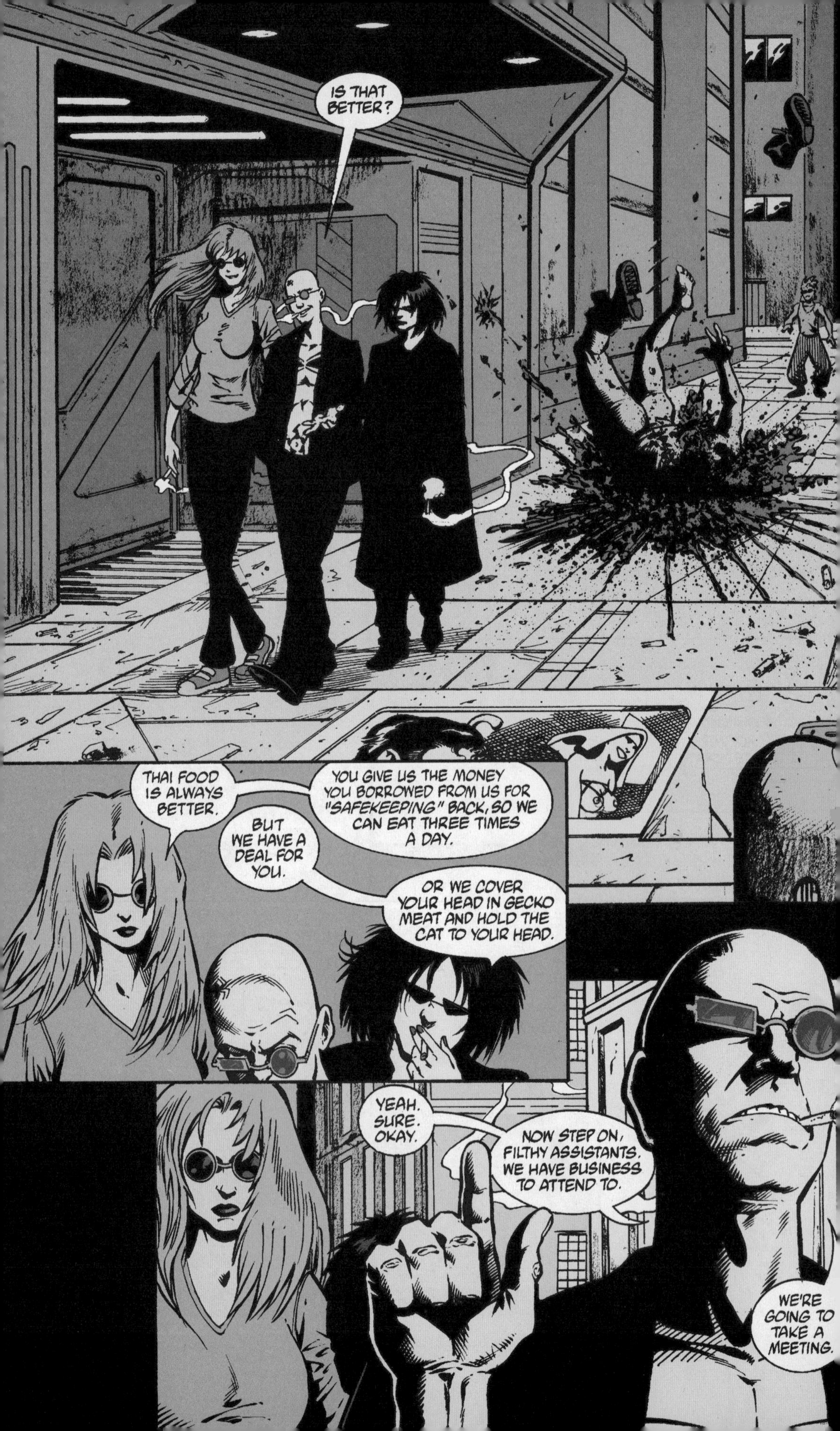
IS THAT BETTER?
THAI FOOD IS ALWAYS BETTER.
YOU GIVE US THE MONEY YOU BORROWED FROM US FOR "SAFEKEEPING" BACK, SO WE CAN EAT THREE TIMES A DAY.
BUT WE HAVE A DEAL FOR YOU.
OR WE COVER YOUR HEAD IN GECKO MEAT AND HOLD THE CAT TO YOUR HEAD.
YEAH. SURE. OKAY.
NOW STEP ON, FILTHY ASSISTANTS. WE HAVE BUSINESS TO ATTEND TO.
WE'RE GOING TO TAKE A MEETING.

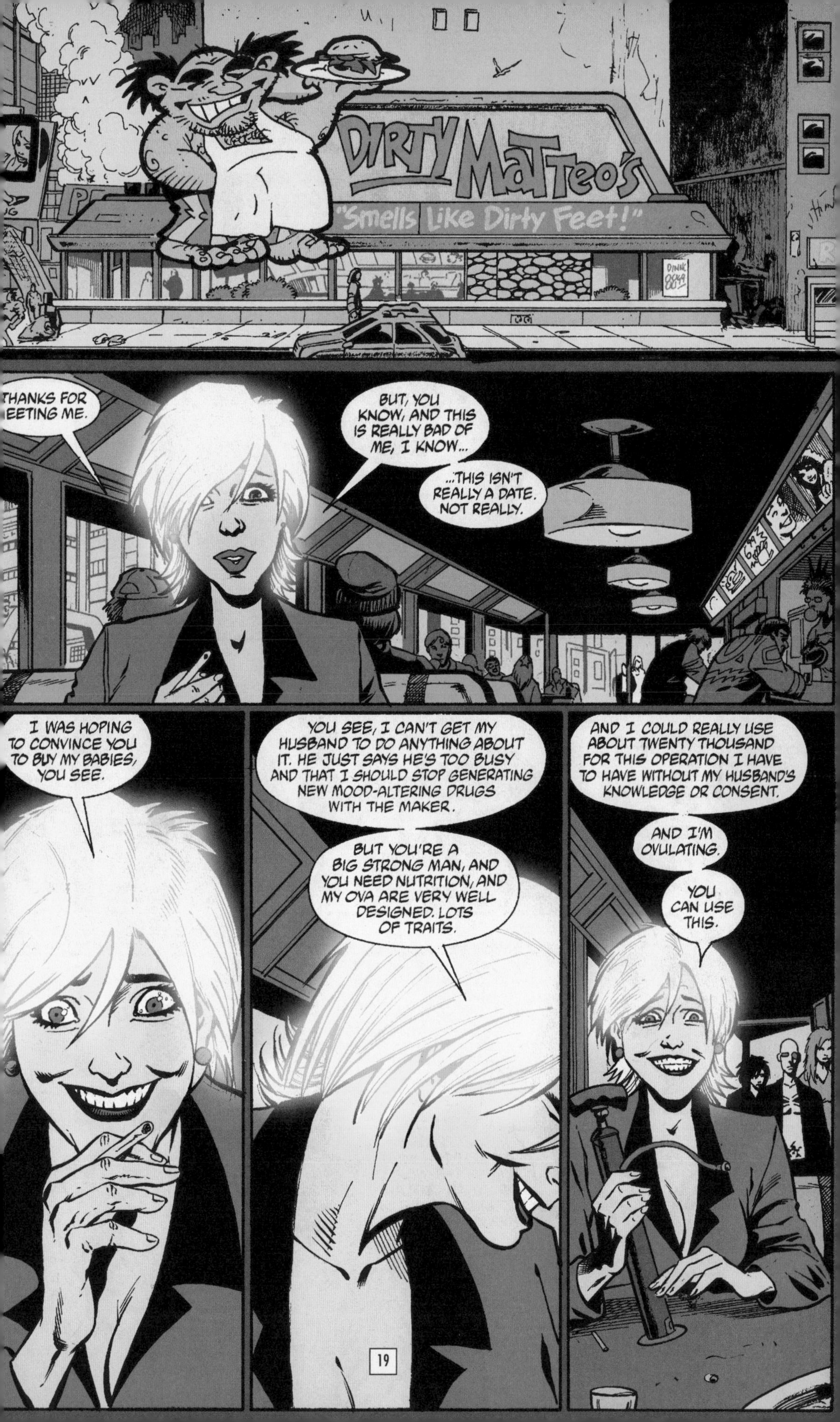
DIRTY MATTEO'S
"Smells Like Dirty Feet!"
THANKS FOR MEETING ME.
BUT, YOU KNOW, AND THIS IS REALLY BAD OF ME, I KNOW...
...THIS ISN'T REALLY A DATE. NOT REALLY.
I WAS HOPING TO CONVINCE YOU TO BUY MY BABIES, YOU SEE.
YOU SEE, I CAN'T GET MY HUSBAND TO DO ANYTHING ABOUT IT. HE JUST SAYS HE'S TOO BUSY AND THAT I SHOULD STOP GENERATING NEW MOOD-ALTERING DRUGS WITH THE MAKER.
BUT YOU'RE A BIG STRONG MAN, AND YOU NEED NUTRITION, AND MY OVA ARE VERY WELL DESIGNED. LOTS OF TRAITS.
AND I COULD REALLY USE ABOUT TWENTY THOUSAND FOR THIS OPERATION I HAVE TO HAVE WITHOUT MY HUSBAND'S KNOWLEDGE OR CONSENT.
AND I'M OVULATING.
YOU CAN USE THIS.

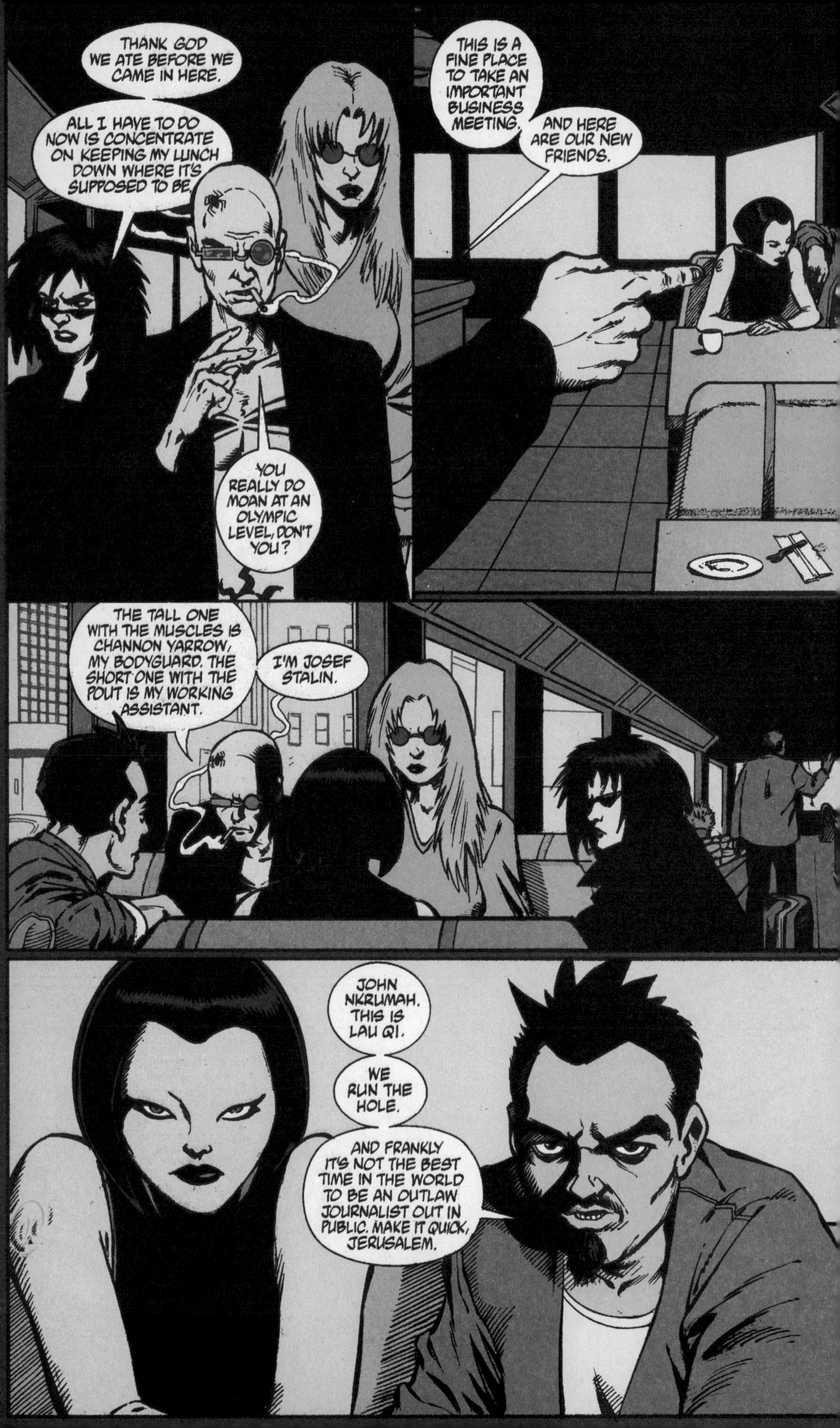
THANK GOD WE ATE BEFORE WE CAME IN HERE.
ALL I HAVE TO DO NOW IS CONCENTRATE ON KEEPING MY LUNCH DOWN WHERE IT'S SUPPOSED TO BE.
YOU REALLY DO MOAN AT AN OLYMPIC LEVEL, DON'T YOU?
THIS IS A FINE PLACE TO TAKE AN IMPORTANT BUSINESS MEETING.
AND HERE ARE OUR NEW FRIENDS.
THE TALL ONE WITH THE MUSCLES IS CHANNON YARROW, MY BODYGUARD. THE SHORT ONE WITH THE POUT IS MY WORKING ASSISTANT.
I'M JOSEF STALIN.
JOHN NKRUMAH. THIS IS LAU QI.
WE RUN THE HOLE.
AND FRANKLY IT'S NOT THE BEST TIME IN THE WORLD TO BE AN OUTLAW JOURNALIST OUT IN PUBLIC. MAKE IT QUICK, JERUSALEM.

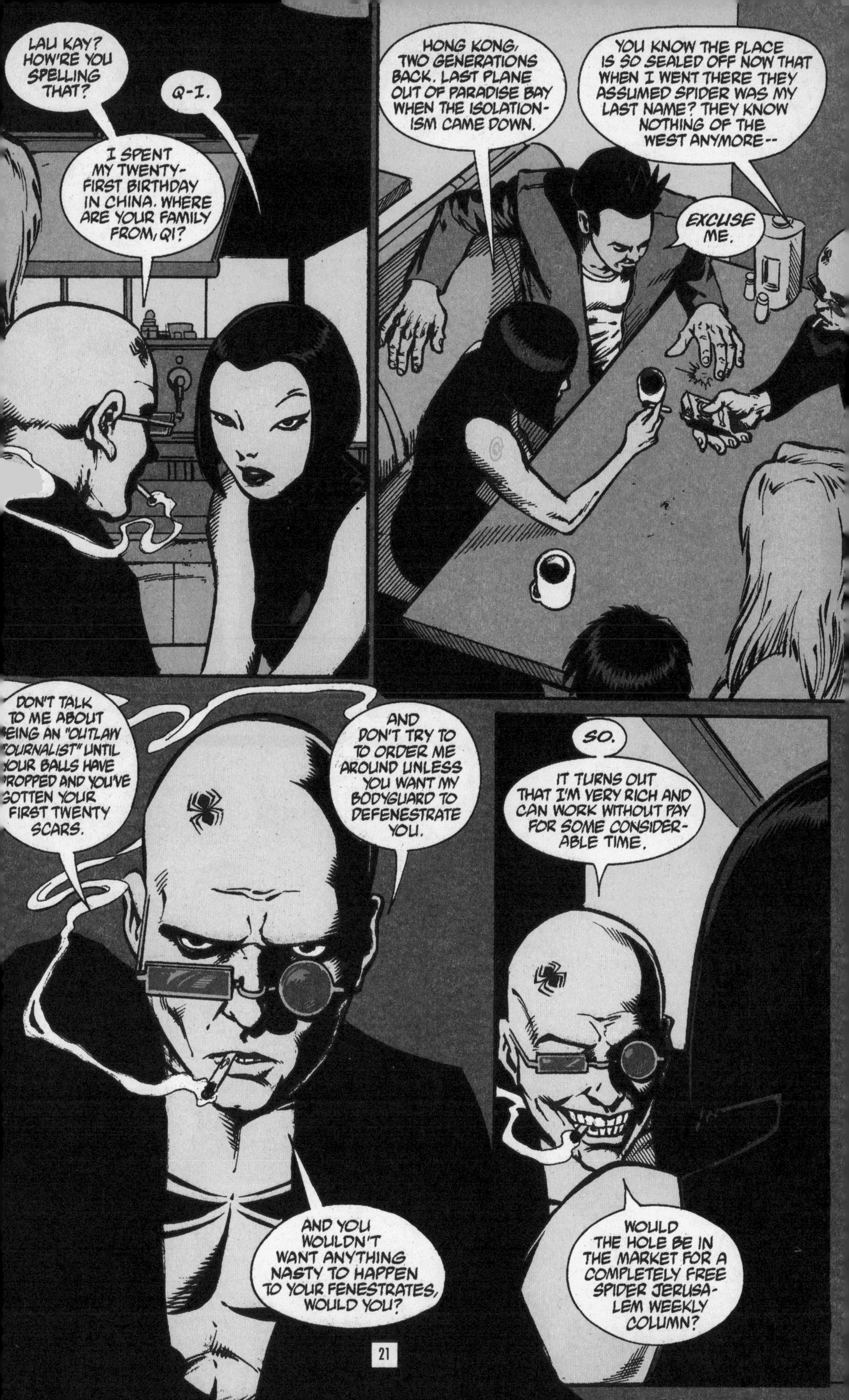
LAU KAY? HOW'RE YOU SPELLING THAT?
Q-I.
I SPENT MY TWENTY-FIRST BIRTHDAY IN CHINA. WHERE ARE YOUR FAMILY FROM, QI?
HONG KONG, TWO GENERATIONS BACK. LAST PLANE OUT OF PARADISE BAY WHEN THE ISOLATION-ISM CAME DOWN.
YOU KNOW THE PLACE IS SO SEALED OFF NOW THAT WHEN I WENT THERE THEY ASSUMED SPIDER WAS MY LAST NAME? THEY KNOW NOTHING OF THE WEST ANYMORE--
EXCUSE ME.
DON'T TALK TO ME ABOUT BEING AN "OUTLAW JOURNALIST" UNTIL YOUR BALLS HAVE DROPPED AND YOU'VE GOTTEN YOUR FIRST TWENTY SCARS.
AND DON'T TRY TO TO ORDER ME AROUND UNLESS YOU WANT MY BODYGUARD TO DEFENESTRATE YOU.
AND YOU WOULDN'T WANT ANYTHING NASTY TO HAPPEN TO YOUR FENESTRATES, WOULD YOU?
SO.
IT TURNS OUT THAT I'M VERY RICH AND CAN WORK WITHOUT PAY FOR SOME CONSIDER-ABLE TIME.
WOULD THE HOLE BE IN THE MARKET FOR A COMPLETELY FREE SPIDER JERUSA-LEM WEEKLY COLUMN?

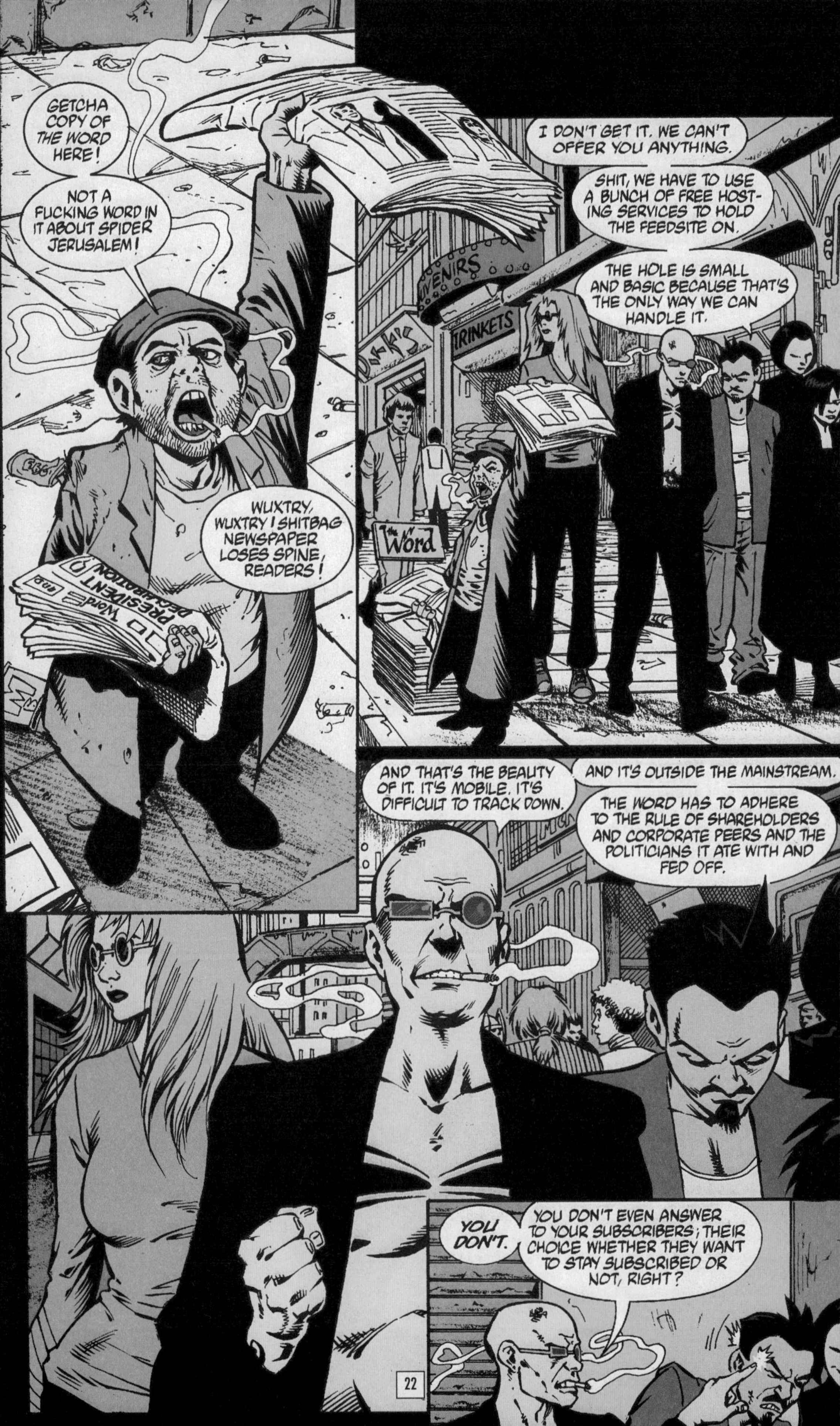
GETCHA COPY OF THE WORD HERE!
NOT A FUCKING WORD IN IT ABOUT SPIDER JERUSALEM!
WUXTRY, WUXTRY! SHITBAG NEWSPAPER LOSES SPINE, READERS!
I DON'T GET IT. WE CAN'T OFFER YOU ANYTHING.
SHIT, WE HAVE TO USE A BUNCH OF FREE HOSTING SERVICES TO HOLD THE FEEDSITE ON.
THE HOLE IS SMALL AND BASIC BECAUSE THAT'S THE ONLY WAY WE CAN HANDLE IT.
TRINKETS
The Word
AND THAT'S THE BEAUTY OF IT. IT'S MOBILE. IT'S DIFFICULT TO TRACK DOWN.
AND IT'S OUTSIDE THE MAINSTREAM.
THE WORD HAS TO ADHERE TO THE RULE OF SHAREHOLDERS AND CORPORATE PEERS AND THE POLITICIANS IT ATE WITH AND FED OFF.
YOU DON'T.
YOU DON'T EVEN ANSWER TO YOUR SUBSCRIBERS; THEIR CHOICE WHETHER THEY WANT TO STAY SUBSCRIBED OR NOT, RIGHT?

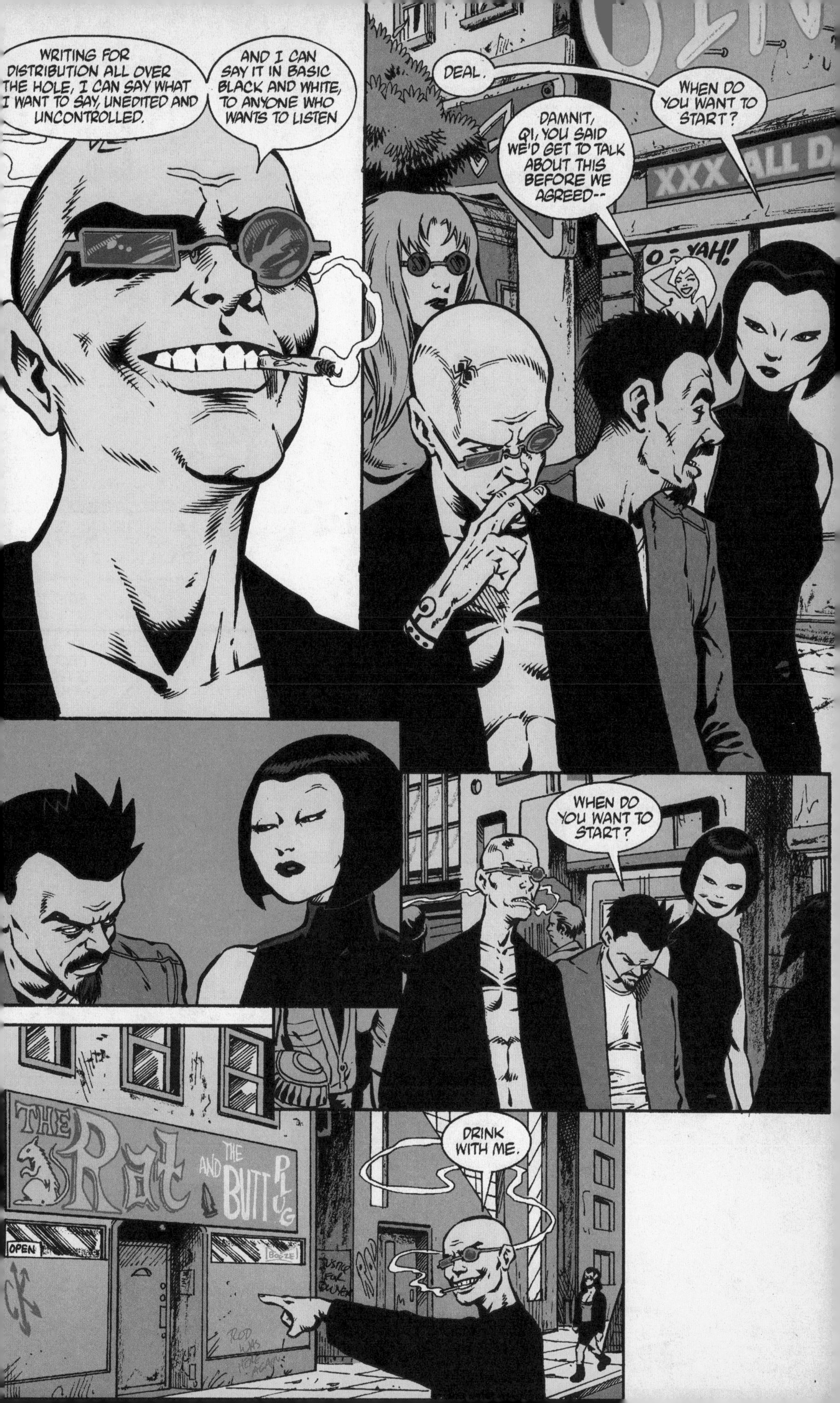
WRITING FOR DISTRIBUTION ALL OVER THE HOLE, I CAN SAY WHAT I WANT TO SAY, UNEDITED AND UNCONTROLLED.
AND I CAN SAY IT IN BASIC BLACK AND WHITE, TO ANYONE WHO WANTS TO LISTEN
DEAL.
WHEN DO YOU WANT TO START?
DAMNIT, QI, YOU SAID WE'D GET TO TALK ABOUT THIS BEFORE WE AGREED--
XXX ALL D
O - YAH!
WHEN DO YOU WANT TO START?
THE Rat AND THE BUTT PLUG
OPEN
BOOZE
DRINK WITH ME.

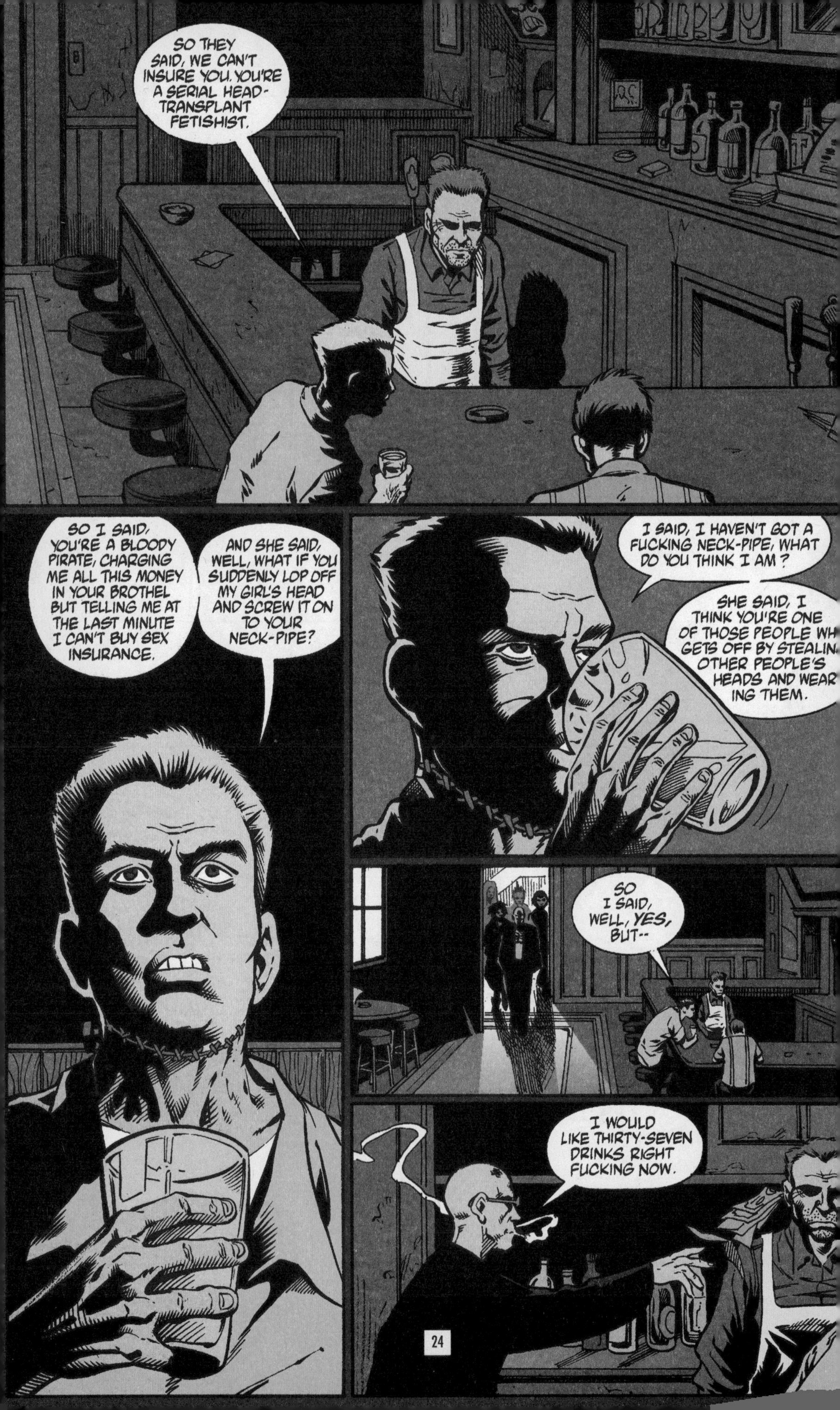
SO THEY SAID, WE CAN'T INSURE YOU. YOU'RE A SERIAL HEAD-TRANSPLANT FETISHIST.
SO I SAID, YOU'RE A BLOODY PIRATE, CHARGING ME ALL THIS MONEY IN YOUR BROTHEL BUT TELLING ME AT THE LAST MINUTE I CAN'T BUY SEX INSURANCE.
AND SHE SAID, WELL, WHAT IF YOU SUDDENLY LOP OFF MY GIRL'S HEAD AND SCREW IT ON TO YOUR NECK-PIPE?
I SAID, I HAVEN'T GOT A FUCKING NECK-PIPE, WHAT DO YOU THINK I AM?
SHE SAID, I THINK YOU'RE ONE OF THOSE PEOPLE WH GETS OFF BY STEALIN OTHER PEOPLE'S HEADS AND WEAR ING THEM.
SO I SAID, WELL, YES, BUT--
I WOULD LIKE THIRTY-SEVEN DRINKS RIGHT FUCKING NOW.

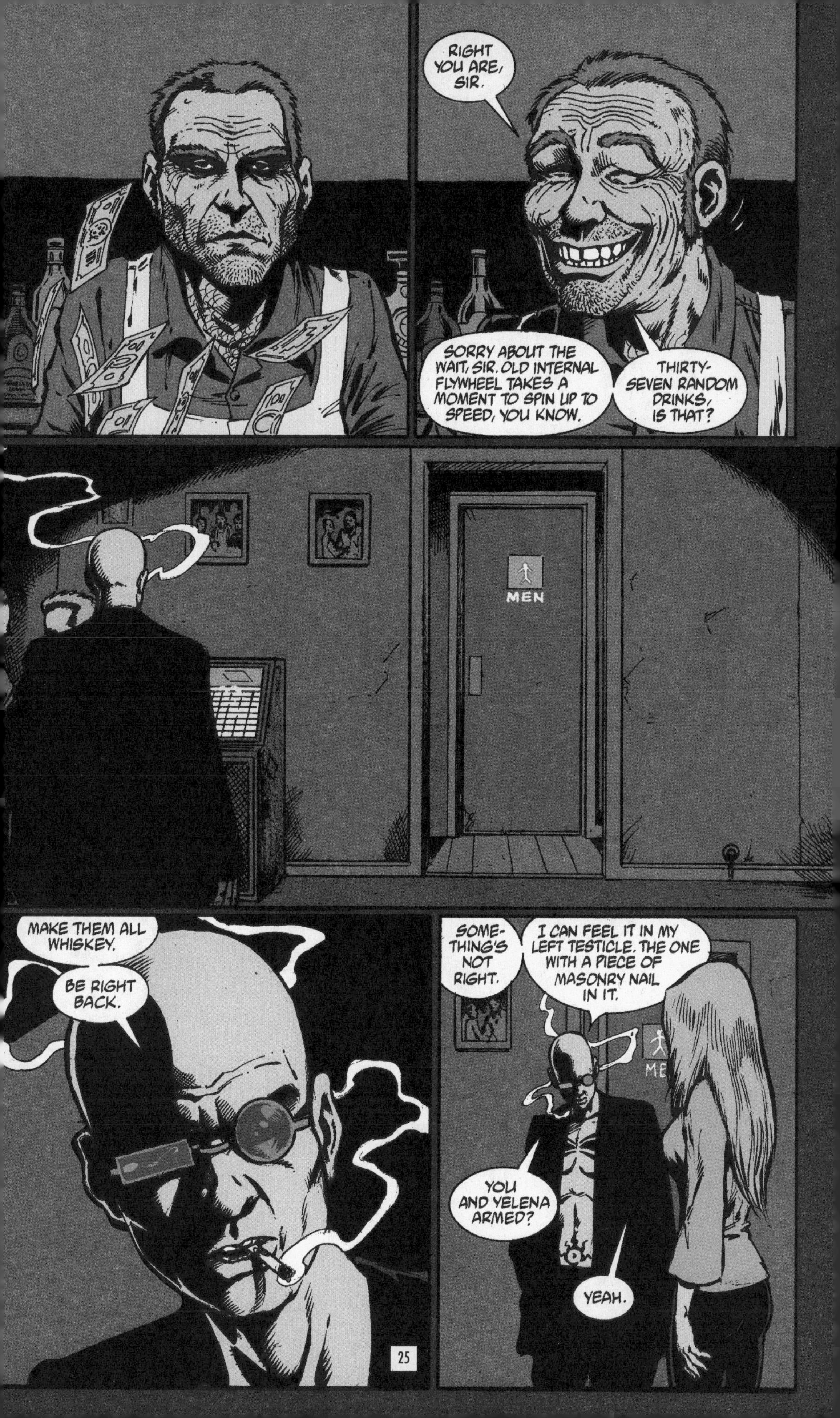
RIGHT YOU ARE, SIR.
SORRY ABOUT THE WAIT, SIR. OLD INTERNAL FLYWHEEL TAKES A MOMENT TO SPIN UP TO SPEED, YOU KNOW.
THIRTY-SEVEN RANDOM DRINKS, IS THAT?
MEN
MAKE THEM ALL WHISKEY.
BE RIGHT BACK.
SOME-THING'S NOT RIGHT.
I CAN FEEL IT IN MY LEFT TESTICLE. THE ONE WITH A PIECE OF MASONRY NAIL IN IT.
YOU AND YELENA ARMED?
YEAH.

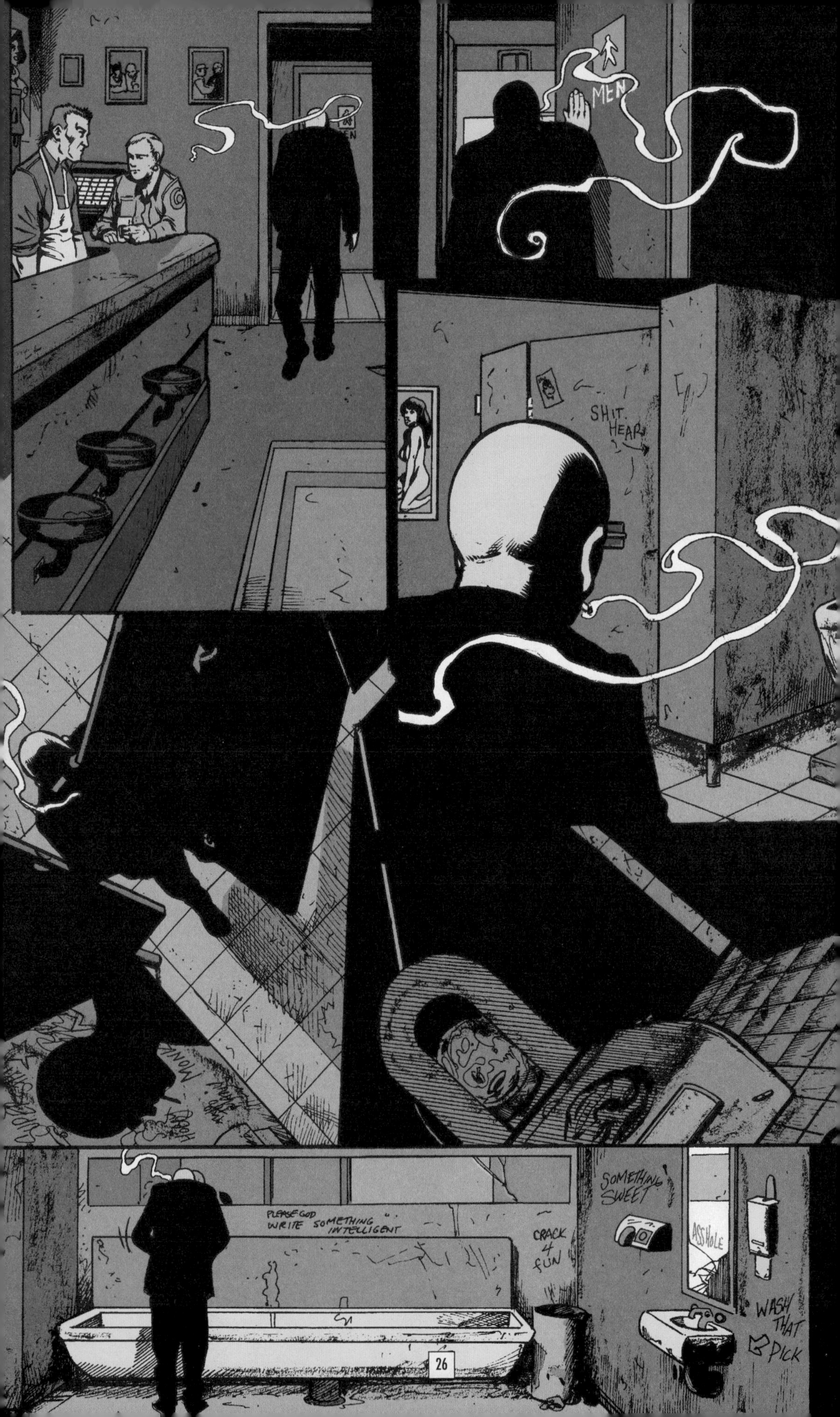
MEN
SHIT HEAR
PLEASE GOD WRITE SOMETHING INTELLIGENT
CRACK 4 FUN
SOMETHING SWEET
ASSHOLE
WASH THAT PICK

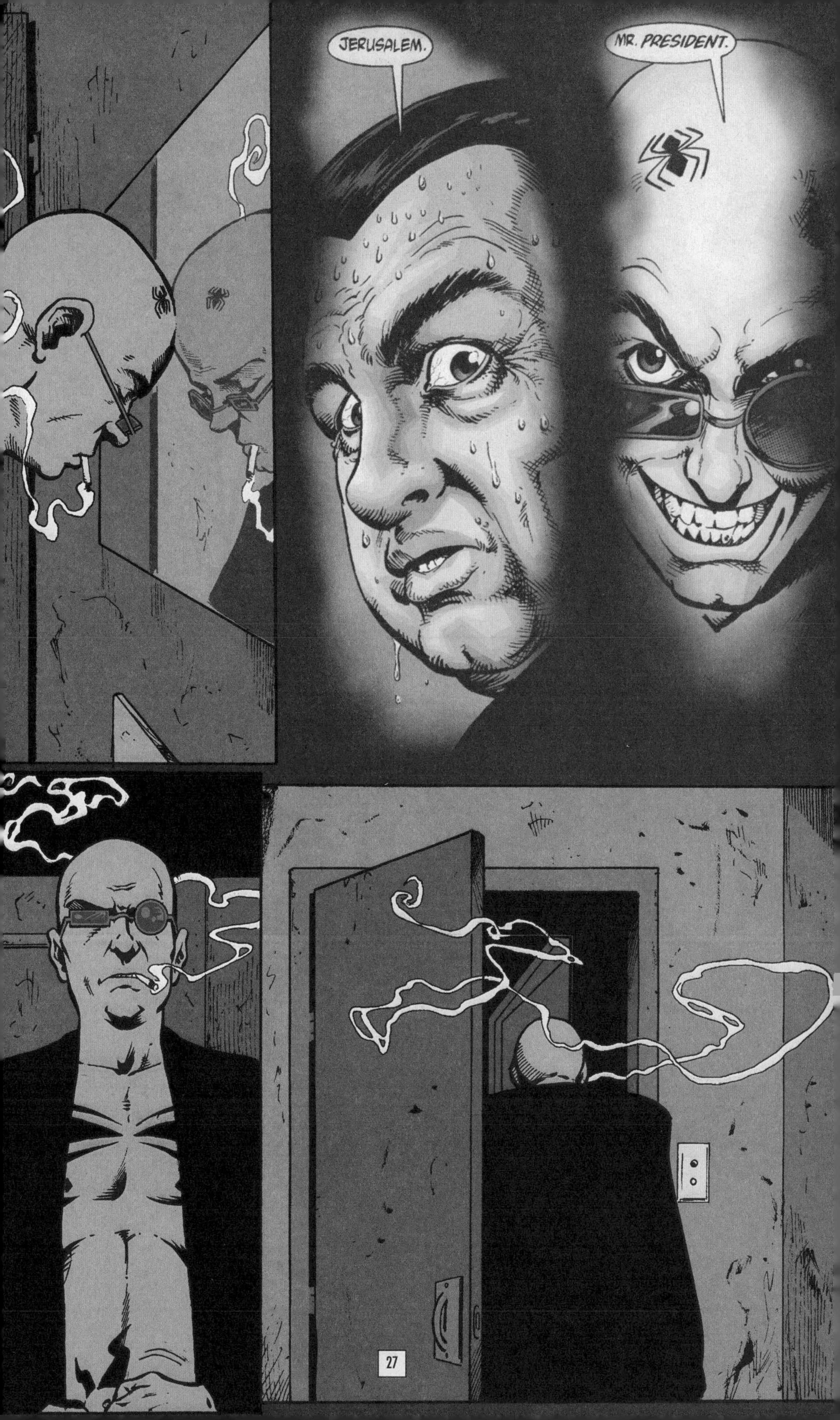
JERUSALEM.
MR. PRESIDENT.

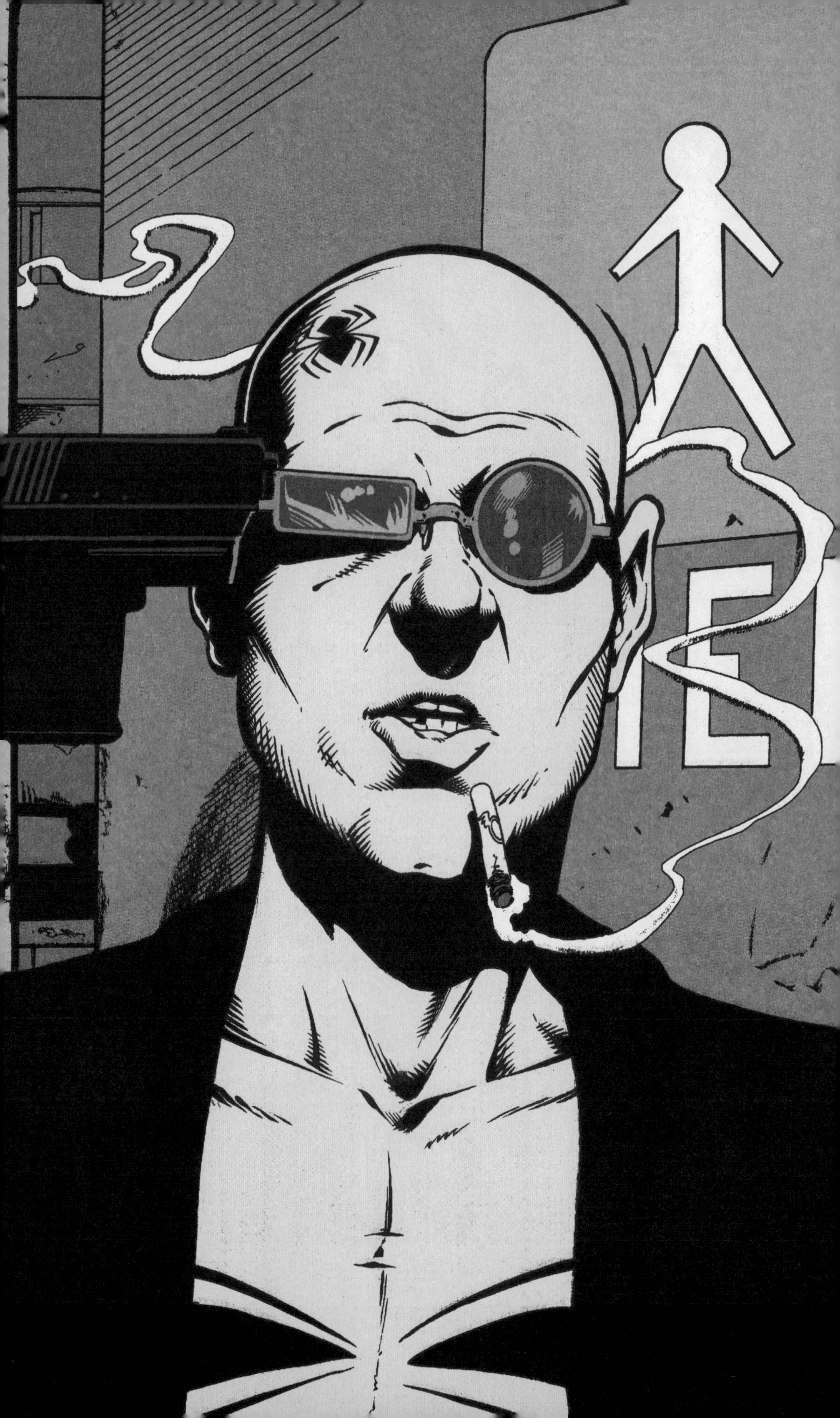

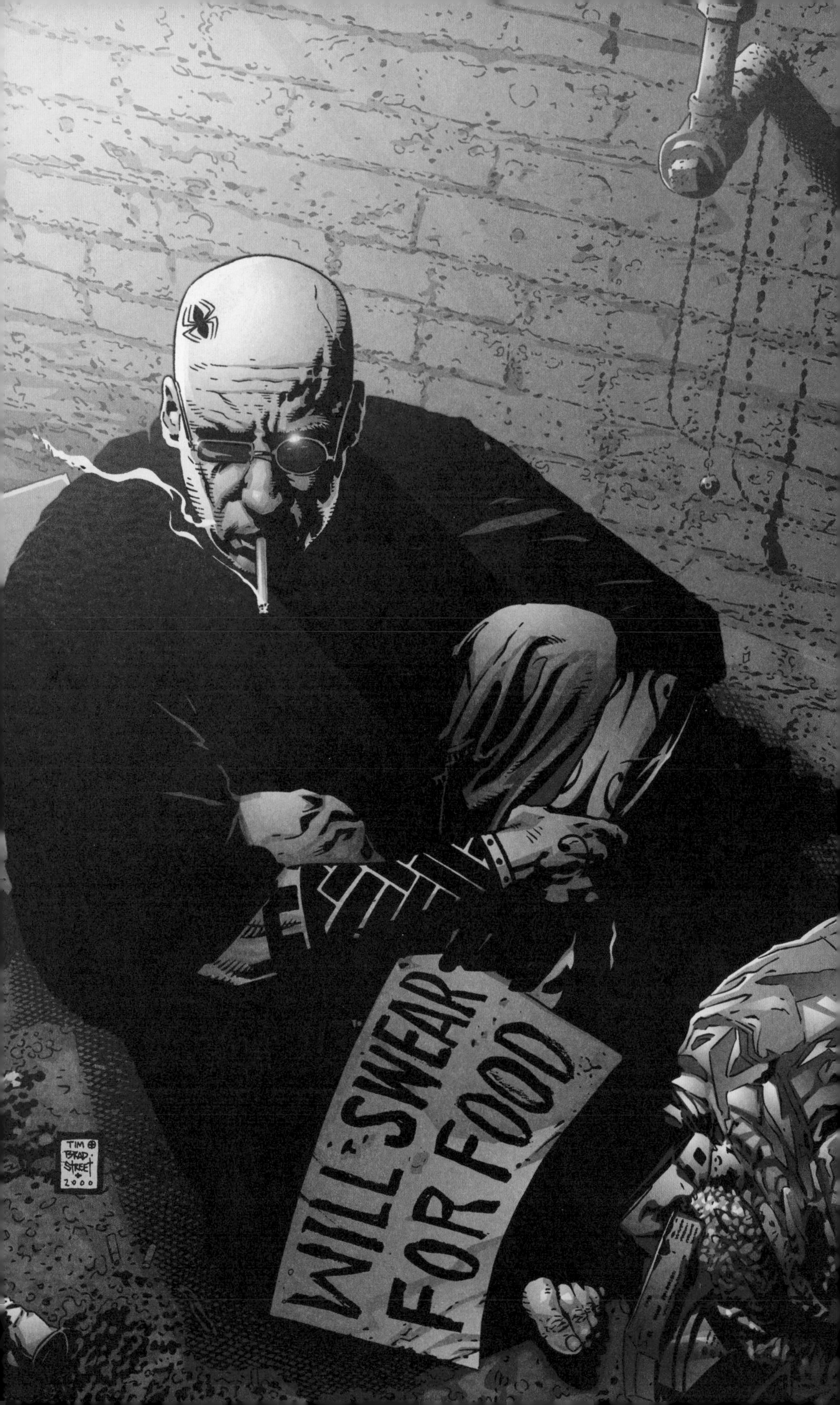
WILL SWEAR
FOR FOOD
TIM BRADSTREET 2000

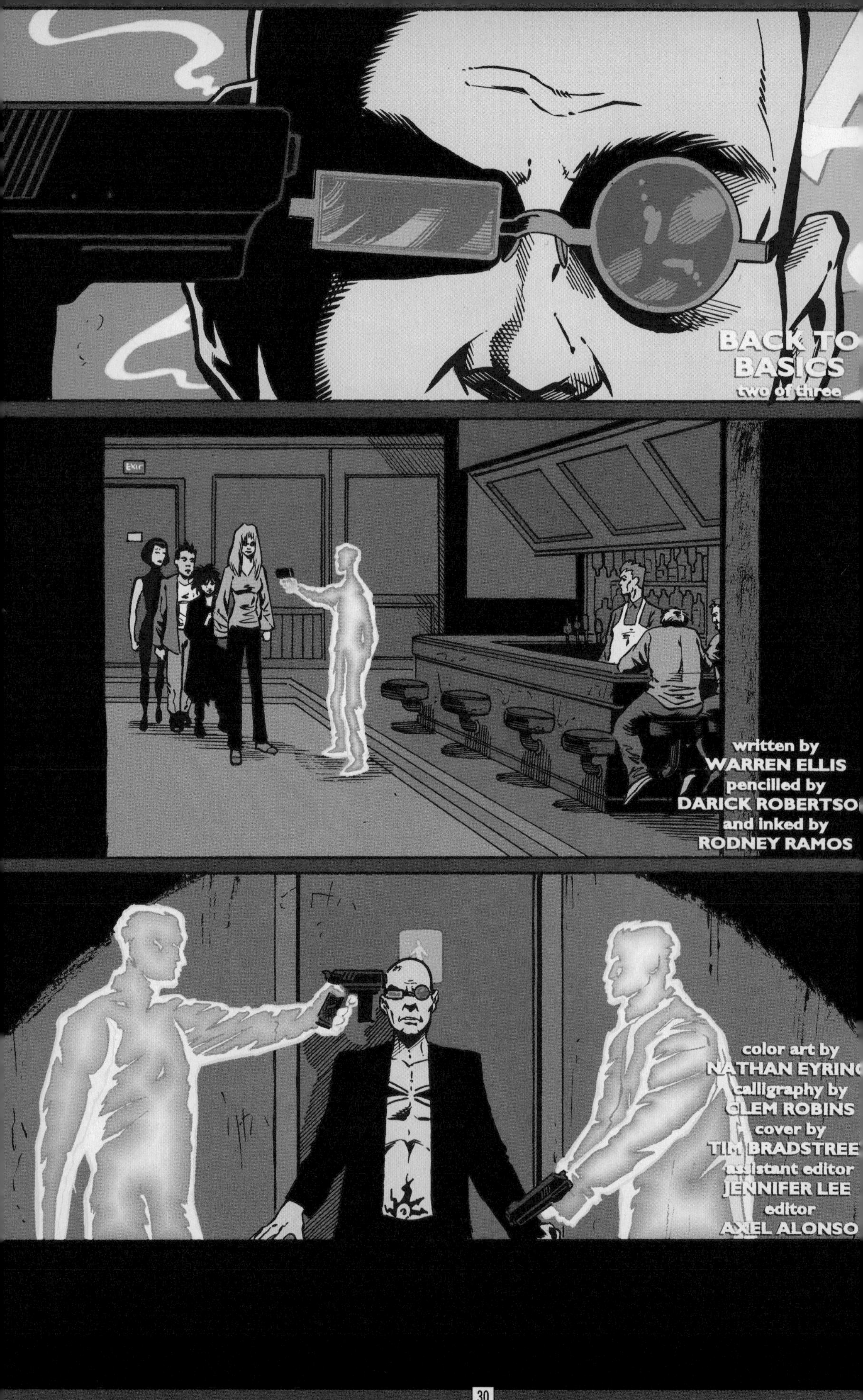
BACK TO BASICS
two of three
written by
WARREN ELLIS
pencilled by
DARICK ROBERTSO
and inked by
RODNEY RAMOS
color art by
NATHAN EYRIN
calligraphy by
CLEM ROBINS
cover by
TIM BRADSTREE
assistant editor
JENNIFER LEE
editor
AXEL ALONSO

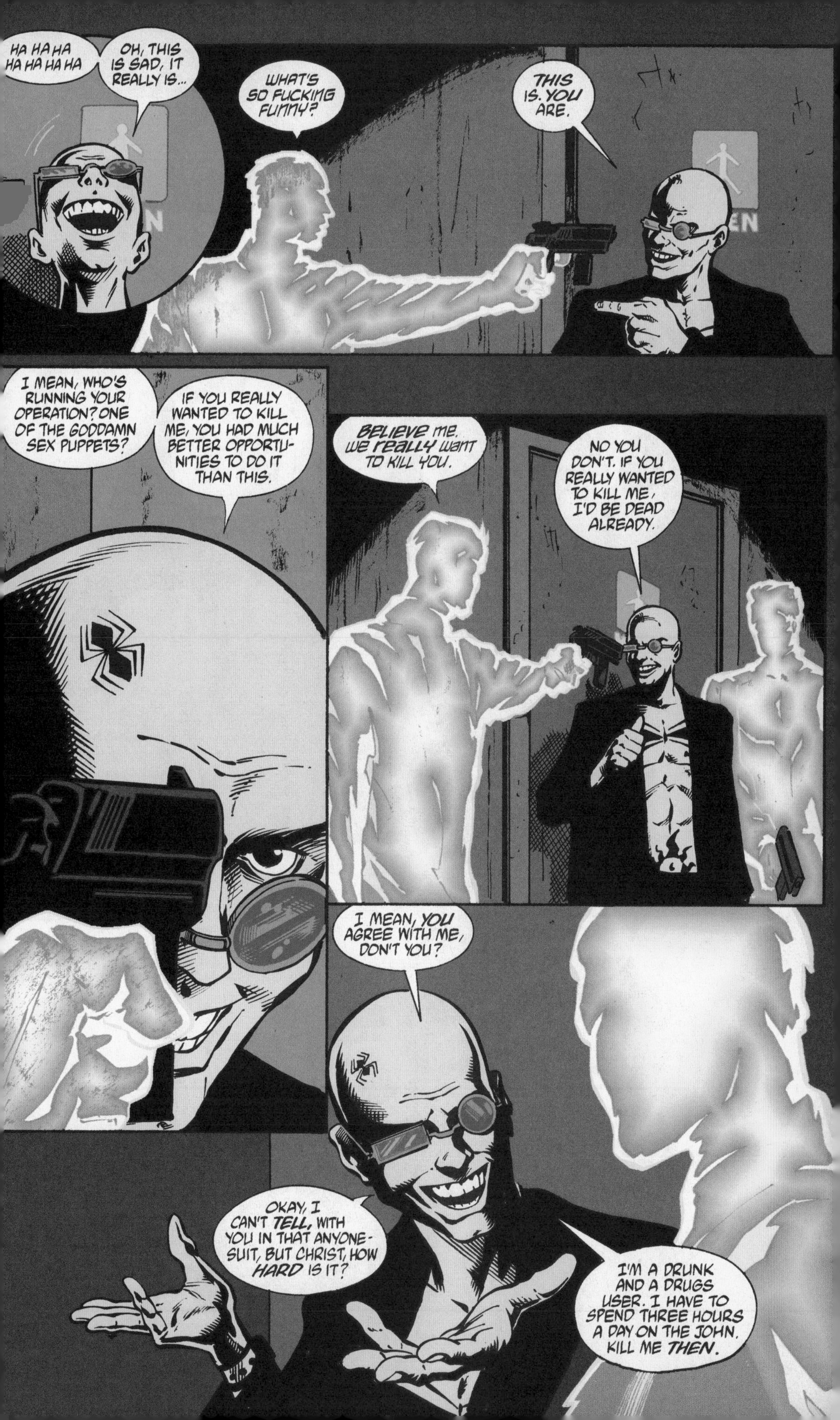
HA HA HA HA HA HA HA HA
OH, THIS IS SAD, IT REALLY IS...
WHAT'S SO FUCKING FUNNY?
THIS IS. YOU ARE.
I MEAN, WHO'S RUNNING YOUR OPERATION? ONE OF THE GODDAMN SEX PUPPETS?
IF YOU REALLY WANTED TO KILL ME, YOU HAD MUCH BETTER OPPORTUNITIES TO DO IT THAN THIS.
BELIEVE ME. WE REALLY WANT TO KILL YOU.
NO YOU DON'T. IF YOU REALLY WANTED TO KILL ME, I'D BE DEAD ALREADY.
I MEAN, YOU AGREE WITH ME, DON'T YOU?
OKAY, I CAN'T TELL, WITH YOU IN THAT ANYONE-SUIT, BUT CHRIST, HOW HARD IS IT?
I'M A DRUNK AND A DRUGS USER. I HAVE TO SPEND THREE HOURS A DAY ON THE JOHN. KILL ME THEN.

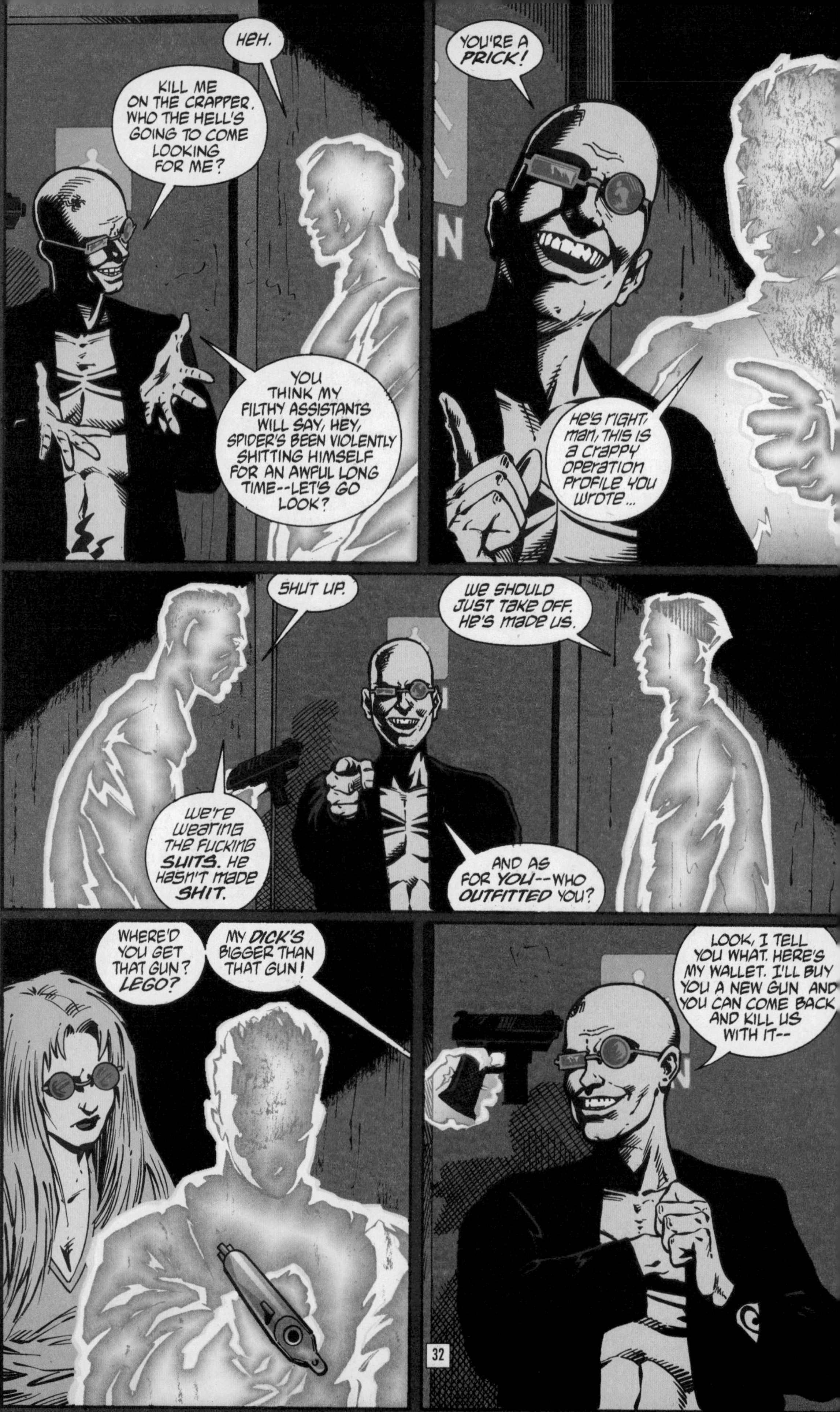
HEH.
KILL ME ON THE CRAPPER. WHO THE HELL'S GOING TO COME LOOKING FOR ME?
YOU THINK MY FILTHY ASSISTANTS WILL SAY, HEY, SPIDER'S BEEN VIOLENTLY SHITTING HIMSELF FOR AN AWFUL LONG TIME--LET'S GO LOOK?
YOU'RE A PRICK!
HE'S RIGHT, MAN, THIS IS A CRAPPY OPERATION PROFILE YOU WROTE...
SHUT UP.
WE SHOULD JUST TAKE OFF. HE'S MADE US.
WE'RE WEARING THE FUCKING SUITS. HE HASN'T MADE SHIT.
AND AS FOR YOU--WHO OUTFITTED YOU?
WHERE'D YOU GET THAT GUN? LEGO?
MY DICK'S BIGGER THAN THAT GUN!
LOOK, I TELL YOU WHAT. HERE'S MY WALLET. I'LL BUY YOU A NEW GUN AND YOU CAN COME BACK AND KILL US WITH IT--

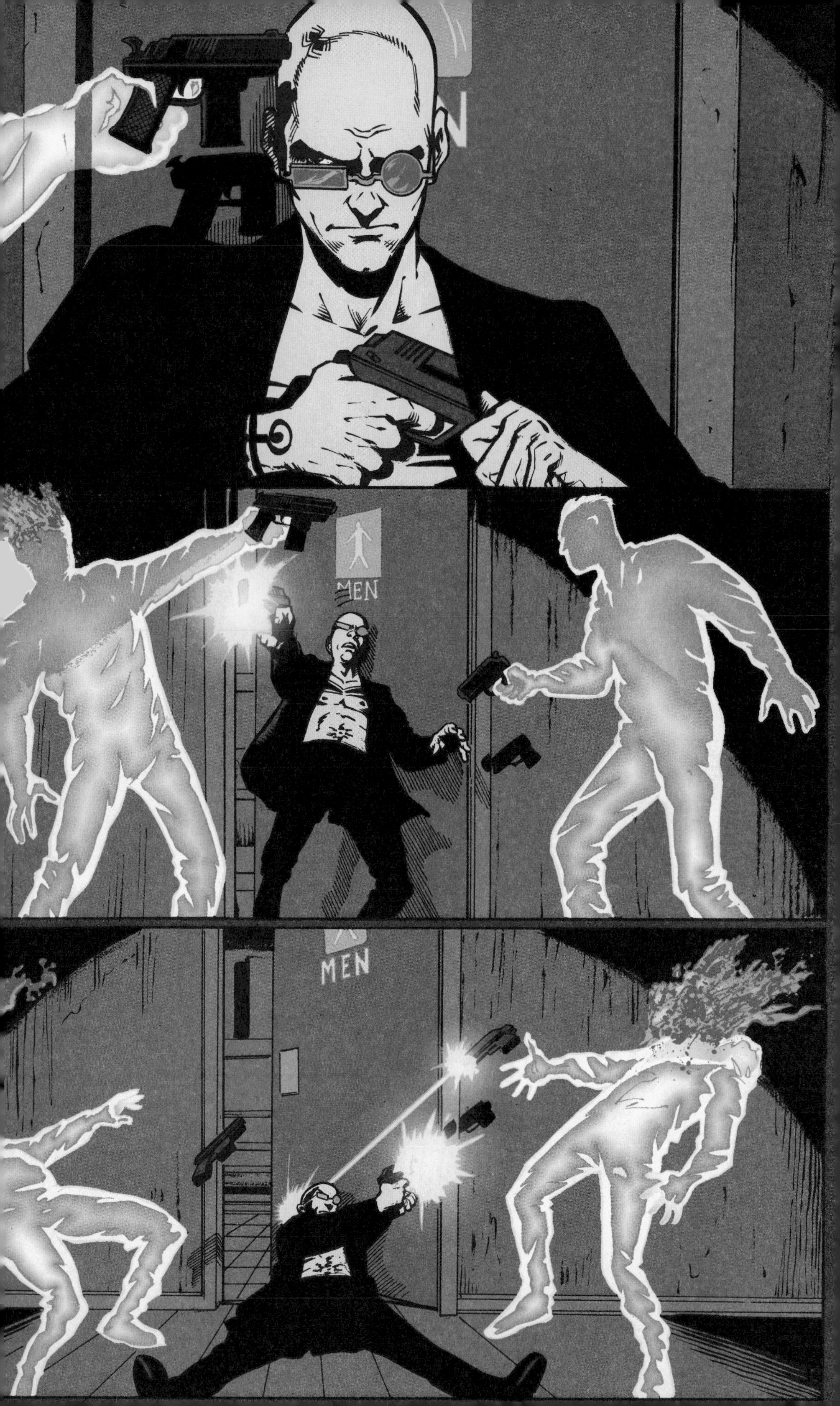
MEN
MEN

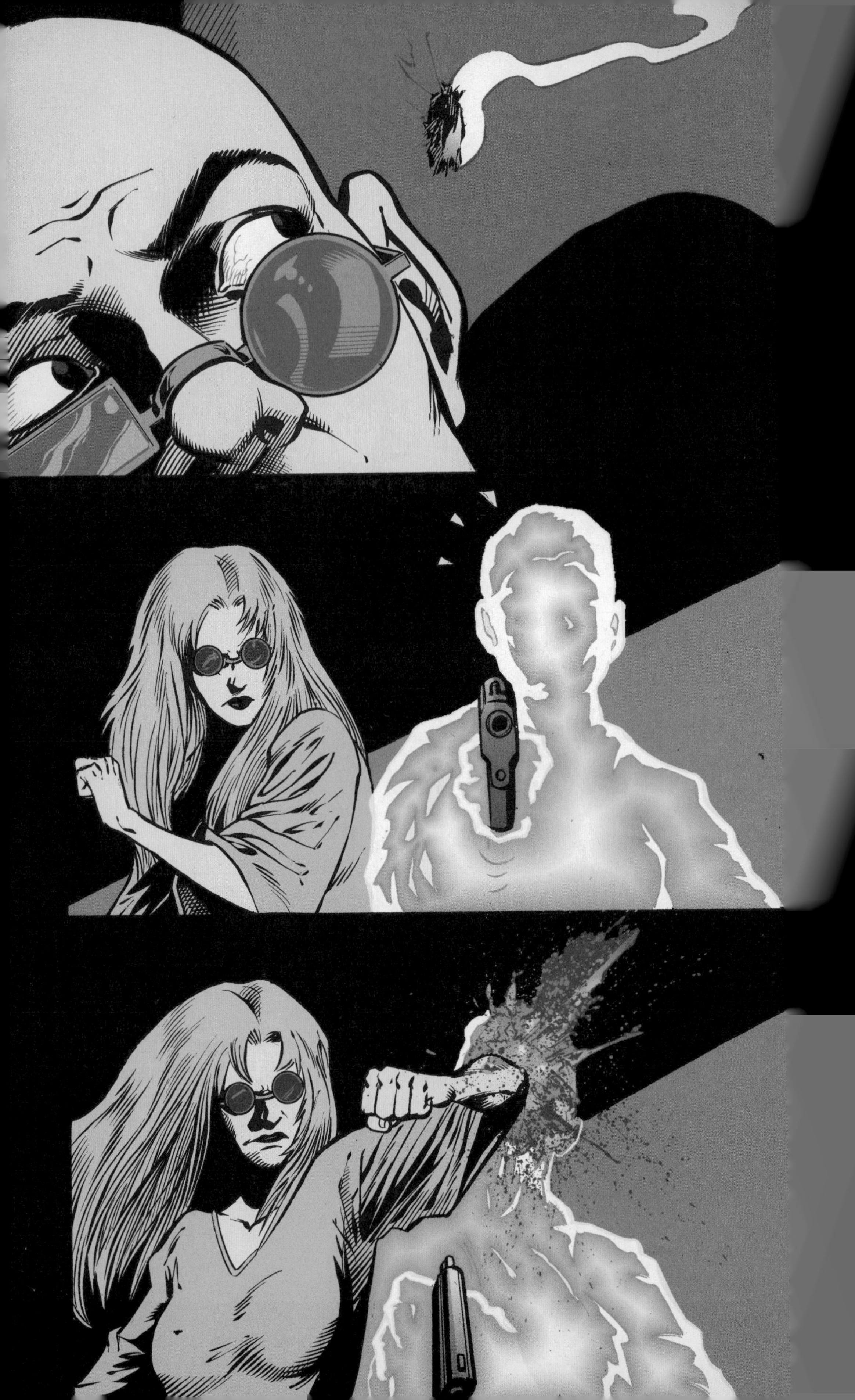

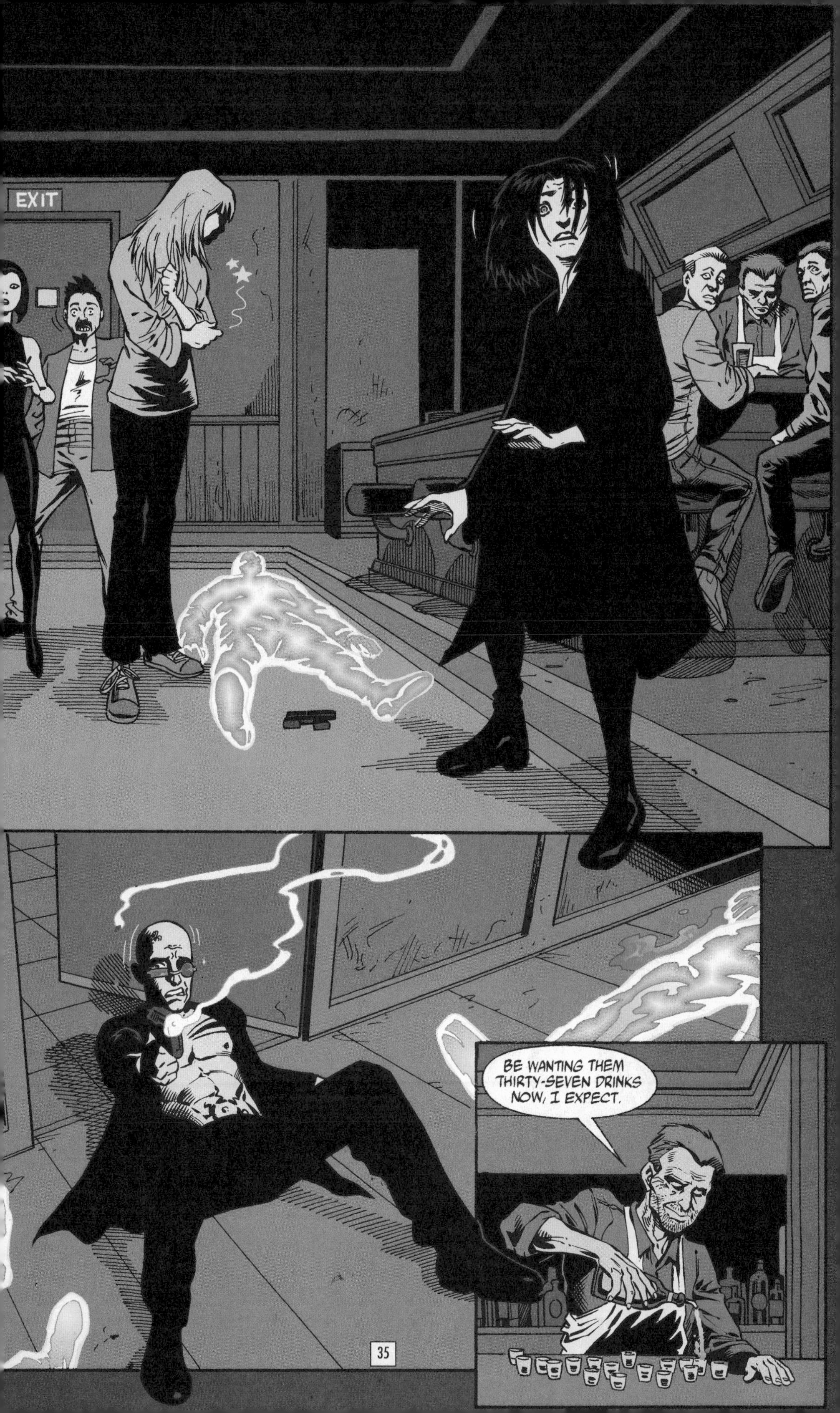
EXIT
BE WANTING THEM THIRTY-SEVEN DRINKS NOW, I EXPECT.

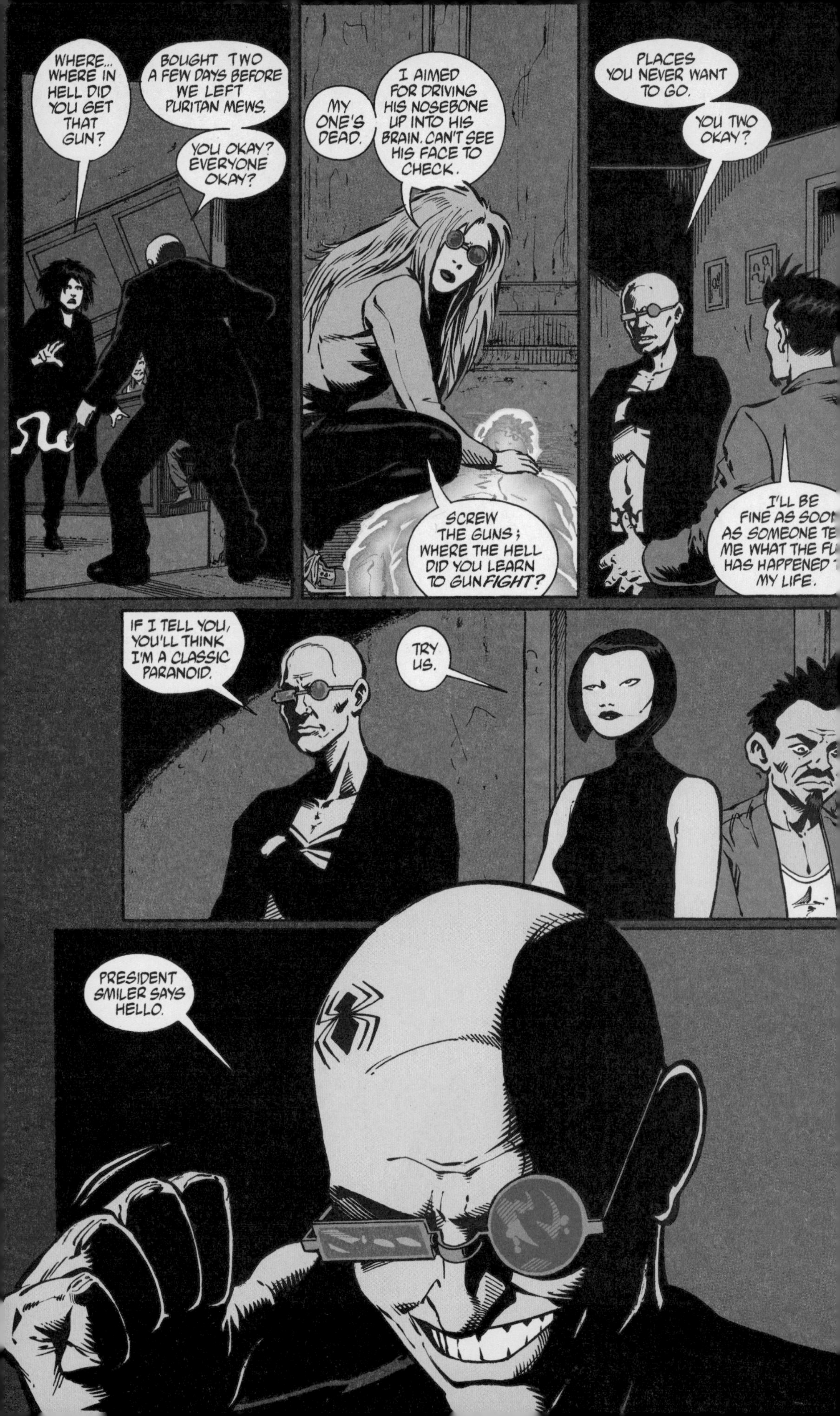
WHERE... WHERE IN HELL DID YOU GET THAT GUN?
BOUGHT TWO A FEW DAYS BEFORE WE LEFT PURITAN MEWS.
YOU OKAY? EVERYONE OKAY?
MY ONE'S DEAD.
I AIMED FOR DRIVING HIS NOSEBONE UP INTO HIS BRAIN. CAN'T SEE HIS FACE TO CHECK.
SCREW THE GUNS; WHERE THE HELL DID YOU LEARN TO GUNFIGHT?
PLACES YOU NEVER WANT TO GO.
YOU TWO OKAY?
I'LL BE FINE AS SOON AS SOMEONE TE ME WHAT THE FU HAS HAPPENED T MY LIFE.
IF I TELL YOU, YOU'LL THINK I'M A CLASSIC PARANOID.
TRY US.
PRESIDENT SMILER SAYS HELLO.

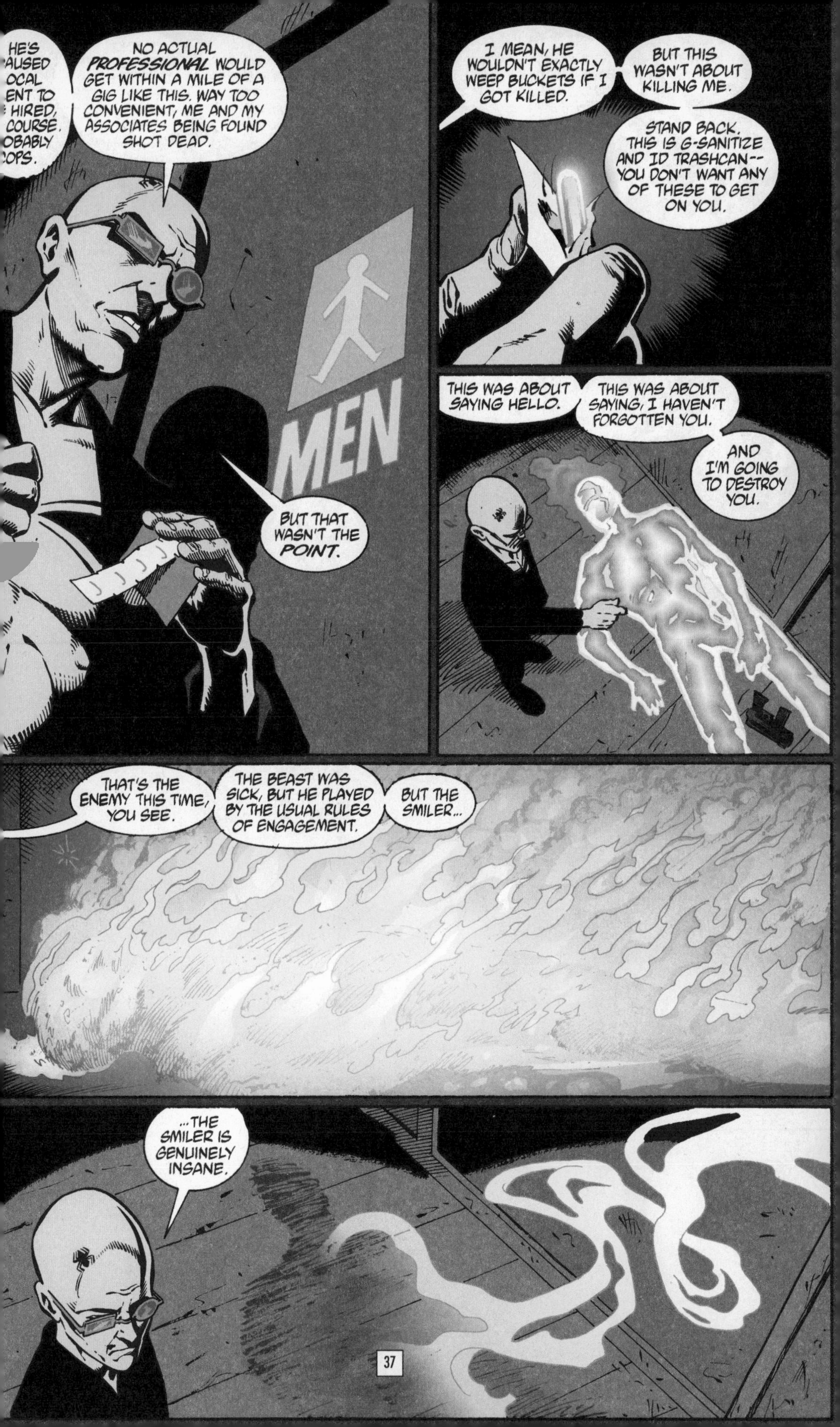

HE'S AUSED OCAL ENT TO HIRED, COURSE. OBABLY COPS.
NO ACTUAL ***PROFESSIONAL*** WOULD GET WITHIN A MILE OF A GIG LIKE THIS. WAY TOO CONVENIENT, ME AND MY ASSOCIATES BEING FOUND SHOT DEAD.
BUT THAT WASN'T THE ***POINT.***
MEN
I MEAN, HE WOULDN'T EXACTLY WEEP BUCKETS IF I GOT KILLED.
BUT THIS WASN'T ABOUT KILLING ME.
STAND BACK. THIS IS G-SANITIZE AND ID TRASHCAN-- YOU DON'T WANT ANY OF THESE TO GET ON YOU.
THIS WAS ABOUT SAYING HELLO.
THIS WAS ABOUT *SAYING,* I HAVEN'T FORGOTTEN YOU.
AND I'M GOING TO DESTROY YOU.
THAT'S THE ENEMY THIS TIME, YOU SEE.
THE BEAST WAS SICK, BUT HE PLAYED BY THE USUAL RULES OF ENGAGEMENT.
BUT THE SMILER...
...THE SMILER IS GENUINELY INSANE.

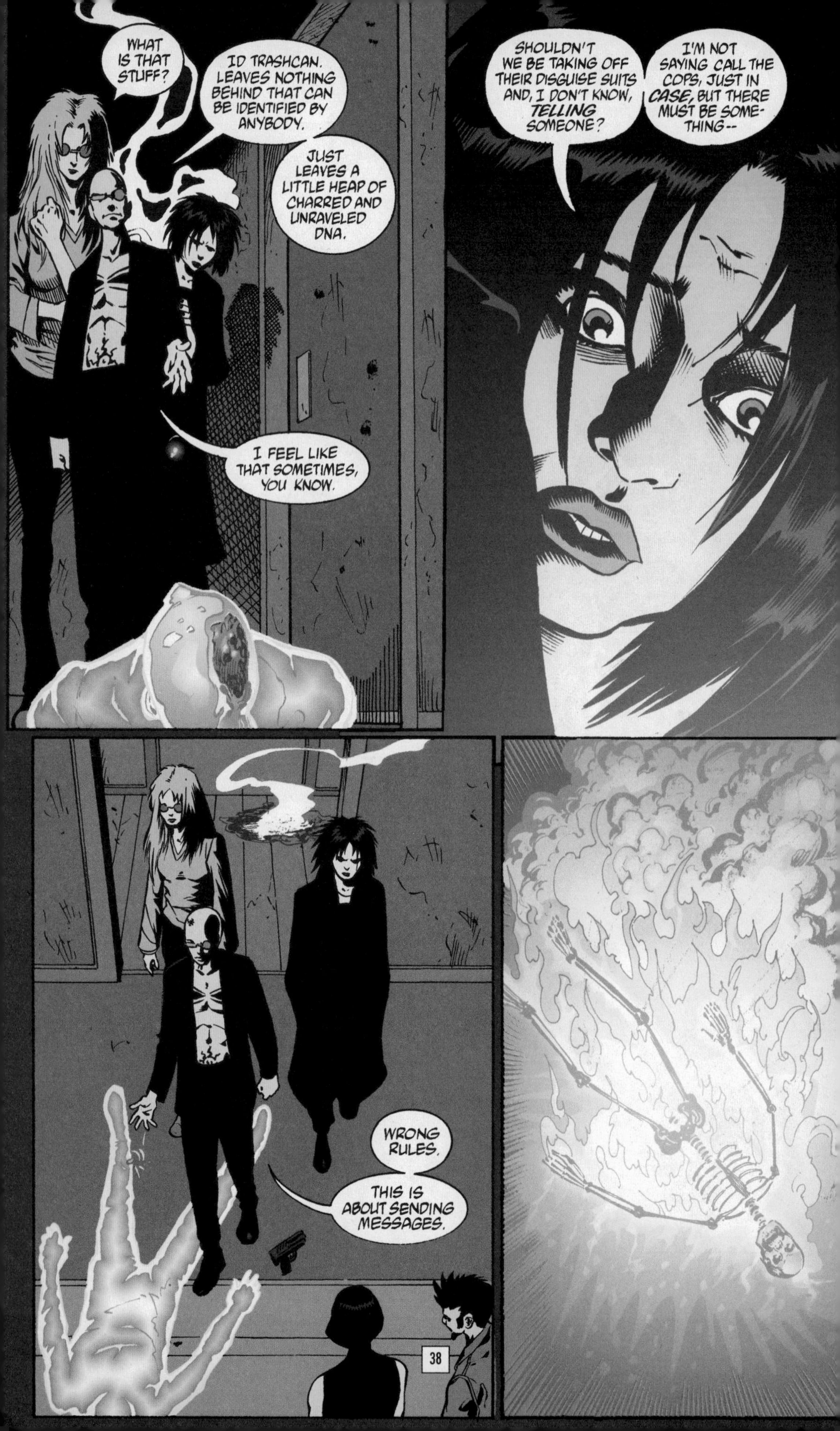
WHAT IS THAT STUFF?
ID TRASHCAN. LEAVES NOTHING BEHIND THAT CAN BE IDENTIFIED BY ANYBODY.
JUST LEAVES A LITTLE HEAP OF CHARRED AND UNRAVELED DNA.
I FEEL LIKE THAT SOMETIMES, YOU KNOW.
SHOULDN'T WE BE TAKING OFF THEIR DISGUISE SUITS AND, I DON'T KNOW, *TELLING* SOMEONE?
I'M NOT SAYING CALL THE COPS, JUST IN *CASE*, BUT THERE MUST BE SOME-THING--
WRONG RULES.
THIS IS ABOUT SENDING MESSAGES.

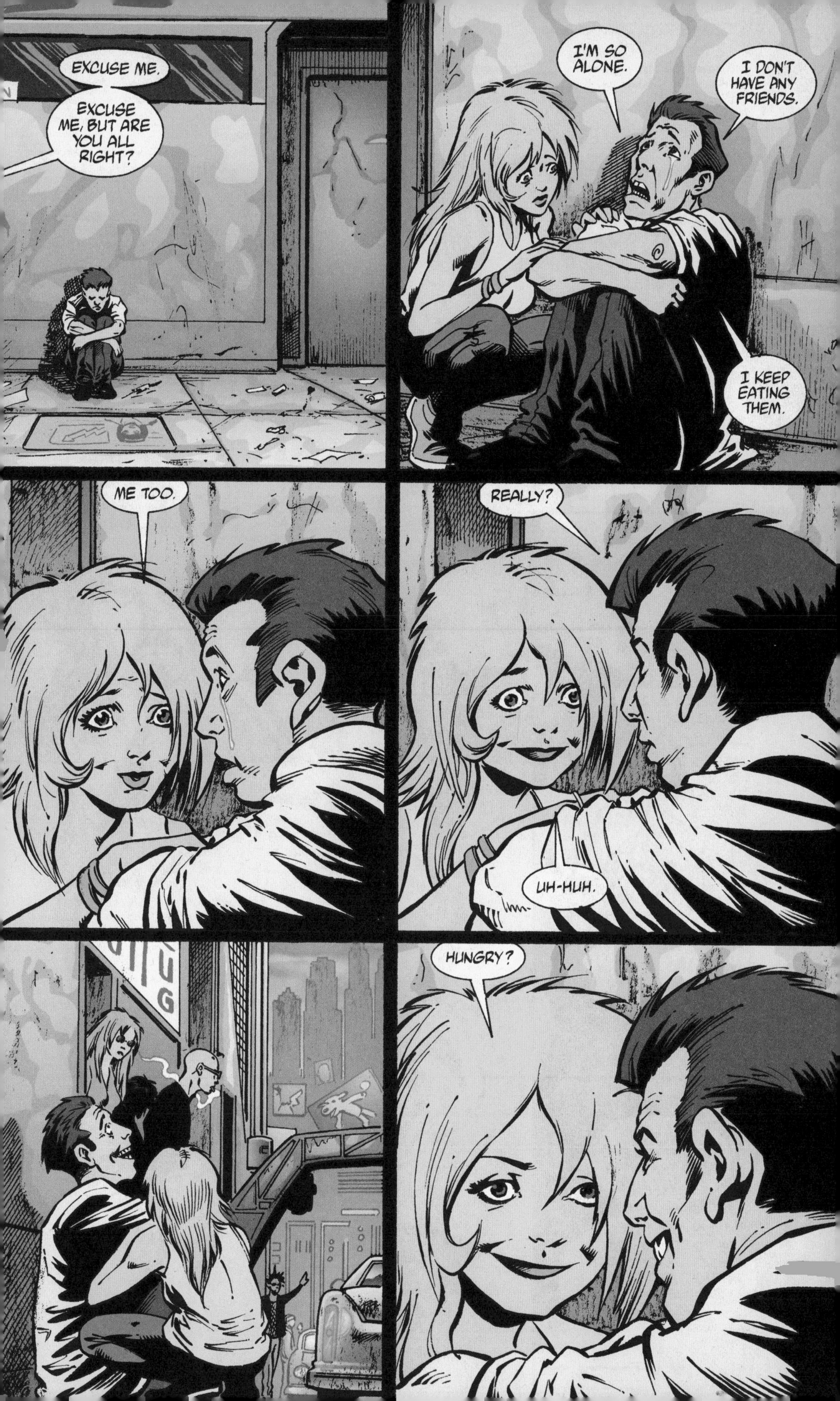
EXCUSE ME.
EXCUSE ME, BUT ARE YOU ALL RIGHT?
I'M SO ALONE.
I DON'T HAVE ANY FRIENDS.
I KEEP EATING THEM.
ME TOO.
REALLY?
UH-HUH.
UG
HUNGRY?

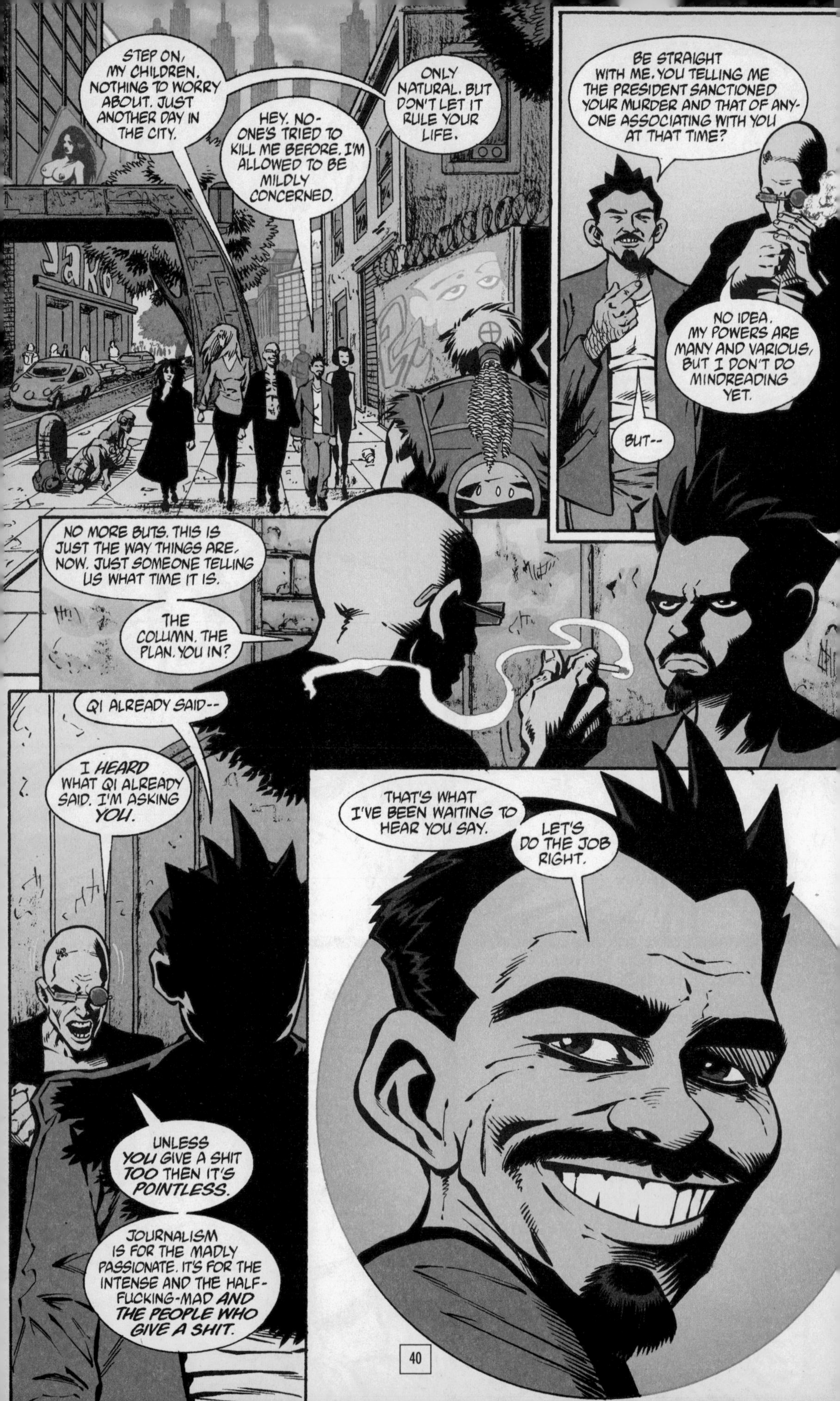
STEP ON, MY CHILDREN. NOTHING TO WORRY ABOUT. JUST ANOTHER DAY IN THE CITY.
HEY. NO-ONE'S TRIED TO KILL ME BEFORE. I'M ALLOWED TO BE MILDLY CONCERNED.
ONLY NATURAL. BUT DON'T LET IT RULE YOUR LIFE.
BE STRAIGHT WITH ME. YOU TELLING ME THE PRESIDENT SANCTIONED YOUR MURDER AND THAT OF ANY-ONE ASSOCIATING WITH YOU AT THAT TIME?
NO IDEA. MY POWERS ARE MANY AND VARIOUS, BUT I DON'T DO MINDREADING YET.
BUT--
NO MORE BUTS. THIS IS JUST THE WAY THINGS ARE, NOW. JUST SOMEONE TELLING US WHAT TIME IT IS.
THE COLUMN. THE PLAN. YOU IN?
QI ALREADY SAID--
I *HEARD* WHAT QI ALREADY SAID. I'M ASKING ***YOU***.
UNLESS ***YOU*** GIVE A SHIT ***TOO*** THEN IT'S ***POINTLESS***.
JOURNALISM IS FOR THE MADLY PASSIONATE. IT'S FOR THE INTENSE AND THE HALF-FUCKING-MAD ***AND THE PEOPLE WHO GIVE A SHIT***.
THAT'S WHAT I'VE BEEN WAITING TO HEAR YOU SAY.
LET'S DO THE JOB RIGHT.

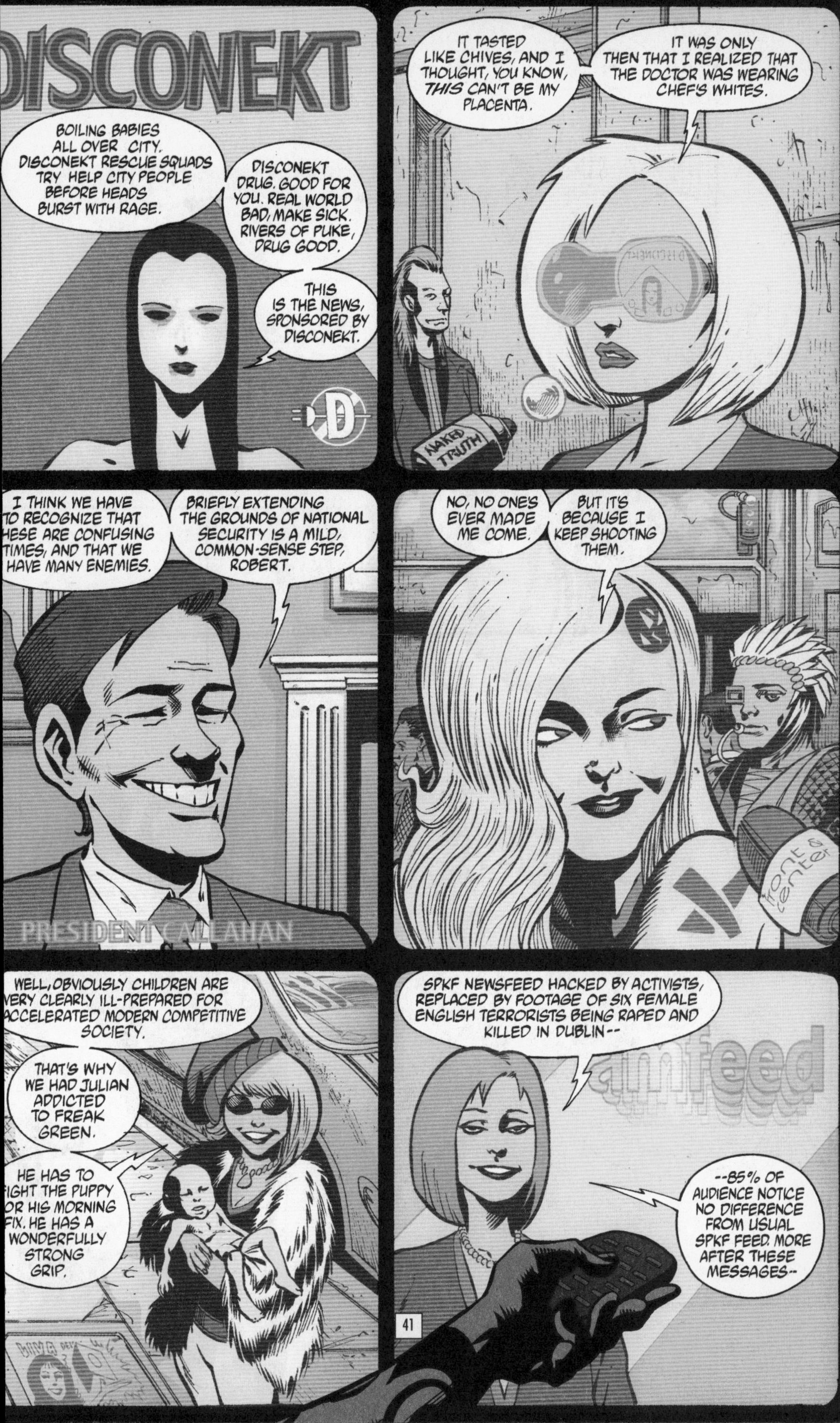
DISCONEKT
BOILING BABIES ALL OVER CITY. DISCONEKT RESCUE SQUADS TRY HELP CITY PEOPLE BEFORE HEADS BURST WITH RAGE.
DISCONEKT DRUG. GOOD FOR YOU. REAL WORLD BAD, MAKE SICK. RIVERS OF PUKE, DRUG GOOD.
THIS IS THE NEWS, SPONSORED BY DISCONEKT.
IT TASTED LIKE CHIVES, AND I THOUGHT, YOU KNOW, THIS CAN'T BE MY PLACENTA.
IT WAS ONLY THEN THAT I REALIZED THAT THE DOCTOR WAS WEARING CHEF'S WHITES.
NAKED TRUTH
I THINK WE HAVE TO RECOGNIZE THAT THESE ARE CONFUSING TIMES, AND THAT WE HAVE MANY ENEMIES.
BRIEFLY EXTENDING THE GROUNDS OF NATIONAL SECURITY IS A MILD, COMMON-SENSE STEP, ROBERT.
PRESIDENT CALLAHAN
NO, NO ONE'S EVER MADE ME COME.
BUT IT'S BECAUSE I KEEP SHOOTING THEM.
front & center
WELL, OBVIOUSLY CHILDREN ARE VERY CLEARLY ILL-PREPARED FOR ACCELERATED MODERN COMPETITIVE SOCIETY.
THAT'S WHY WE HAD JULIAN ADDICTED TO FREAK GREEN.
HE HAS TO FIGHT THE PUPPY FOR HIS MORNING FIX. HE HAS A WONDERFULLY STRONG GRIP.
SPKF NEWSFEED HACKED BY ACTIVISTS, REPLACED BY FOOTAGE OF SIX FEMALE ENGLISH TERRORISTS BEING RAPED AND KILLED IN DUBLIN--
--85% OF AUDIENCE NOTICE NO DIFFERENCE FROM USUAL SPKF FEED. MORE AFTER THESE MESSAGES--

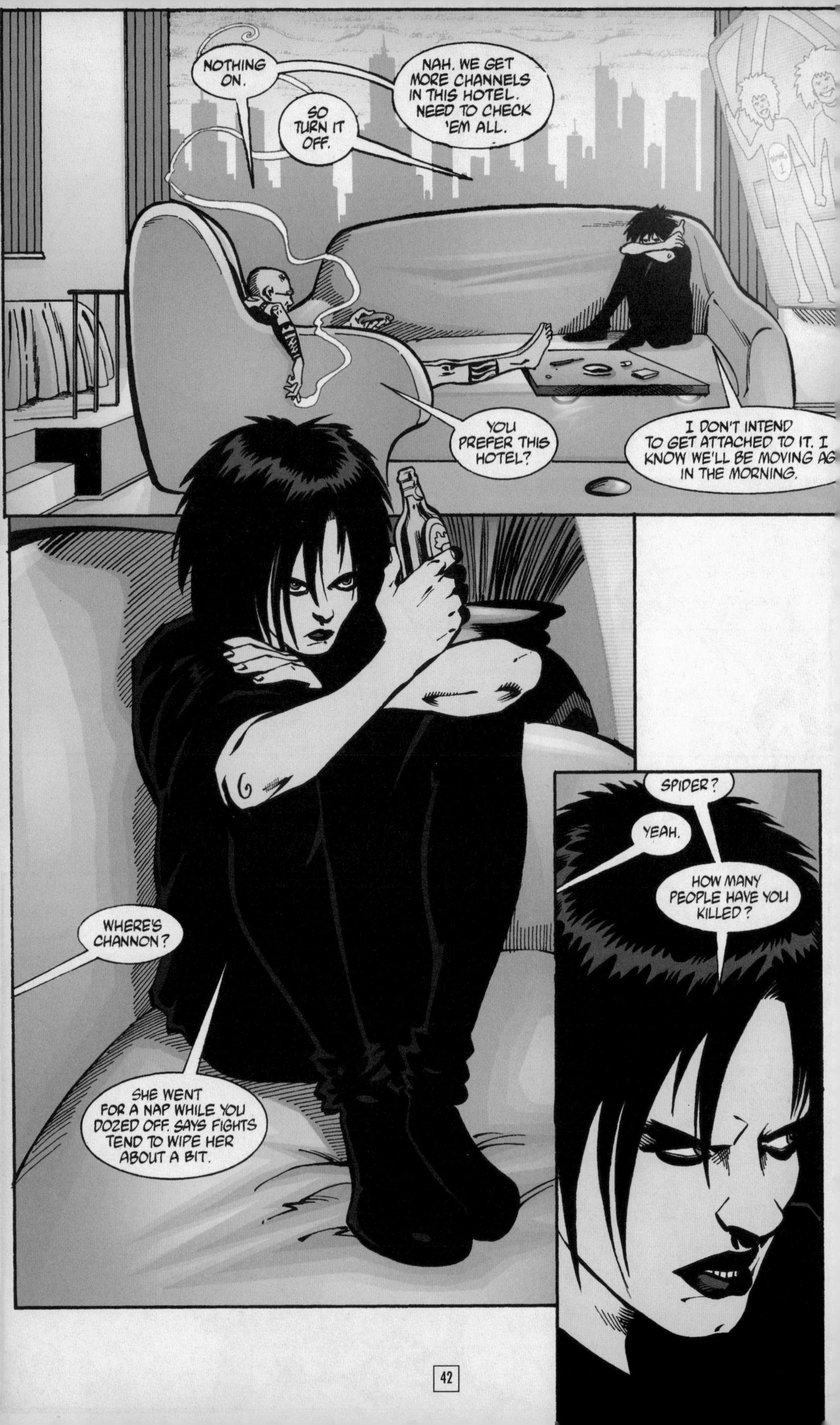
NOTHING ON.
SO TURN IT OFF.
NAH. WE GET MORE CHANNELS IN THIS HOTEL. NEED TO CHECK 'EM ALL.
YOU PREFER THIS HOTEL?
I DON'T INTEND TO GET ATTACHED TO IT. I KNOW WE'LL BE MOVING AG
IN THE MORNING.
WHERE'S CHANNON?
SHE WENT FOR A NAP WHILE YOU DOZED OFF. SAYS FIGHTS TEND TO WIPE HER ABOUT A BIT.
SPIDER?
YEAH.
HOW MANY PEOPLE HAVE YOU KILLED?

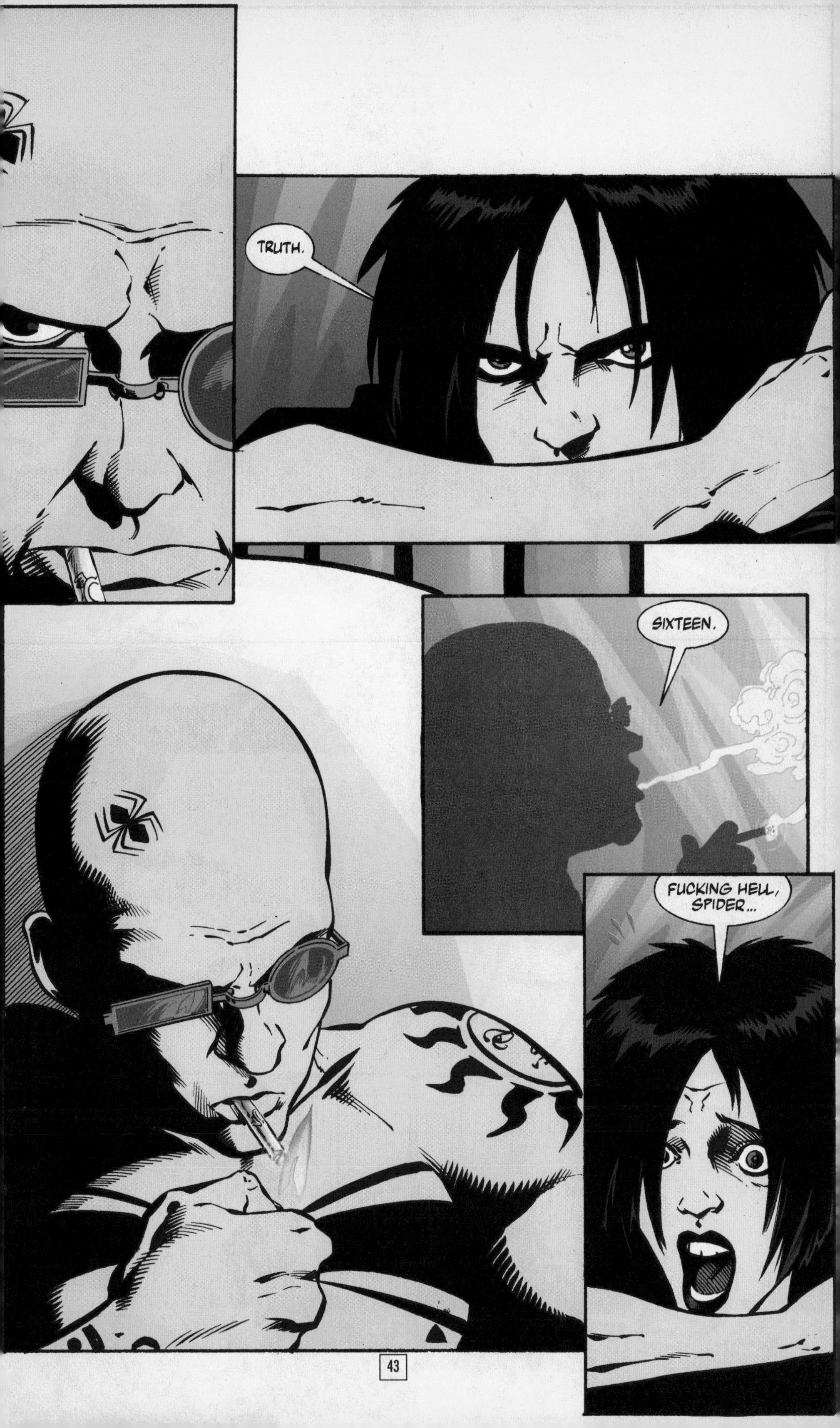
TRUTH.
SIXTEEN.
FUCKING HELL, SPIDER...

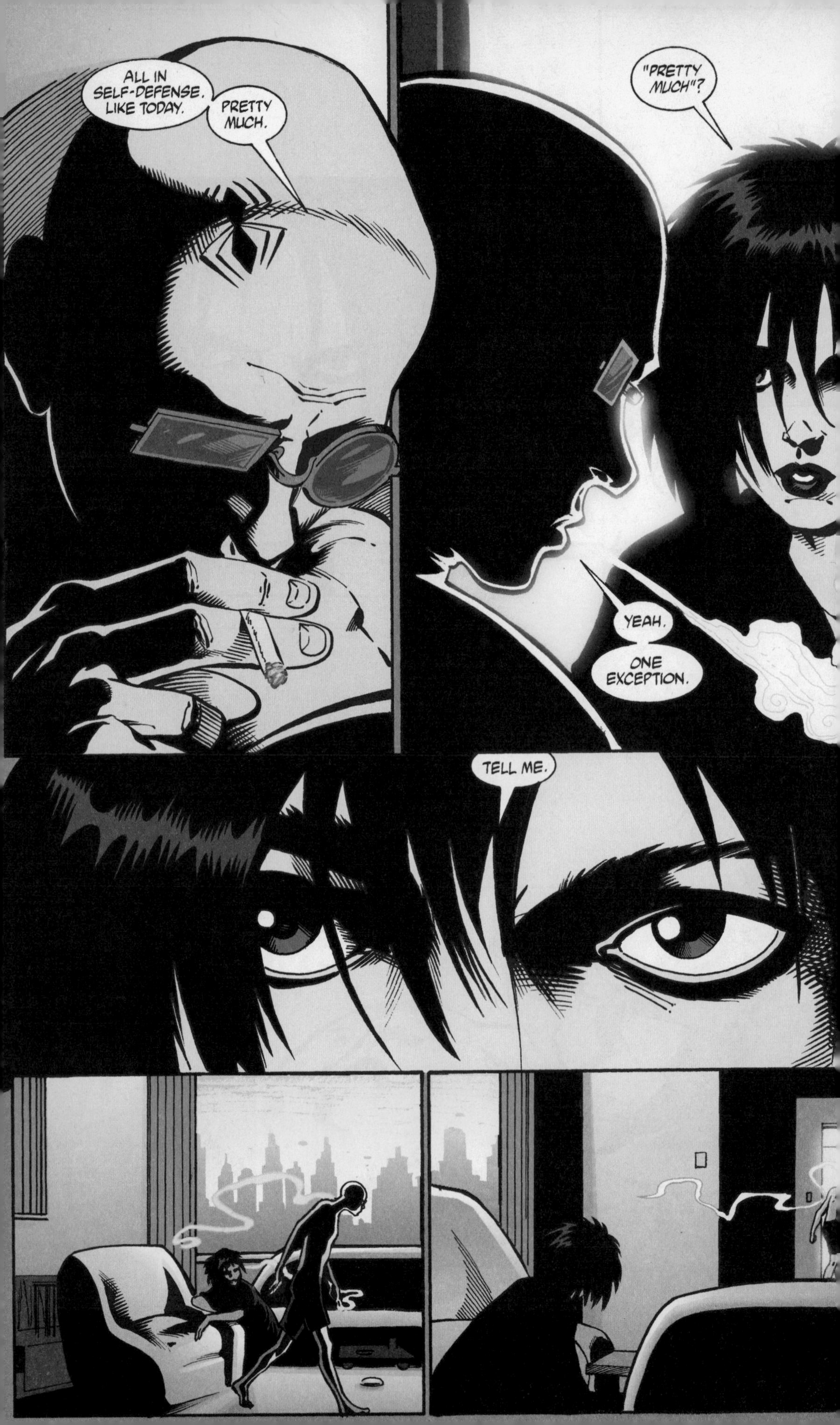
ALL IN SELF-DEFENSE. LIKE TODAY.
PRETTY MUCH.
"PRETTY MUCH"?
YEAH.
ONE EXCEPTION.
TELL ME.

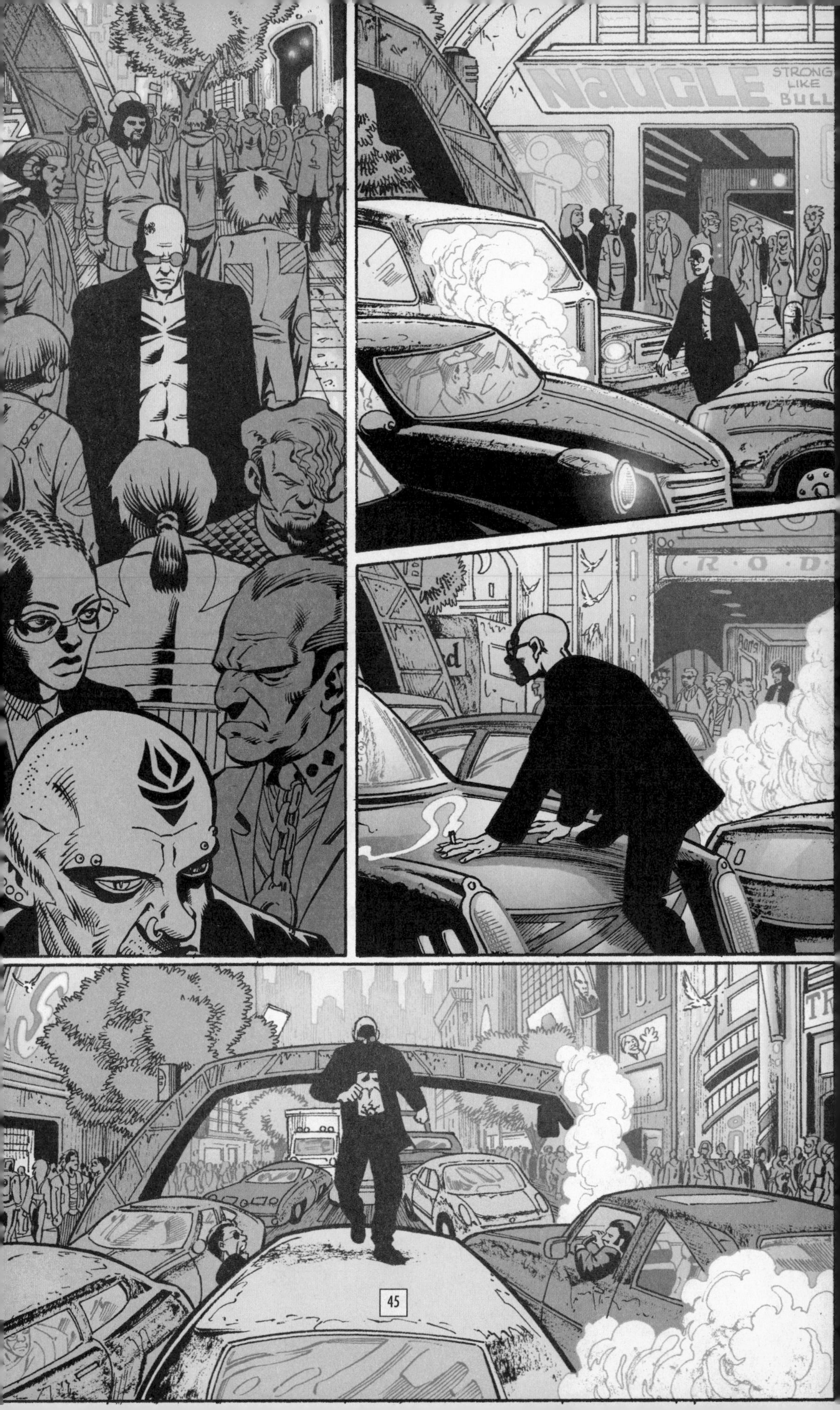
NAUGLE
STRONG LIKE BULL
R O D

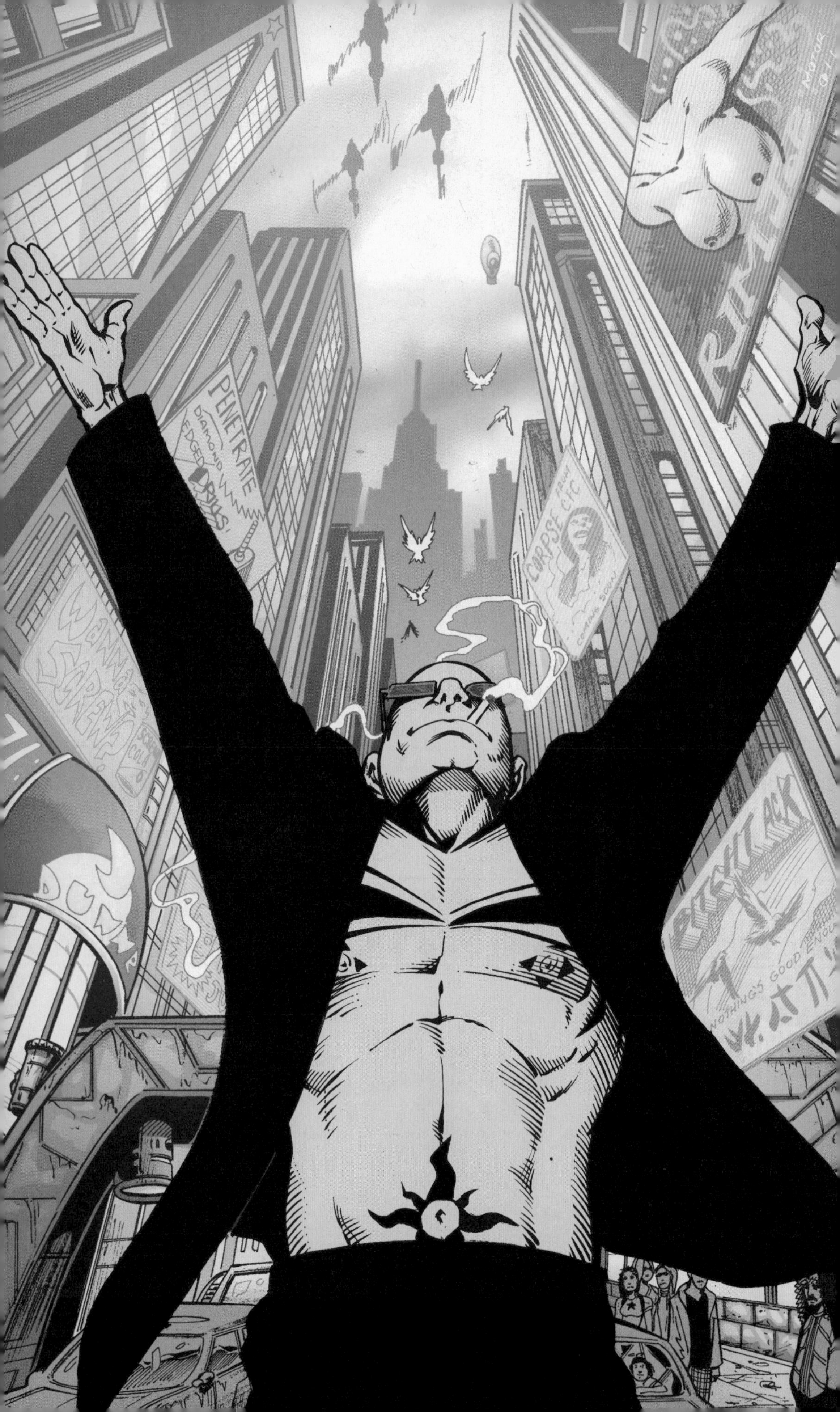
PENETRATE
DIAMOND
EDGED
CORPSE
FROM CFC
COMING SOON

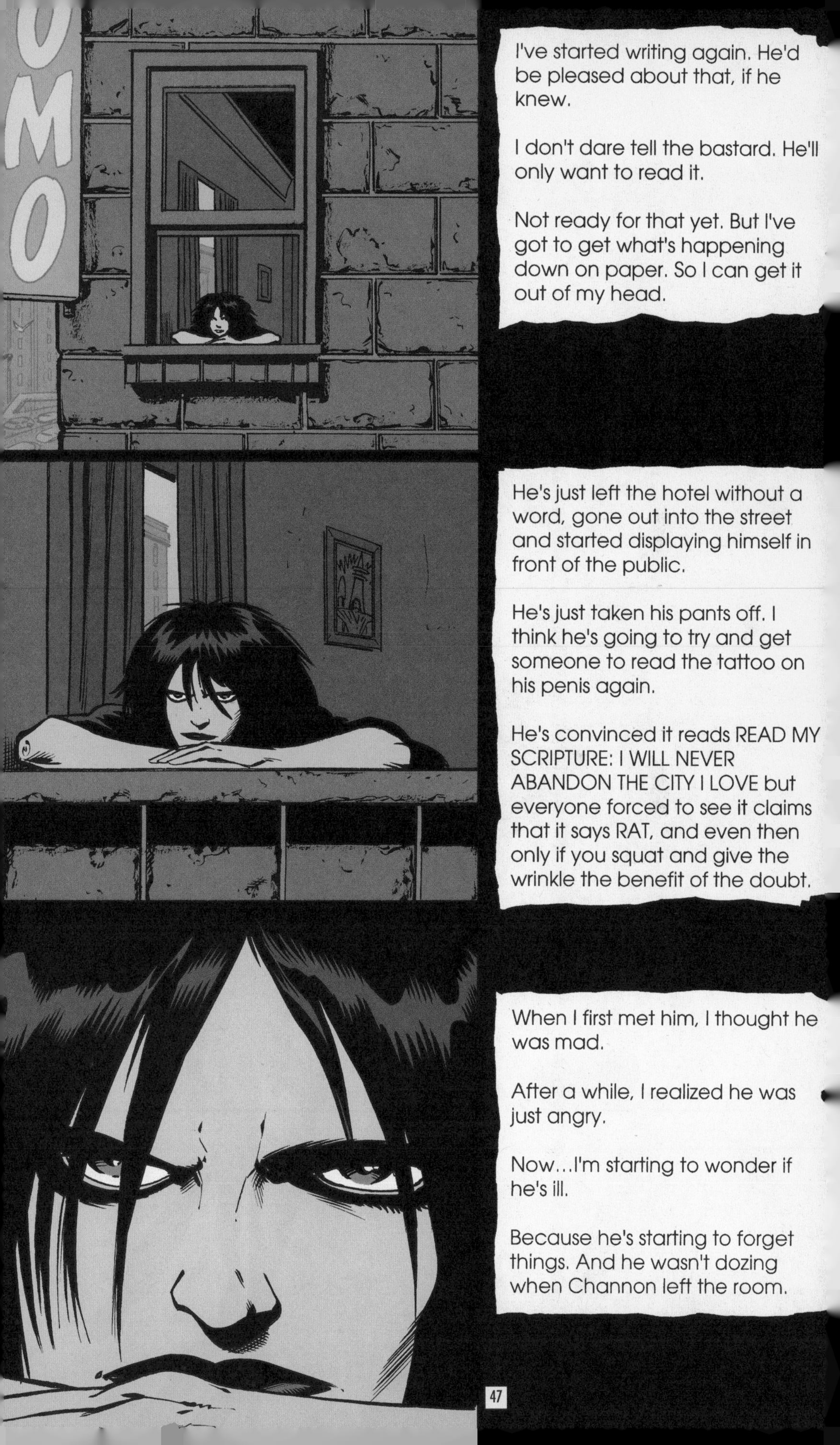
OMO
I've started writing again. He'd be pleased about that, if he knew.
I don't dare tell the bastard. He'll only want to read it.
Not ready for that yet. But I've got to get what's happening down on paper. So I can get it out of my head.
He's just left the hotel without a word, gone out into the street and started displaying himself in front of the public.
He's just taken his pants off. I think he's going to try and get someone to read the tattoo on his penis again.
He's convinced it reads READ MY SCRIPTURE: I WILL NEVER ABANDON THE CITY I LOVE but everyone forced to see it claims that it says RAT, and even then only if you squat and give the wrinkle the benefit of the doubt.
When I first met him, I thought he was mad.
After a while, I realized he was just angry.
Now...I'm starting to wonder if he's ill.
Because he's starting to forget things. And he wasn't dozing when Channon left the room.

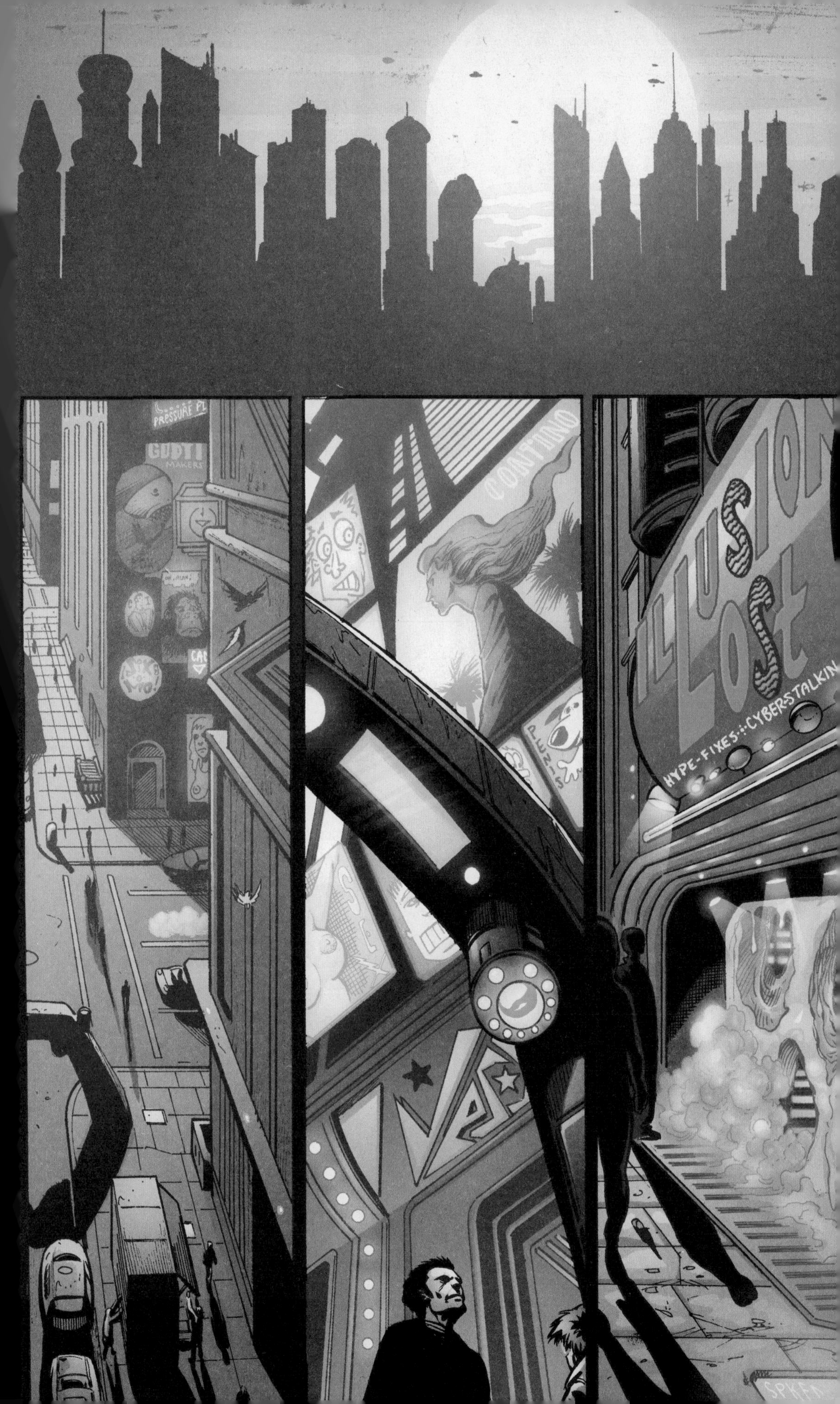
PRESSURE PL
ILLUSION Lost
HYPE-FIXES-:-CYBERSTALKIN

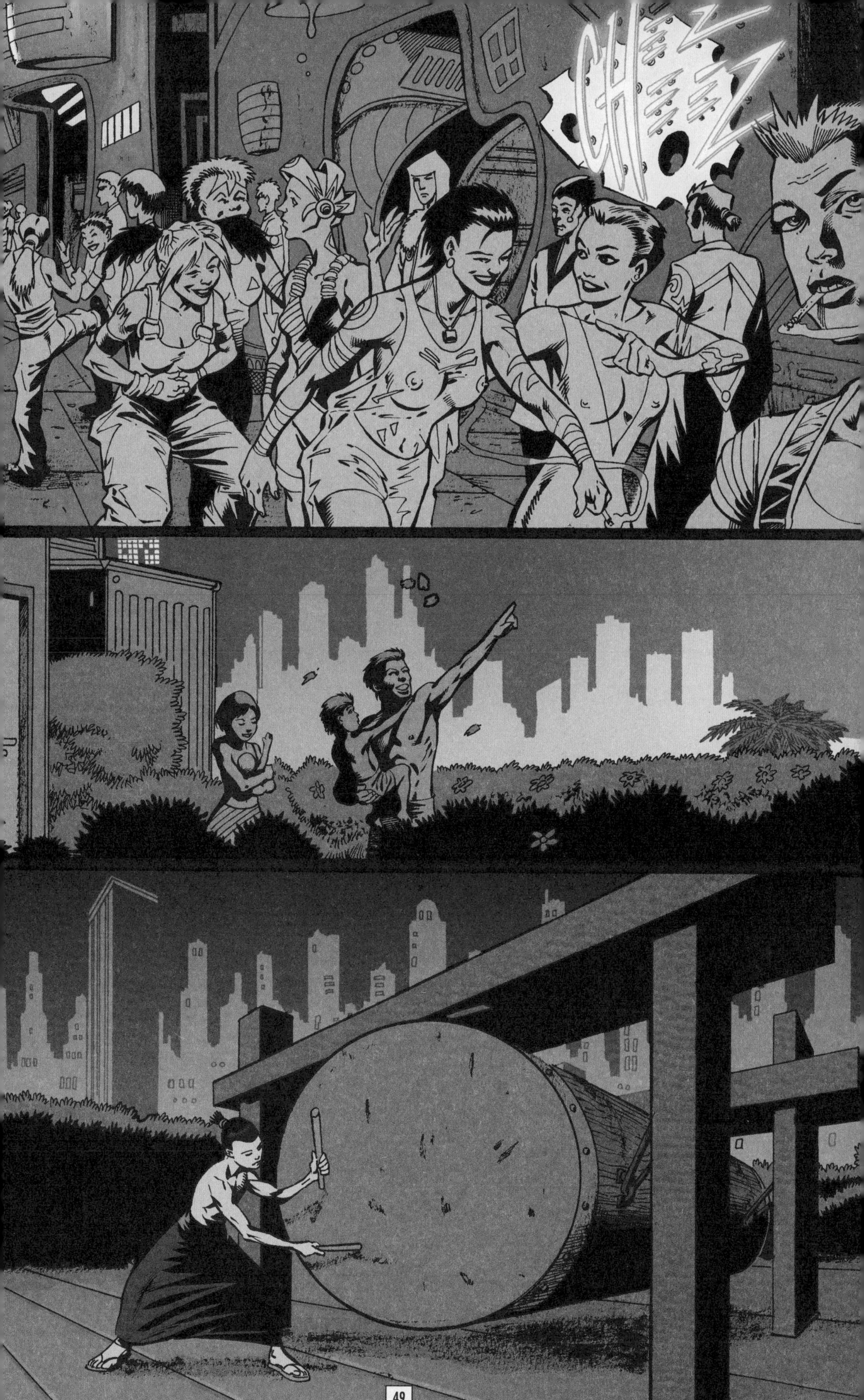
CHEEZZ

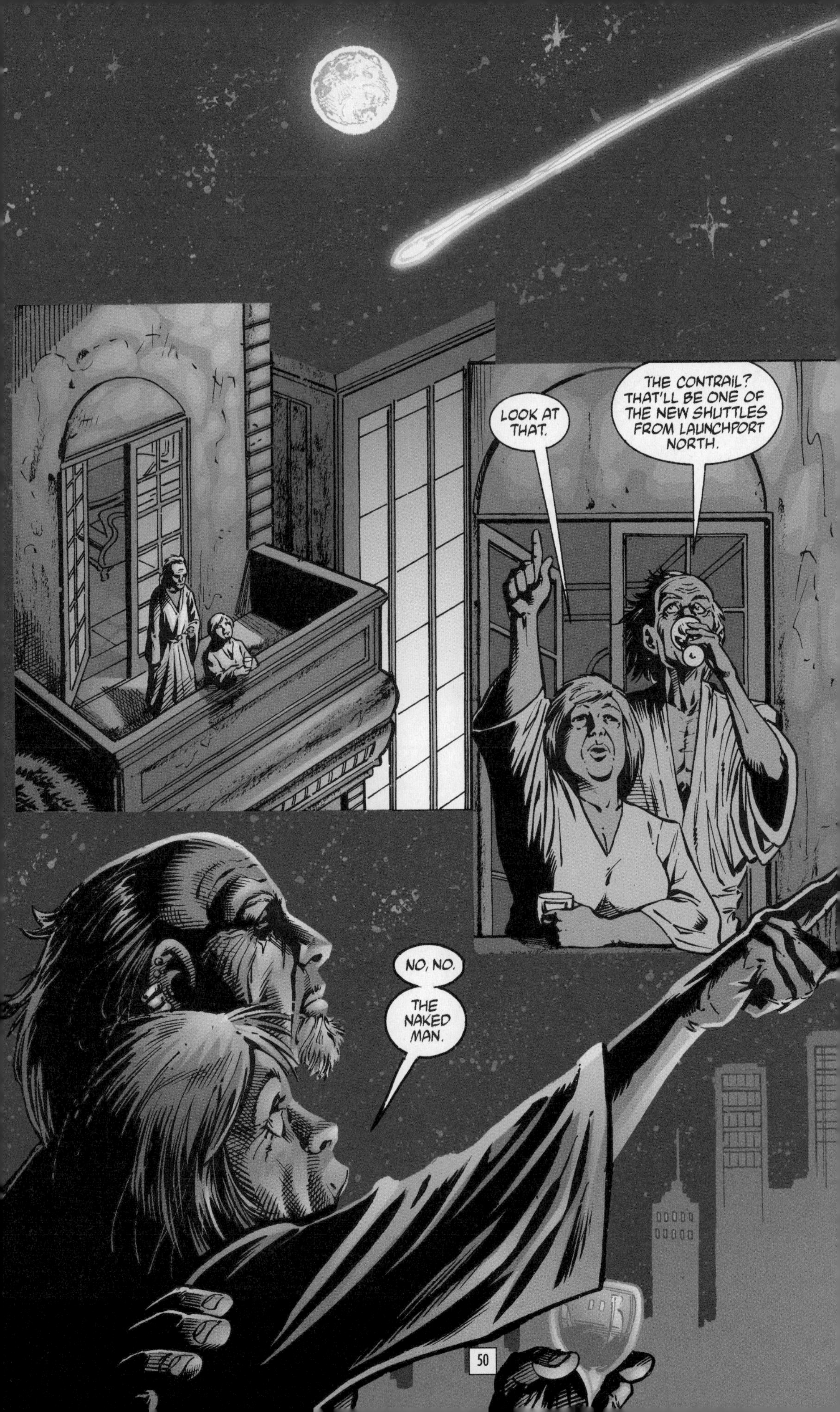
LOOK AT THAT.
THE CONTRAIL? THAT'LL BE ONE OF THE NEW SHUTTLES FROM LAUNCHPORT NORTH.
NO, NO.
THE NAKED MAN.

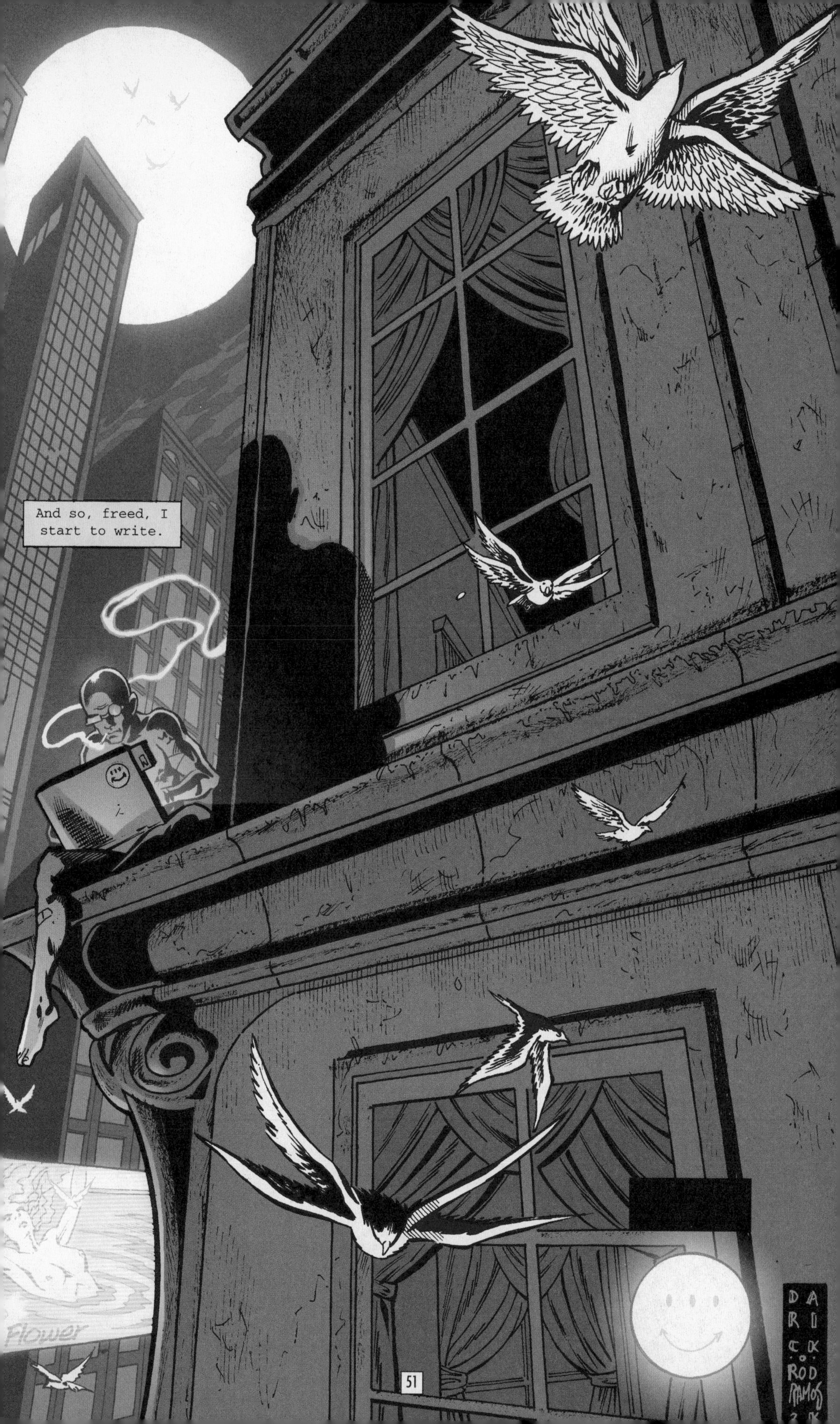
And so, freed, I start to write.
Flower
DARICK
ROD RAMOS 2K

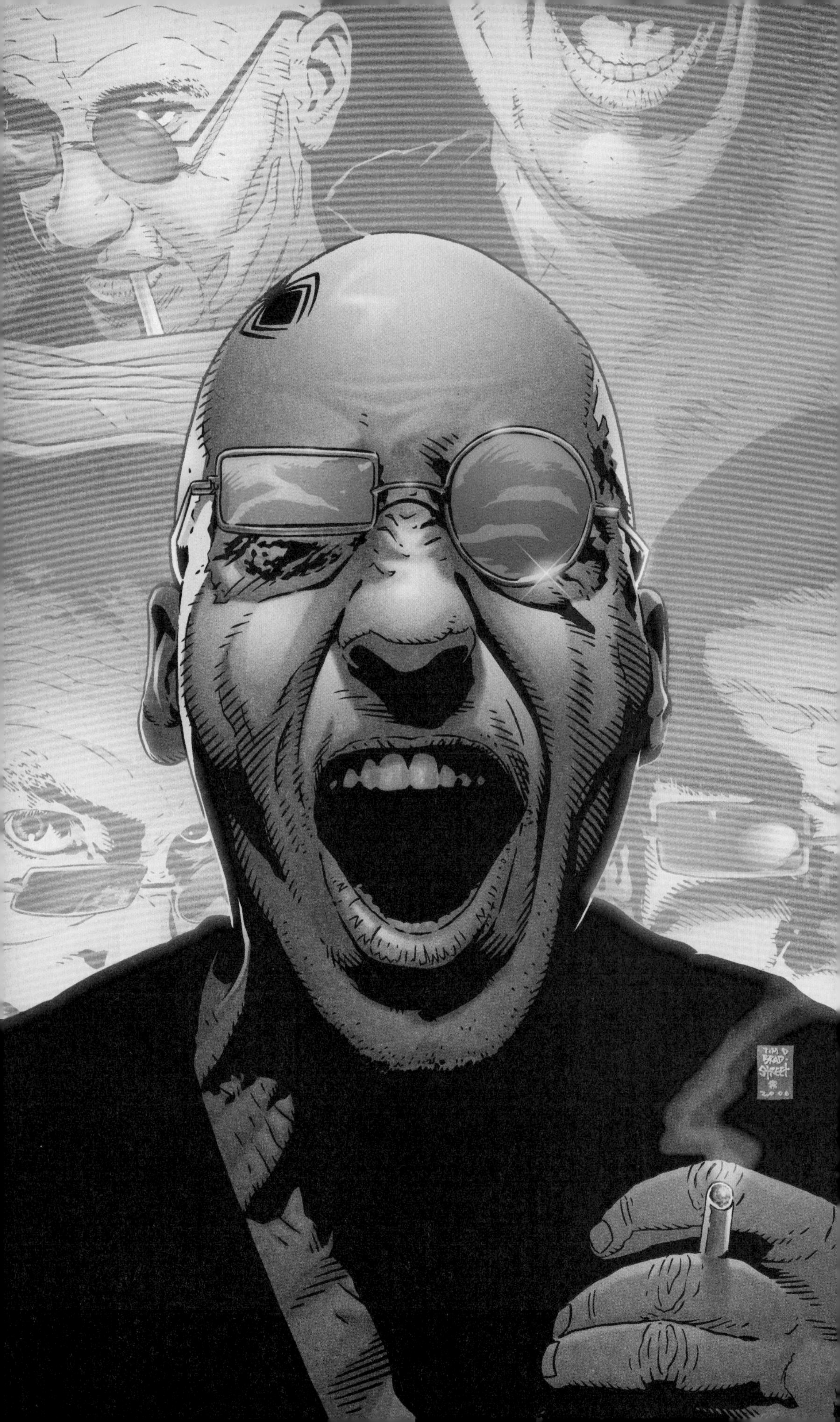
TIM BRAD-STREET
2000

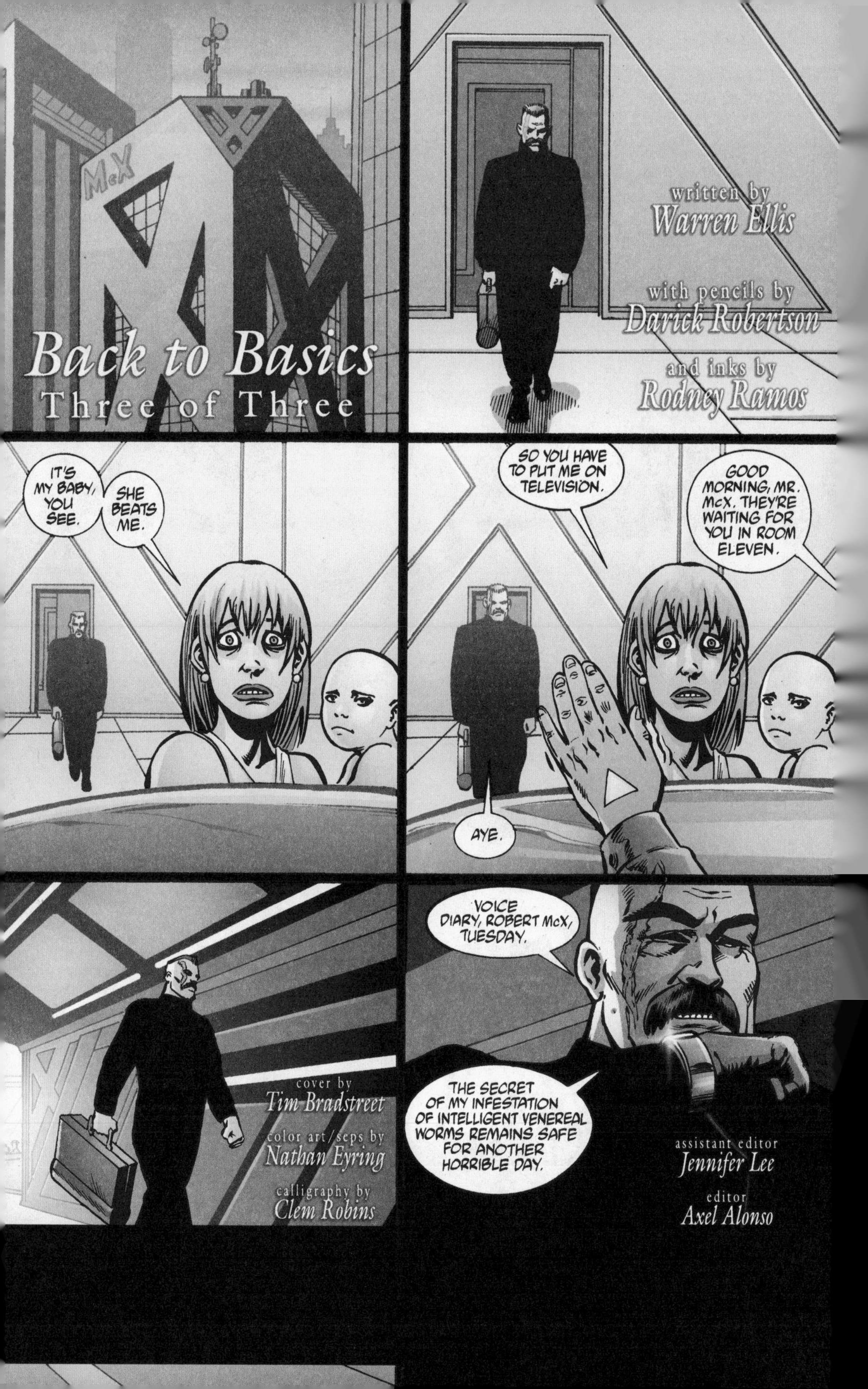
McX
Back to Basics
Three of Three
written by
Warren Ellis
with pencils by
Darick Robertson
and inks by
Rodney Ramos
IT'S MY BABY, YOU SEE.
SHE BEATS ME.
SO YOU HAVE TO PUT ME ON TELEVISION.
GOOD MORNING, MR. McX. THEY'RE WAITING FOR YOU IN ROOM ELEVEN.
AYE.
cover by
Tim Bradstreet
color art/seps by
Nathan Eyring
calligraphy by
Clem Robins
VOICE DIARY, ROBERT McX, TUESDAY.
THE SECRET OF MY INFESTATION OF INTELLIGENT VENEREAL WORMS REMAINS SAFE FOR ANOTHER HORRIBLE DAY.
assistant editor
Jennifer Lee
editor
Axel Alonso

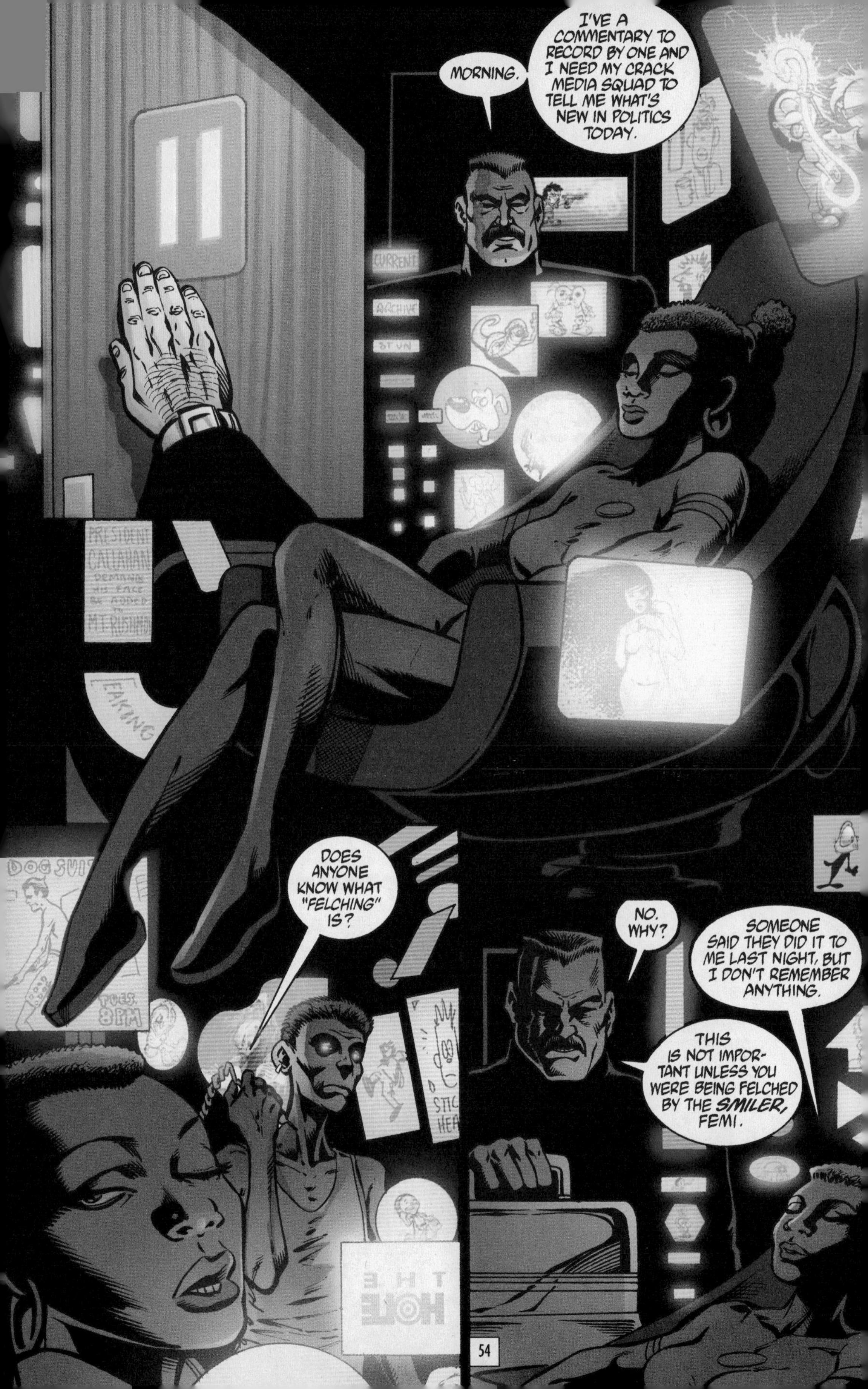
MORNING.
I'VE A COMMENTARY TO RECORD BY ONE AND I NEED MY CRACK MEDIA SQUAD TO TELL ME WHAT'S NEW IN POLITICS TODAY.
CURRENT
ARCHIVE
PRESIDENT CALLAHAN
DOES ANYONE KNOW WHAT "FELCHING" IS?
NO. WHY?
SOMEONE SAID THEY DID IT TO ME LAST NIGHT, BUT I DON'T REMEMBER ANYTHING.
THIS IS NOT IMPORTANT UNLESS YOU WERE BEING FELCHED BY THE *SMILER,* FEMI.
TUES. 8PM

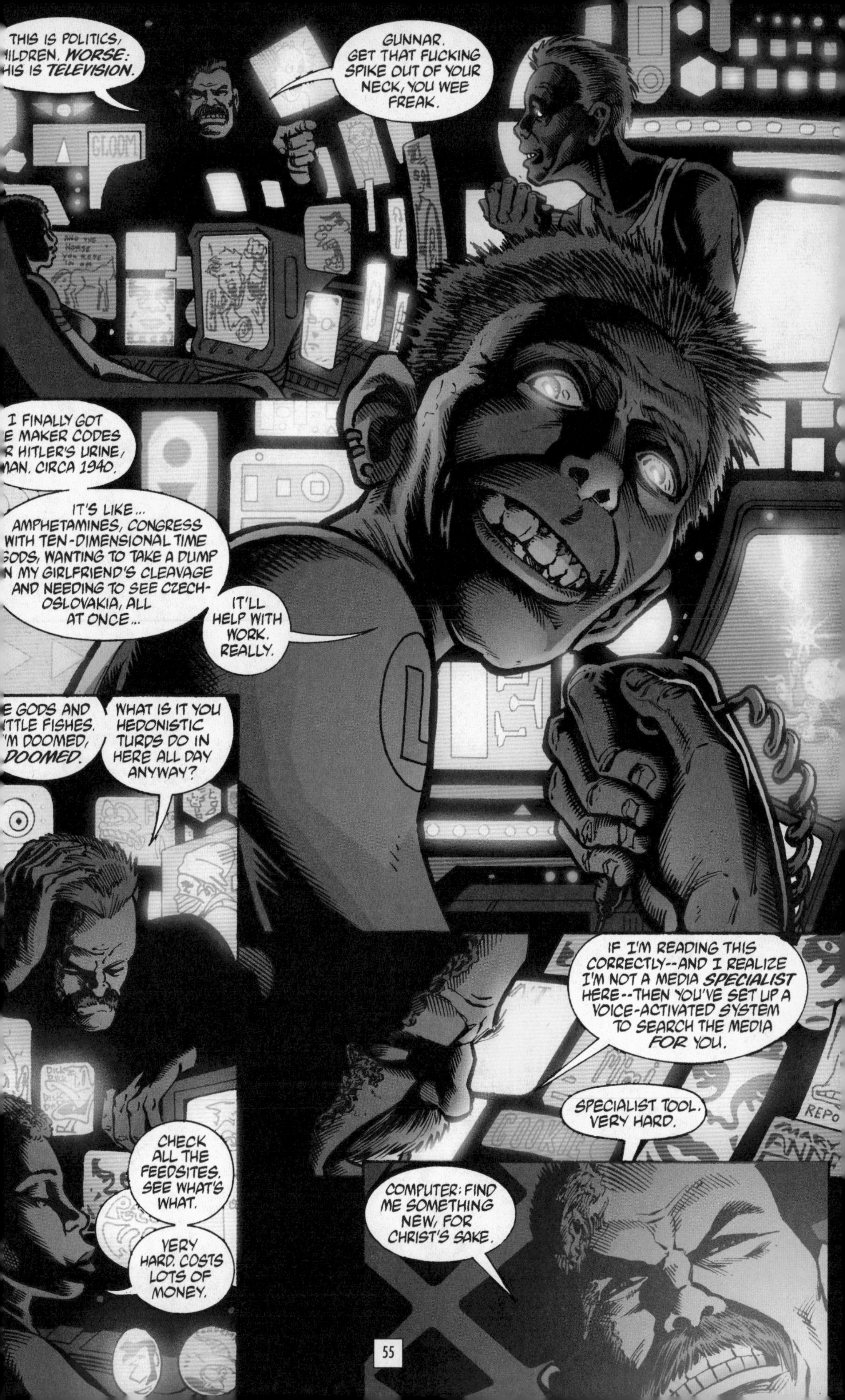
THIS IS POLITICS, ILDREN. WORSE: HIS IS TELEVISION.
GUNNAR. GET THAT FUCKING SPIKE OUT OF YOUR NECK, YOU WEE FREAK.
I FINALLY GOT E MAKER CODES R HITLER'S URINE, MAN. CIRCA 1940.
IT'S LIKE... AMPHETAMINES, CONGRESS WITH TEN-DIMENSIONAL TIME GODS, WANTING TO TAKE A DUMP N MY GIRLFRIEND'S CLEAVAGE AND NEEDING TO SEE CZECH-OSLOVAKIA, ALL AT ONCE...
IT'LL HELP WITH WORK. REALLY.
E GODS AND ITTLE FISHES. 'M DOOMED, DOOMED.
WHAT IS IT YOU HEDONISTIC TURDS DO IN HERE ALL DAY ANYWAY?
IF I'M READING THIS CORRECTLY--AND I REALIZE I'M NOT A MEDIA SPECIALIST HERE--THEN YOU'VE SET UP A VOICE-ACTIVATED SYSTEM TO SEARCH THE MEDIA FOR YOU.
SPECIALIST TOOL. VERY HARD.
CHECK ALL THE FEEDSITES. SEE WHAT'S WHAT.
VERY HARD. COSTS LOTS OF MONEY.
COMPUTER: FIND ME SOMETHING NEW, FOR CHRIST'S SAKE.

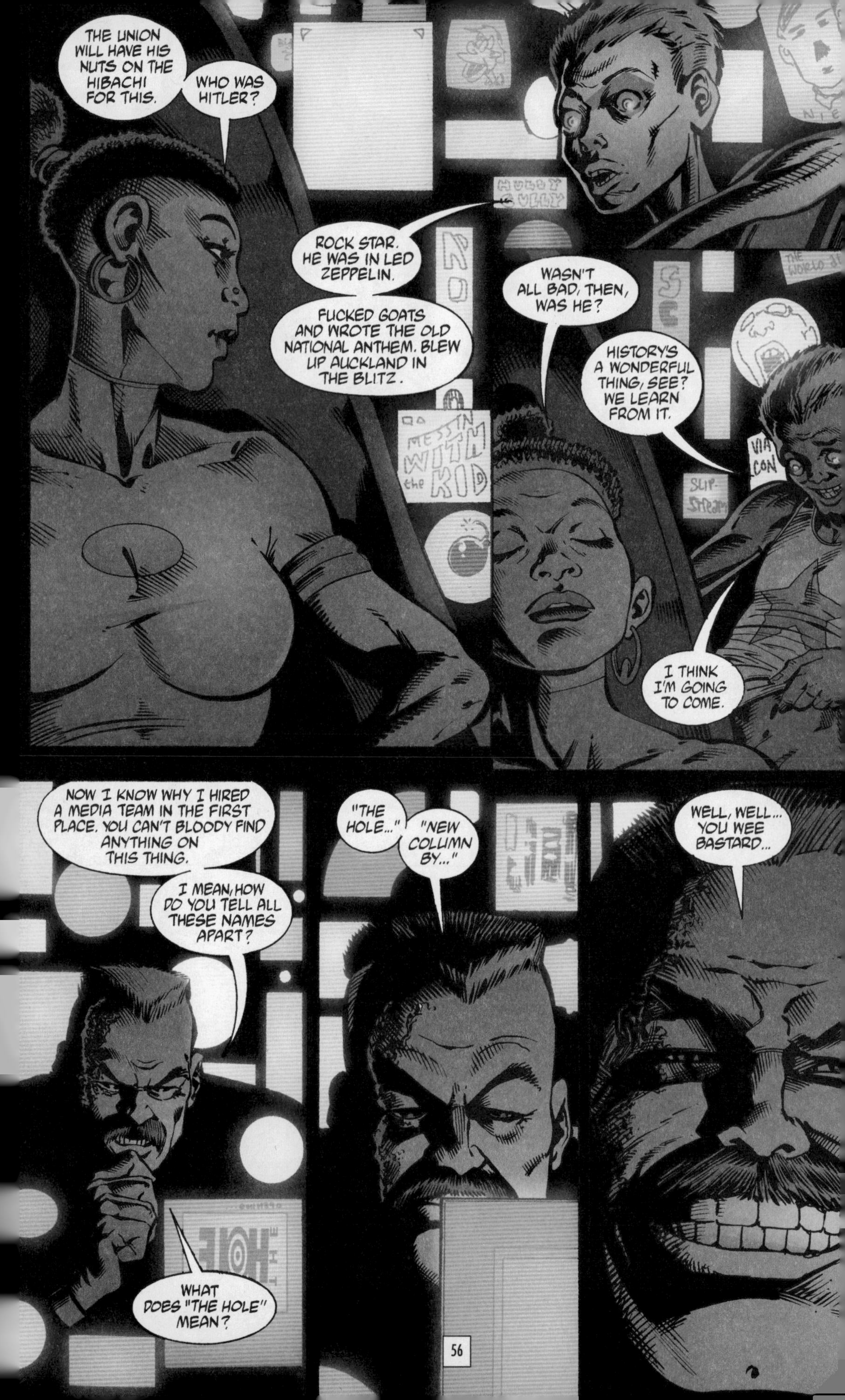
THE UNION WILL HAVE HIS NUTS ON THE HIBACHI FOR THIS.
WHO WAS HITLER?
ROCK STAR. HE WAS IN LED ZEPPELIN.
FUCKED GOATS AND WROTE THE OLD NATIONAL ANTHEM. BLEW UP AUCKLAND IN THE BLITZ.
WASN'T ALL BAD, THEN, WAS HE?
HISTORY'S A WONDERFUL THING, SEE? WE LEARN FROM IT.
I THINK I'M GOING TO COME.
MESSIN WITH the KID
SLIP-STREAM
NOW I KNOW WHY I HIRED A MEDIA TEAM IN THE FIRST PLACE. YOU CAN'T BLOODY FIND ANYTHING ON THIS THING.
I MEAN, HOW DO YOU TELL ALL THESE NAMES APART?
WHAT DOES "THE HOLE" MEAN?
"THE HOLE..."
"NEW COLUMN BY..."
WELL, WELL... YOU WEE BASTARD...

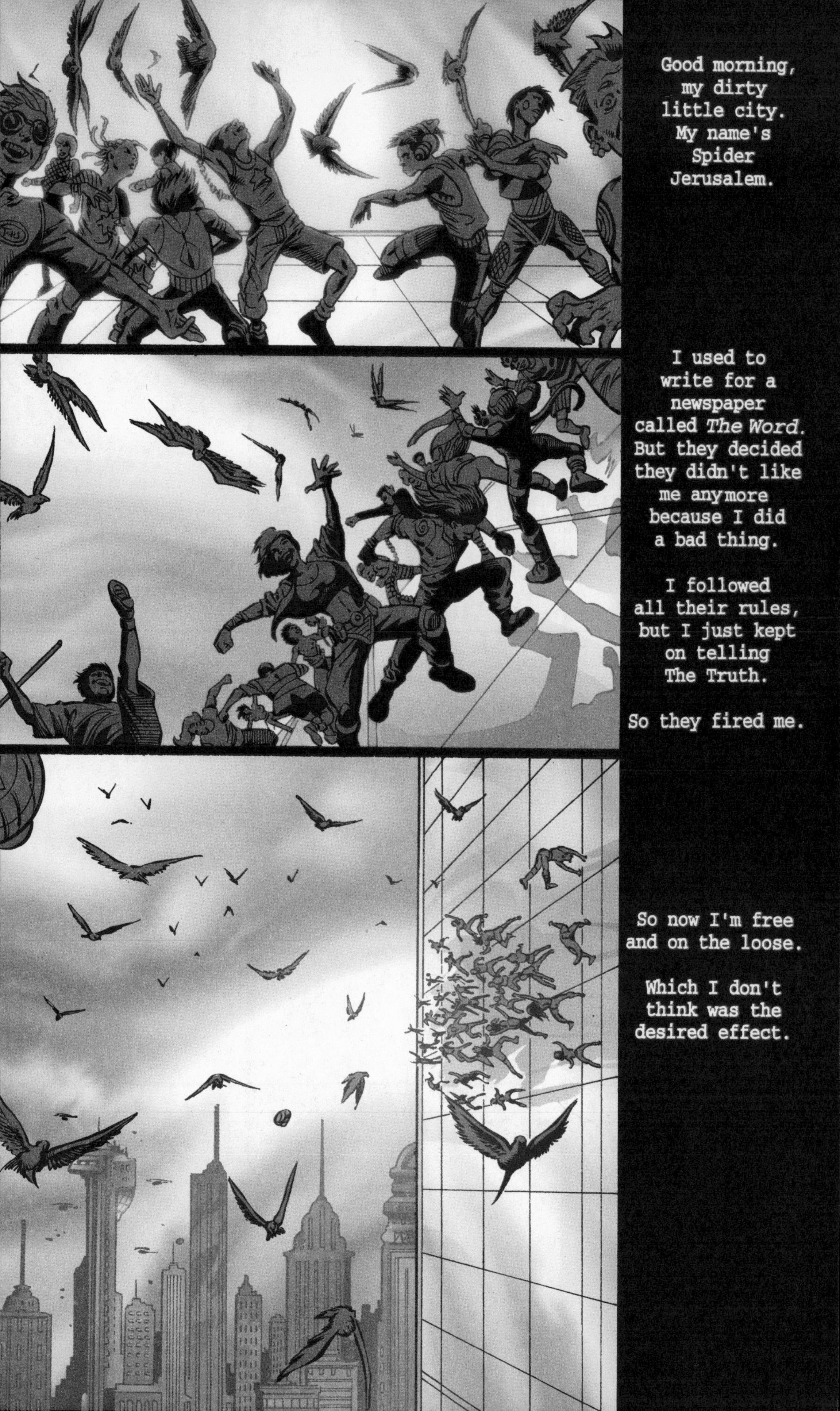
Good morning, my dirty little city. My name's Spider Jerusalem.
I used to write for a newspaper called *The Word*. But they decided they didn't like me anymore because I did a bad thing.
I followed all their rules, but I just kept on telling The Truth.
So they fired me.
So now I'm free and on the loose.
Which I don't think was the desired effect.

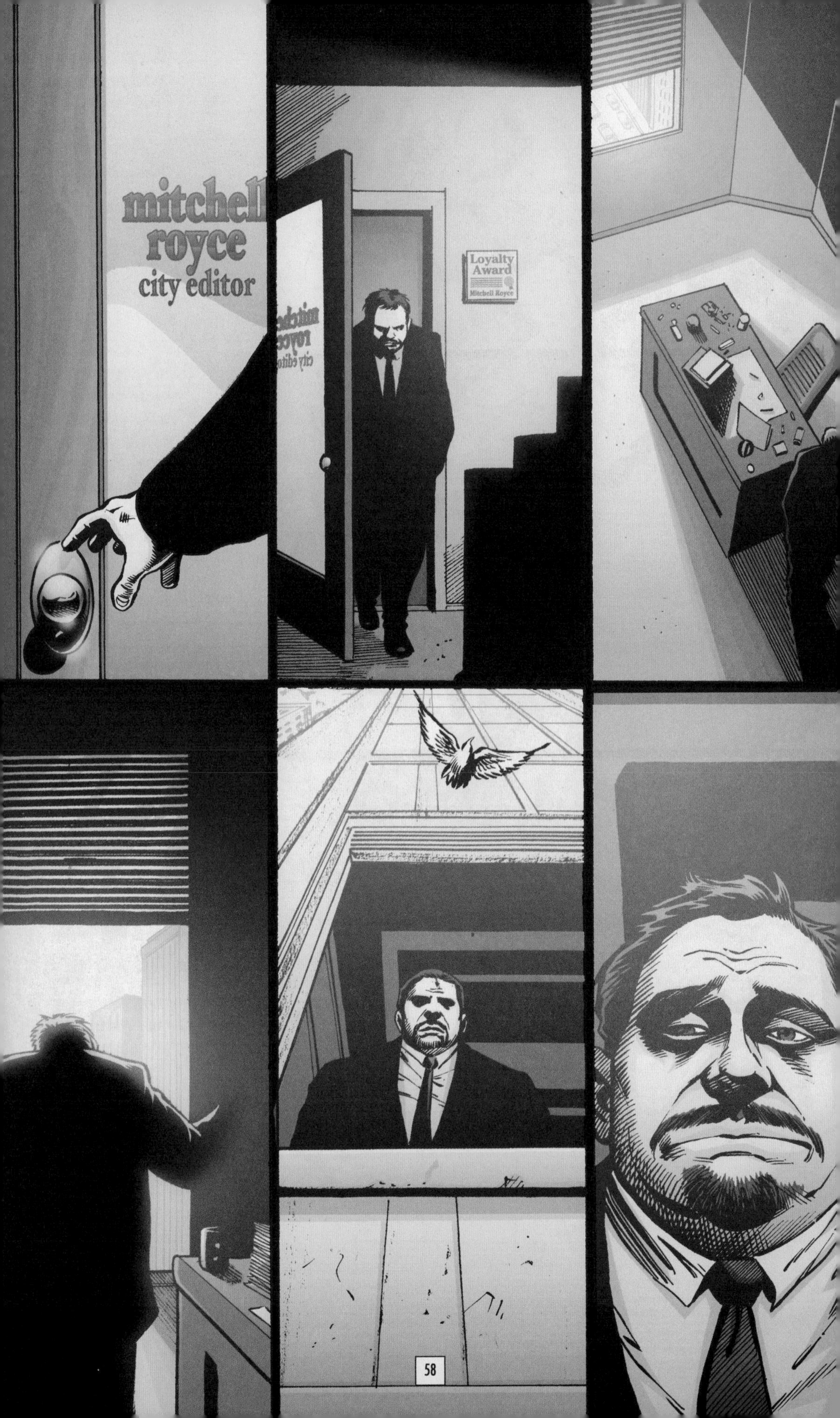
mitchell
royce
city editor
Loyalty
Award
Mitchell Royce

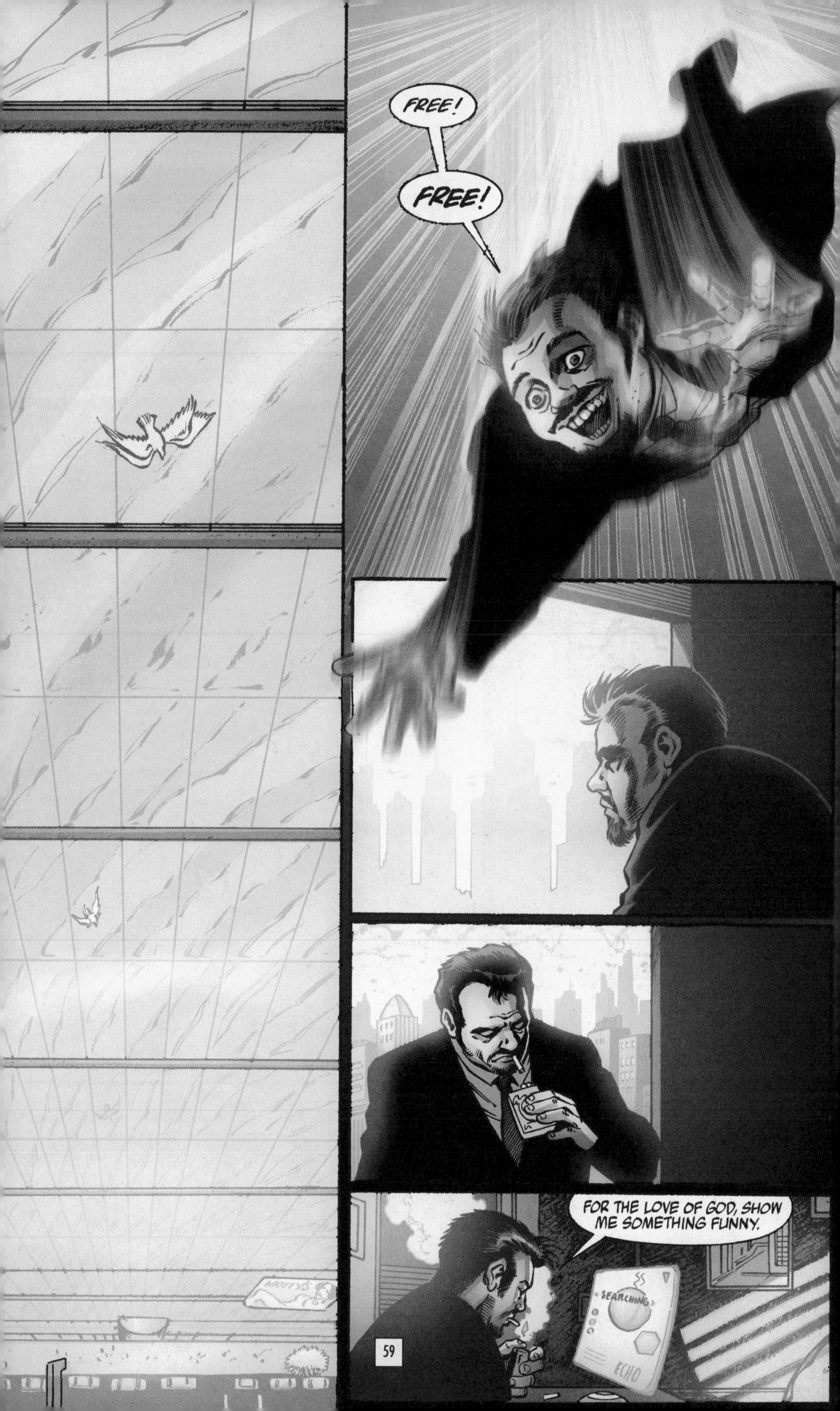
FREE!
FREE!
FOR THE LOVE OF GOD, SHOW ME SOMETHING FUNNY.
SEARCHING
ECHO

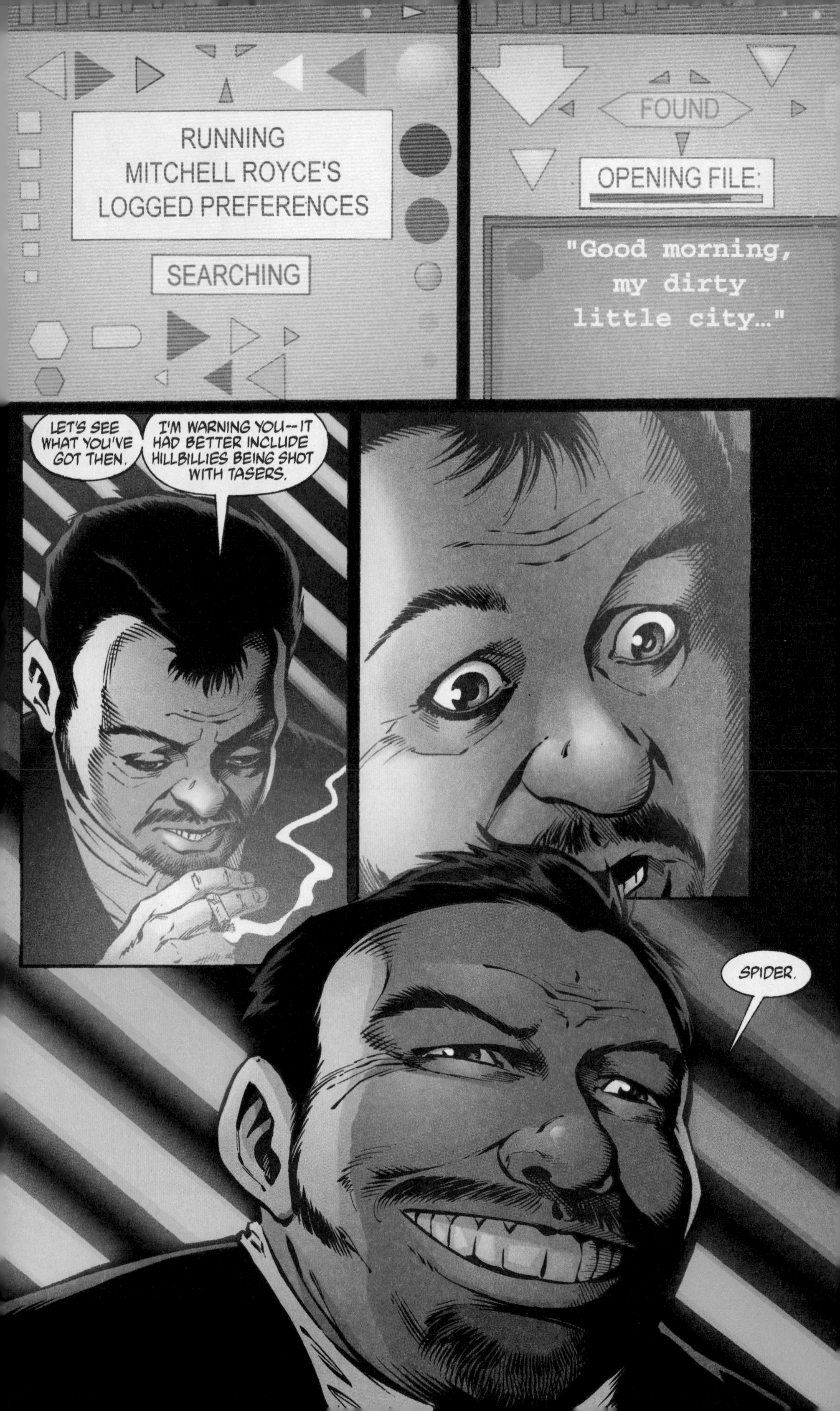
RUNNING
MITCHELL ROYCE'S
LOGGED PREFERENCES
SEARCHING
FOUND
OPENING FILE:
"Good morning,
my dirty
little city..."
LET'S SEE WHAT YOU'VE GOT THEN.
I'M WARNING YOU--IT HAD BETTER INCLUDE HILLBILLIES BEING SHOT WITH TASERS.
SPIDER.

There are now people all over town muttering, "He's not dead? Shit, this is awkward.."

No, I'm not dead. I cannot be killed. My own assistants have tried to kill me, but, like Rasputin, I notice not the poison and laugh at their icepicks. Shoot me in the lungs and I'll snarl and spit nicotine tar at you from the bulletholes.

You thought I was dead, but I sailed away, on a wave of mutilation.

And now I'm back, the big rock in front of the cave rolled away; gnawing on my nailholes and wondering which Roman ass to kick first.

Because I'm not back to have fun, oh no. I'm back to do business.

I am in a fine tradition of City businessmen with sickening motives, though, do not fear. Take, for instance, political resurrectee Fred Christ—humiliated one-time Transient activist turned Transient religious supremo.

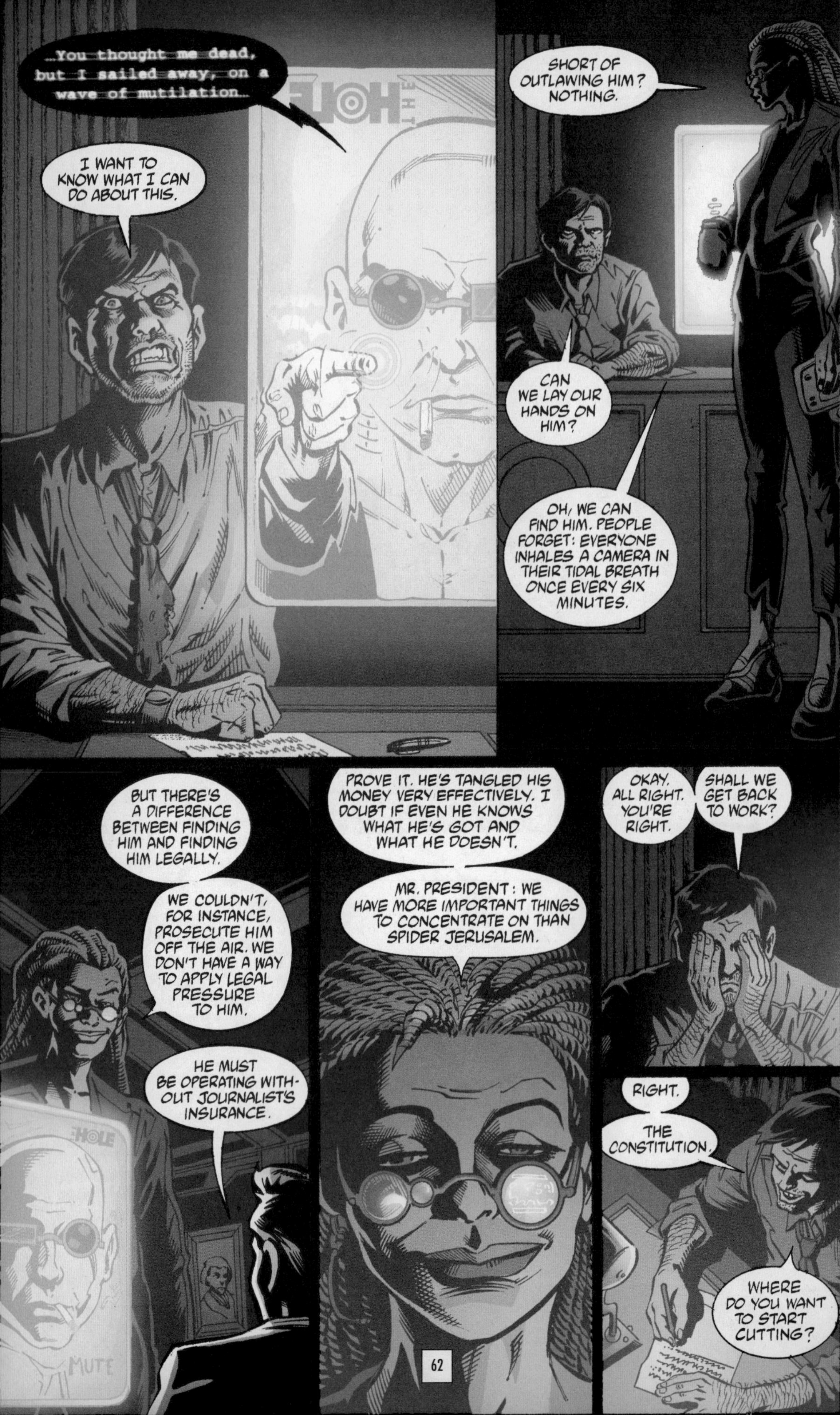
...You thought me dead, but I sailed away, on a wave of mutilation...
THE HOLE
I WANT TO KNOW WHAT I CAN DO ABOUT THIS.
SHORT OF OUTLAWING HIM? NOTHING.
CAN WE LAY OUR HANDS ON HIM?
OH, WE CAN FIND HIM. PEOPLE FORGET: EVERYONE INHALES A CAMERA IN THEIR TIDAL BREATH ONCE EVERY SIX MINUTES.
BUT THERE'S A DIFFERENCE BETWEEN FINDING HIM AND FINDING HIM LEGALLY.
WE COULDN'T, FOR INSTANCE, PROSECUTE HIM OFF THE AIR. WE DON'T HAVE A WAY TO APPLY LEGAL PRESSURE TO HIM.
HE MUST BE OPERATING WITHOUT JOURNALIST'S INSURANCE.
HOLE
MUTE
PROVE IT. HE'S TANGLED HIS MONEY VERY EFFECTIVELY. I DOUBT IF EVEN HE KNOWS WHAT HE'S GOT AND WHAT HE DOESN'T.
MR. PRESIDENT: WE HAVE MORE IMPORTANT THINGS TO CONCENTRATE ON THAN SPIDER JERUSALEM.
OKAY. ALL RIGHT. YOU'RE RIGHT.
SHALL WE GET BACK TO WORK?
RIGHT.
THE CONSTITUTION.
WHERE DO YOU WANT TO START CUTTING?

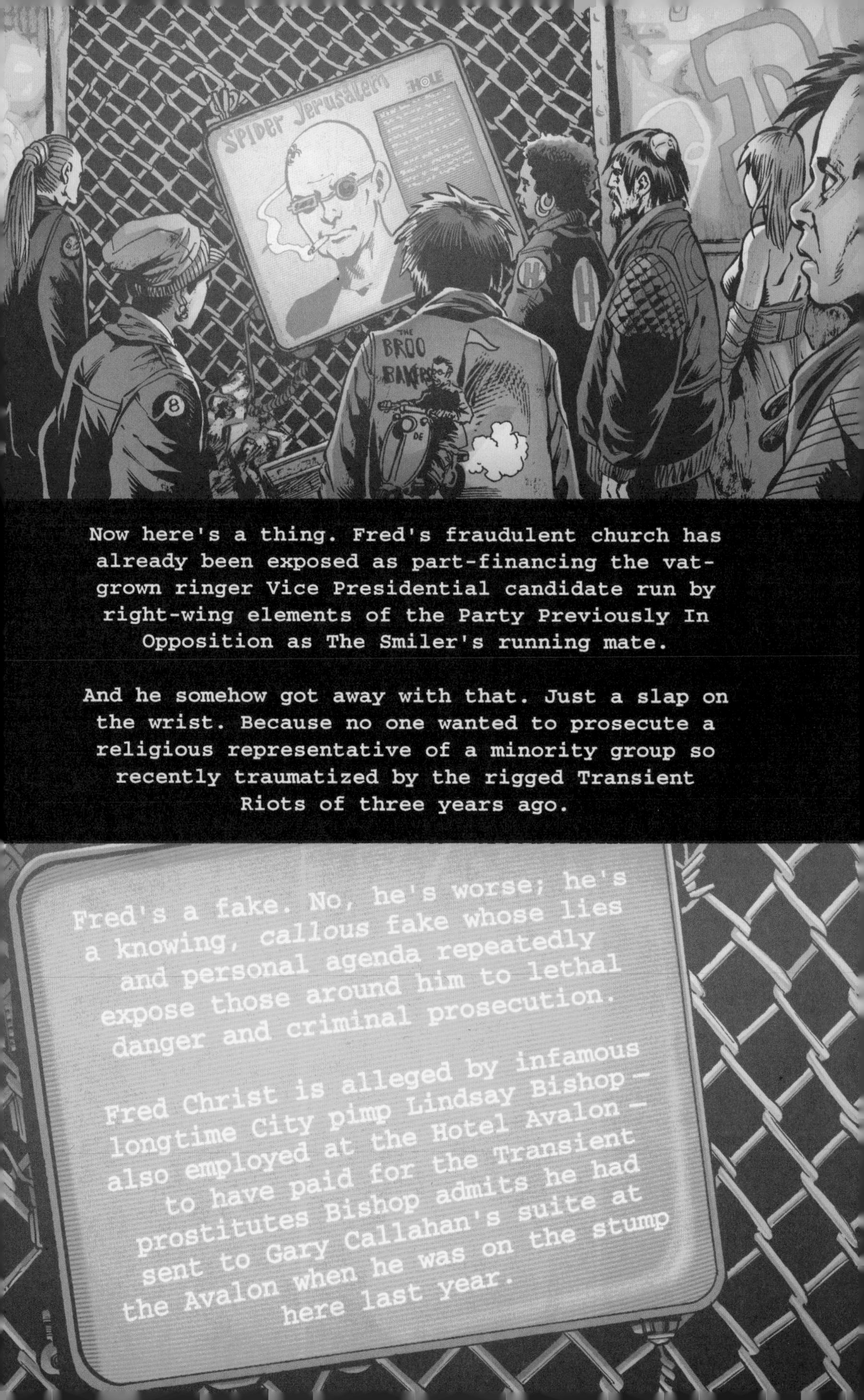
Spider Jerusalem
Now here's a thing. Fred's fraudulent church has already been exposed as part-financing the vat-grown ringer Vice Presidential candidate run by right-wing elements of the Party Previously In Opposition as The Smiler's running mate.
And he somehow got away with that. Just a slap on the wrist. Because no one wanted to prosecute a religious representative of a minority group so recently traumatized by the rigged Transient Riots of three years ago.
Fred's a fake. No, he's worse; he's a knowing, callous fake whose lies and personal agenda repeatedly expose those around him to lethal danger and criminal prosecution.
Fred Christ is alleged by infamous longtime City pimp Lindsay Bishop – also employed at the Hotel Avalon – to have paid for the Transient prostitutes Bishop admits he had sent to Gary Callahan's suite at the Avalon when he was on the stump here last year.

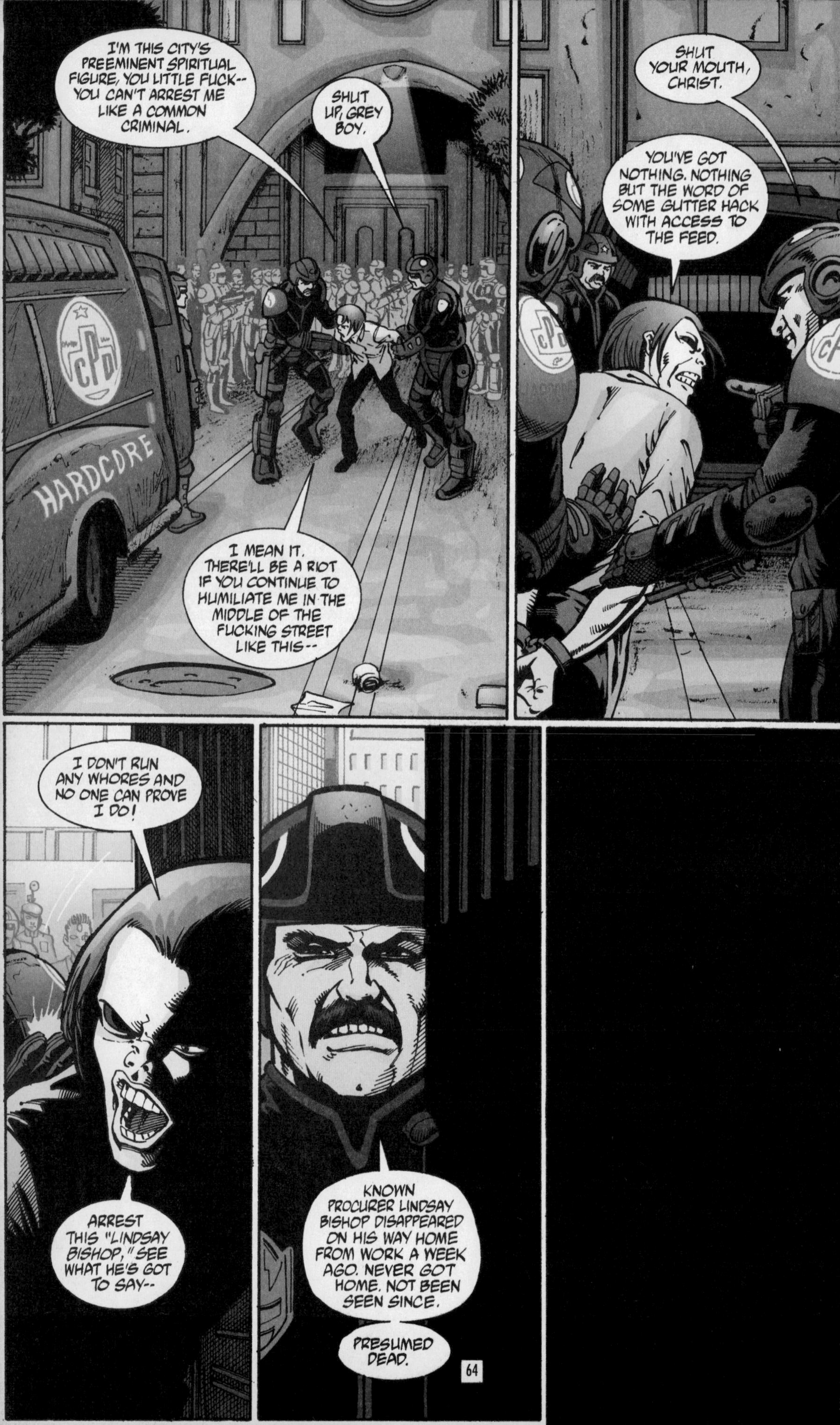
I'M THIS CITY'S PREEMINENT SPIRITUAL FIGURE, YOU LITTLE FUCK-- YOU CAN'T ARREST ME LIKE A COMMON CRIMINAL.
SHUT UP, GREY BOY.
HARDCORE
I MEAN IT. THERE'LL BE A RIOT IF YOU CONTINUE TO HUMILIATE ME IN THE MIDDLE OF THE FUCKING STREET LIKE THIS--
SHUT YOUR MOUTH, CHRIST.
YOU'VE GOT NOTHING. NOTHING BUT THE WORD OF SOME GUTTER HACK WITH ACCESS TO THE FEED.
I DON'T RUN ANY WHORES AND NO ONE CAN PROVE I DO!
ARREST THIS "LINDSAY BISHOP," SEE WHAT HE'S GOT TO SAY--
KNOWN PROCURER LINDSAY BISHOP DISAPPEARED ON HIS WAY HOME FROM WORK A WEEK AGO. NEVER GOT HOME. NOT BEEN SEEN SINCE.
PRESUMED DEAD.

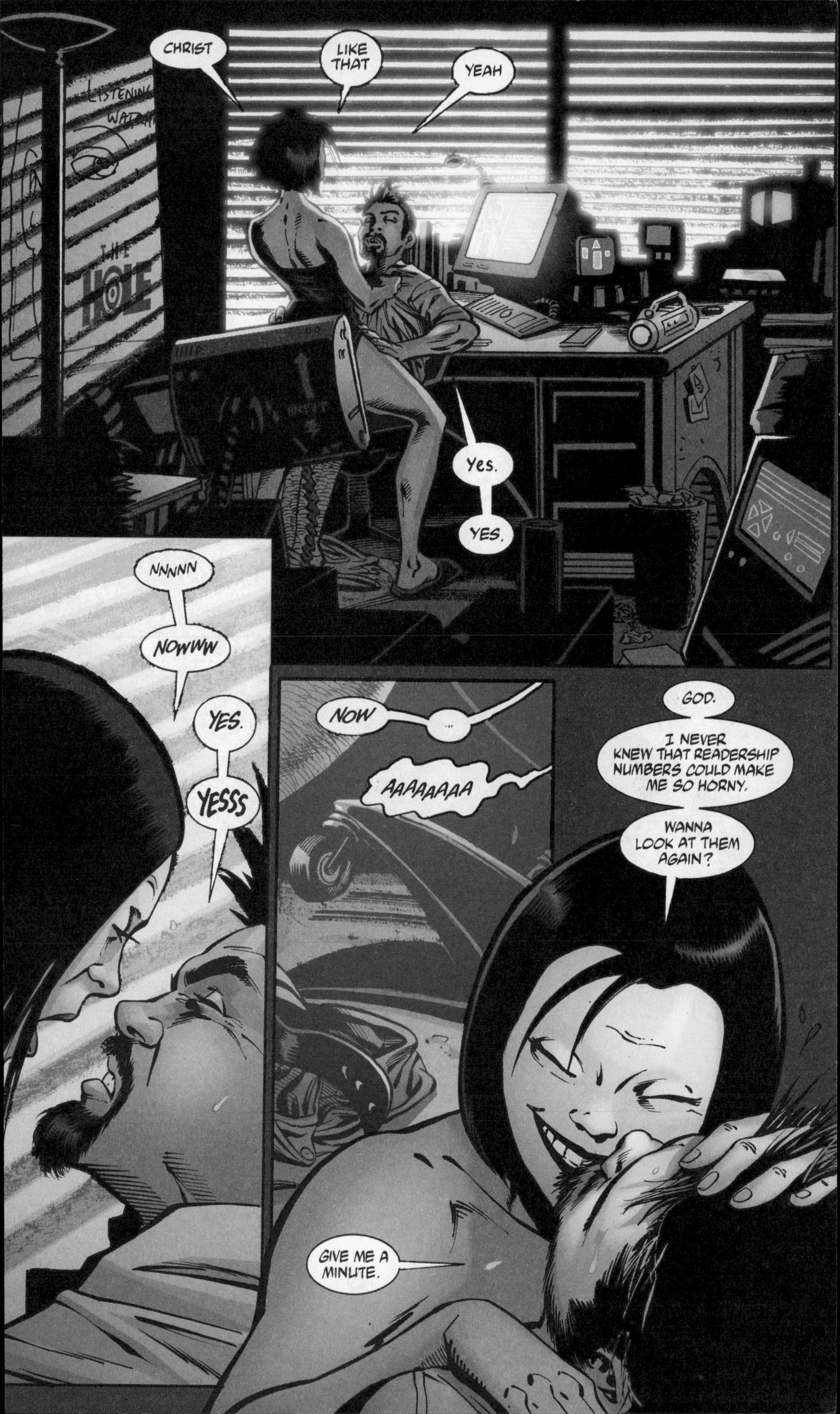
CHRIST
LIKE THAT
YEAH
Yes.
YES.
NNNNN
NOWWW
YES.
YESSS
NOW
...
AAAAAAAA
GOD.
I NEVER KNEW THAT READERSHIP NUMBERS COULD MAKE ME SO HORNY.
WANNA LOOK AT THEM AGAIN?
GIVE ME A MINUTE.

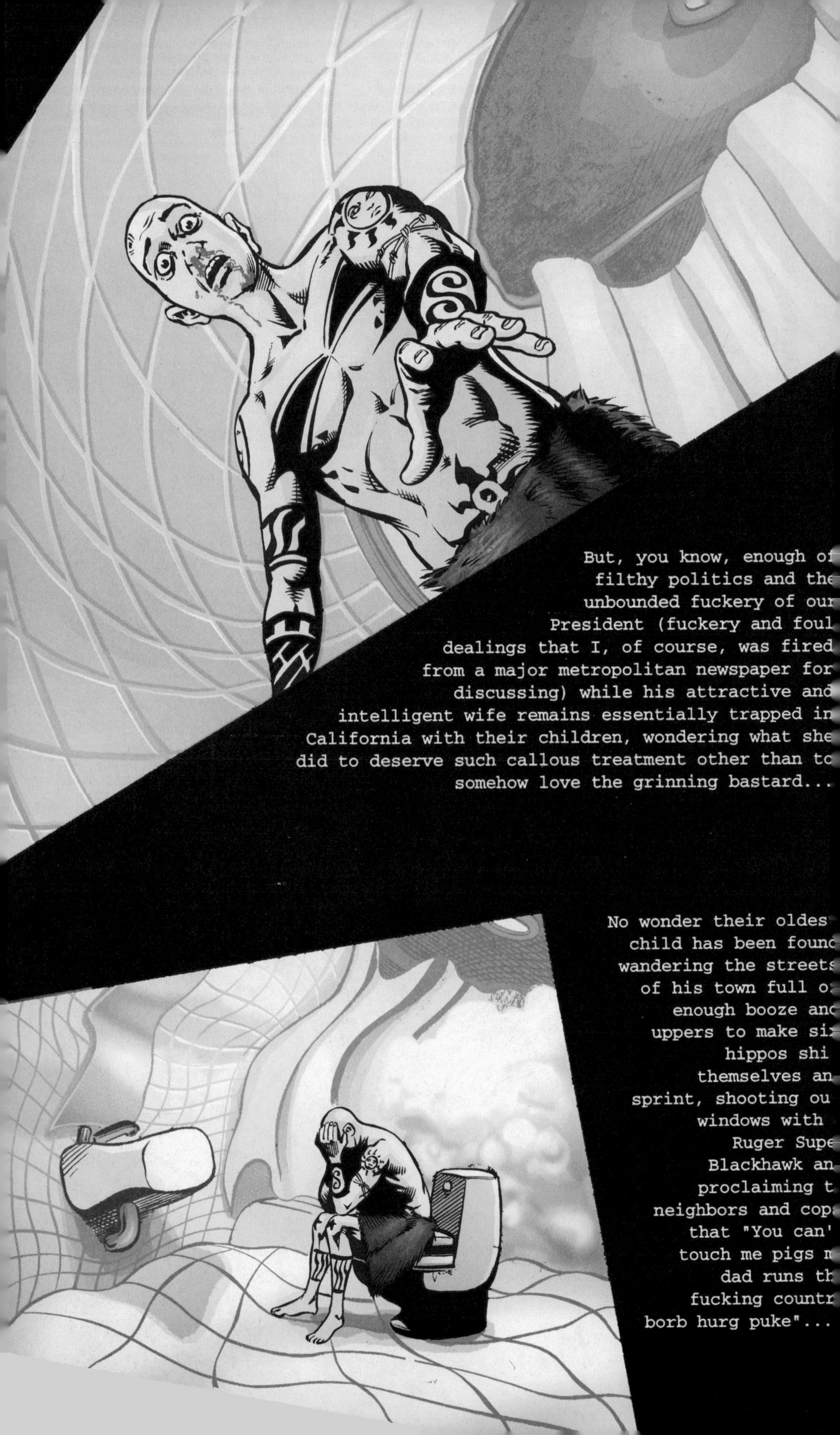

But, you know, enough of
filthy politics and the
unbounded fuckery of our
President (fuckery and foul
dealings that I, of course, was fired
from a major metropolitan newspaper for
discussing) while his attractive and
intelligent wife remains essentially trapped in
California with their children, wondering what she
did to deserve such callous treatment other than to
somehow love the grinning bastard...
No wonder their oldes
child has been found
wandering the streets
of his town full o
enough booze and
uppers to make si
hippos shi
themselves an
sprint, shooting ou
windows with
Ruger Supe
Blackhawk an
proclaiming t
neighbors and cop
that "You can'
touch me pigs m
dad runs th
fucking countr
borb hurg puke"...

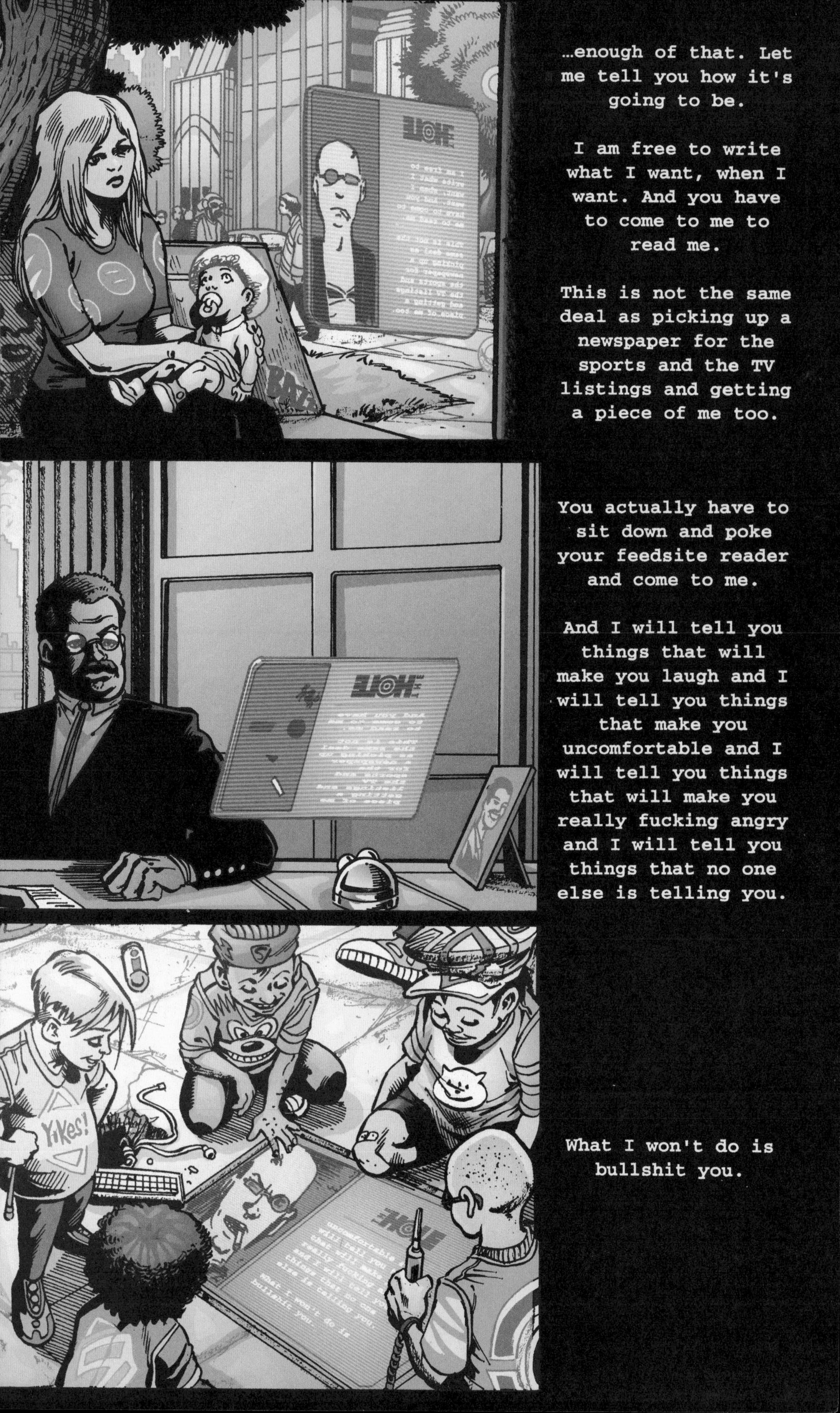
...enough of that. Let me tell you how it's going to be.
I am free to write what I want, when I want. And you have to come to me to read me.
This is not the same deal as picking up a newspaper for the sports and the TV listings and getting a piece of me too.
You actually have to sit down and poke your feedsite reader and come to me.
And I will tell you things that will make you laugh and I will tell you things that make you uncomfortable and I will tell you things that will make you really fucking angry and I will tell you things that no one else is telling you.
Yikes!
What I won't do is bullshit you.

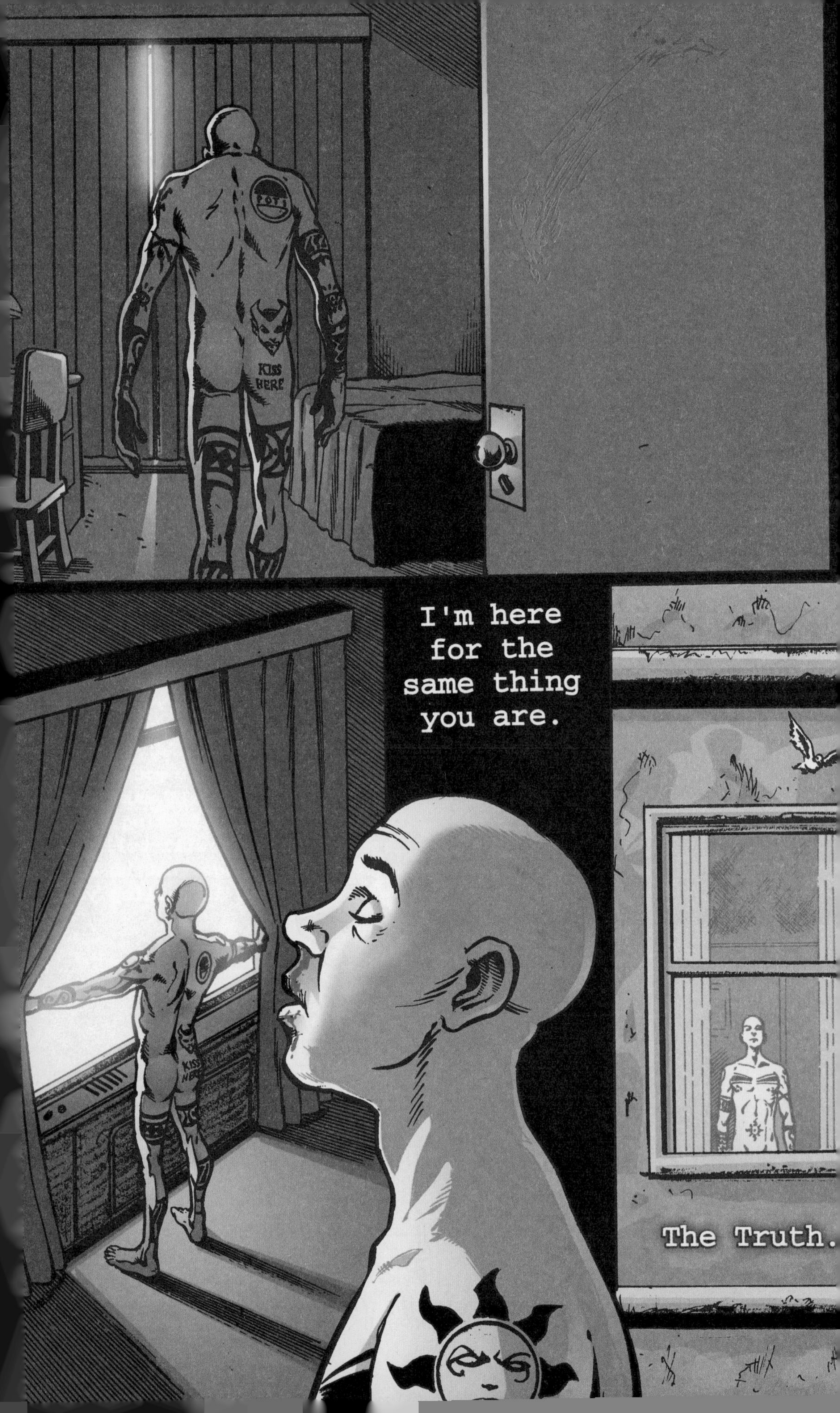
POTS
KISS HERE
I'm here for the same thing you are.
The Truth.

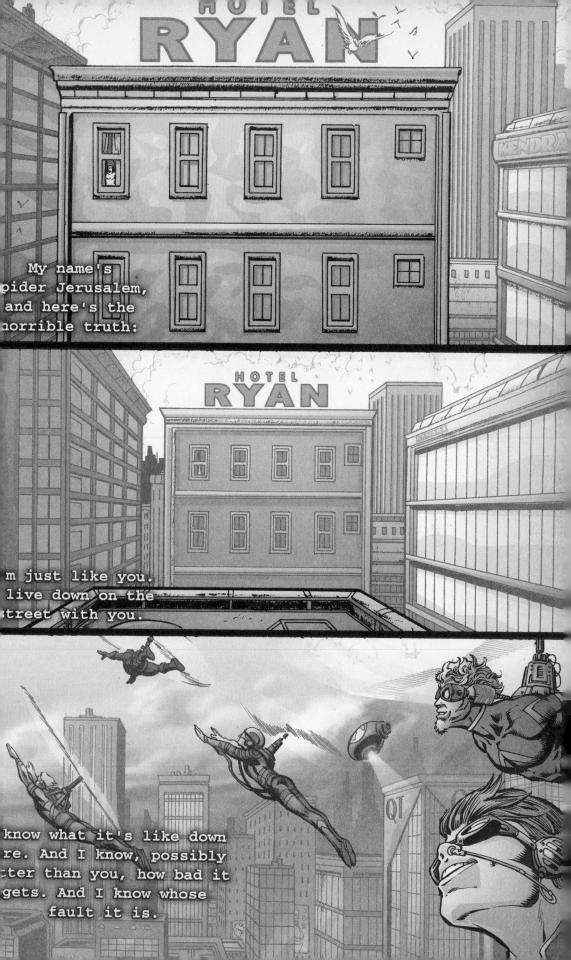

My name's
Spider Jerusalem,
and here's the
horrible truth:

I'm just like you.
I live down on the
street with you.

I know what it's like down
here. And I know, possibly
better than you, how bad it
gets. And I know whose
fault it is.

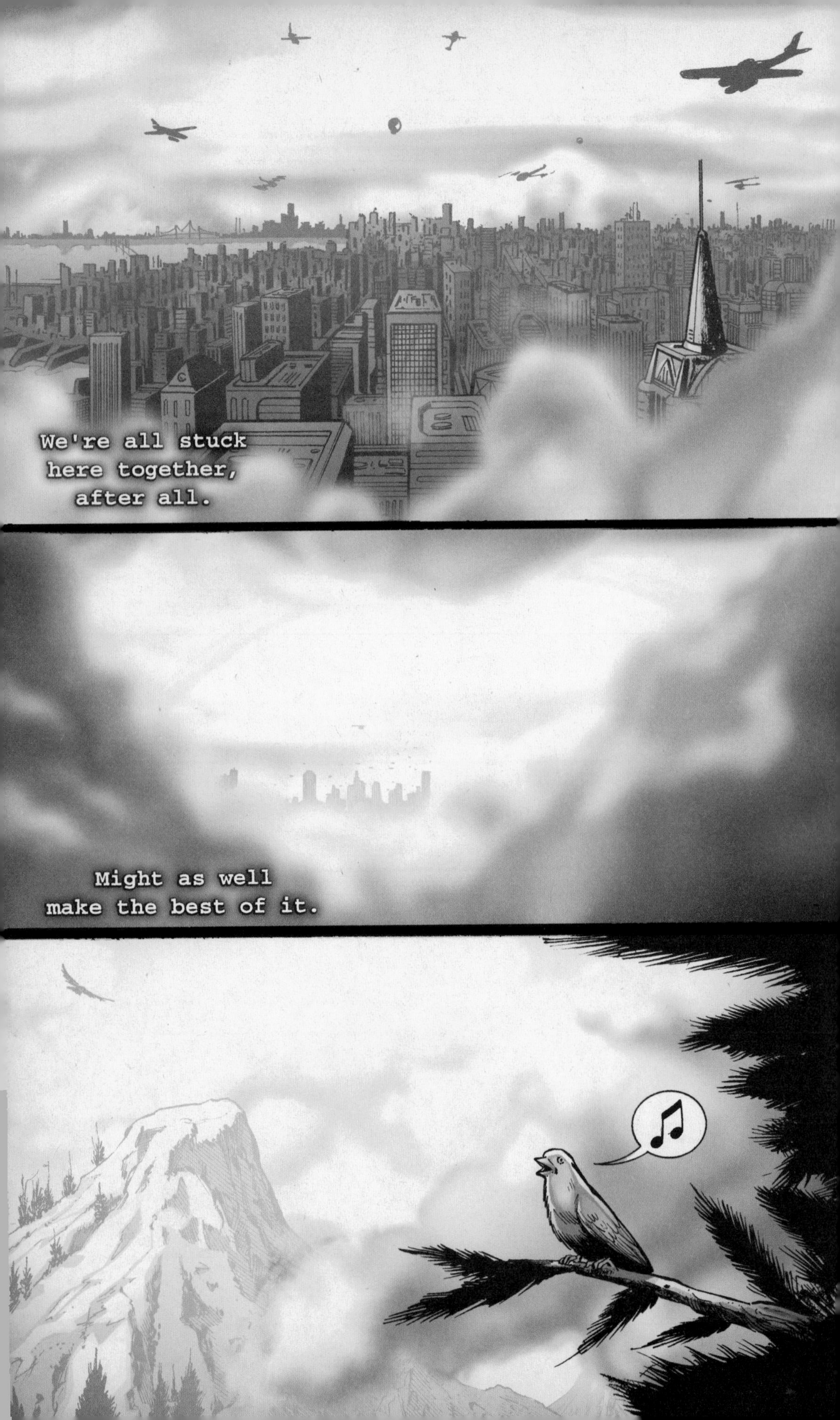
We're all stuck here together, after all.
Might as well make the best of it.
♫

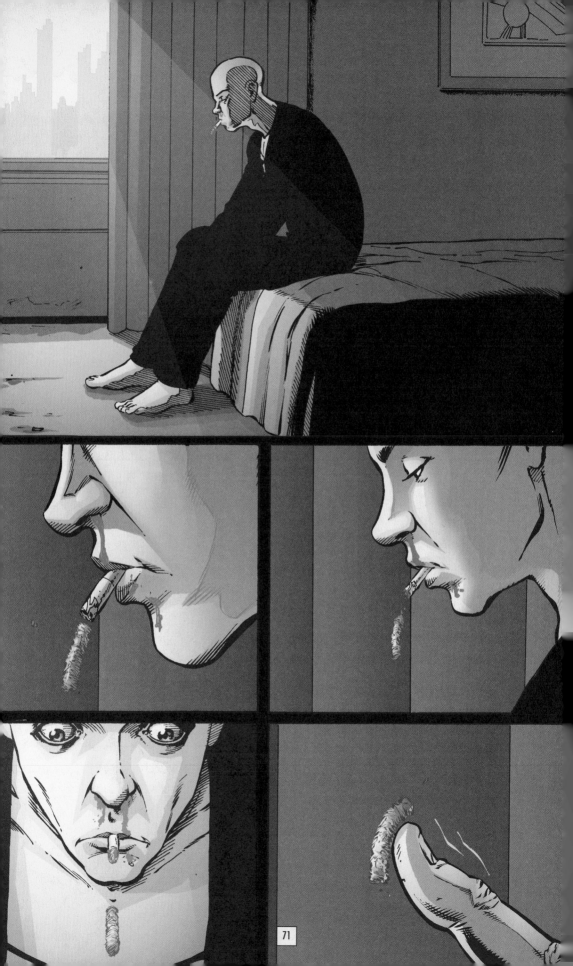

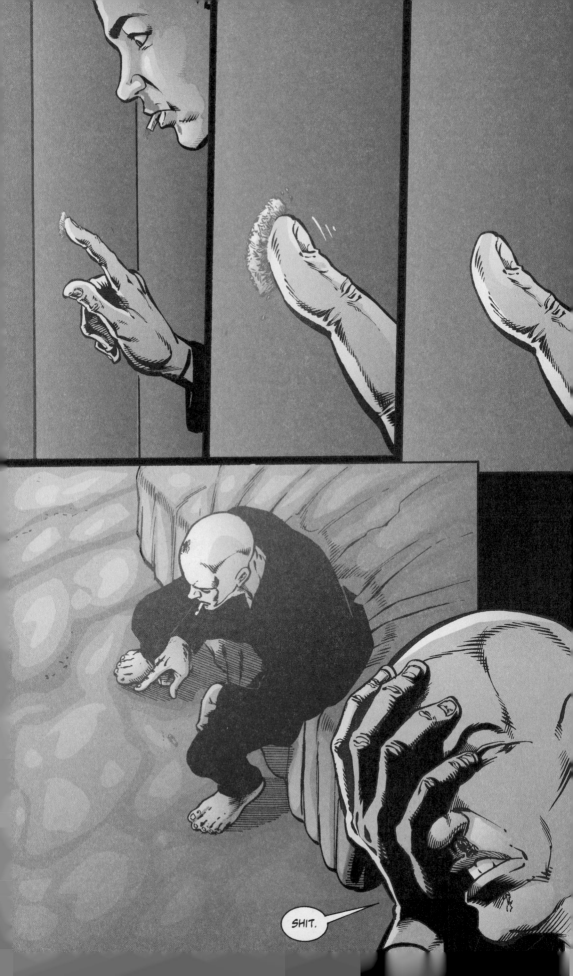

SHIT.

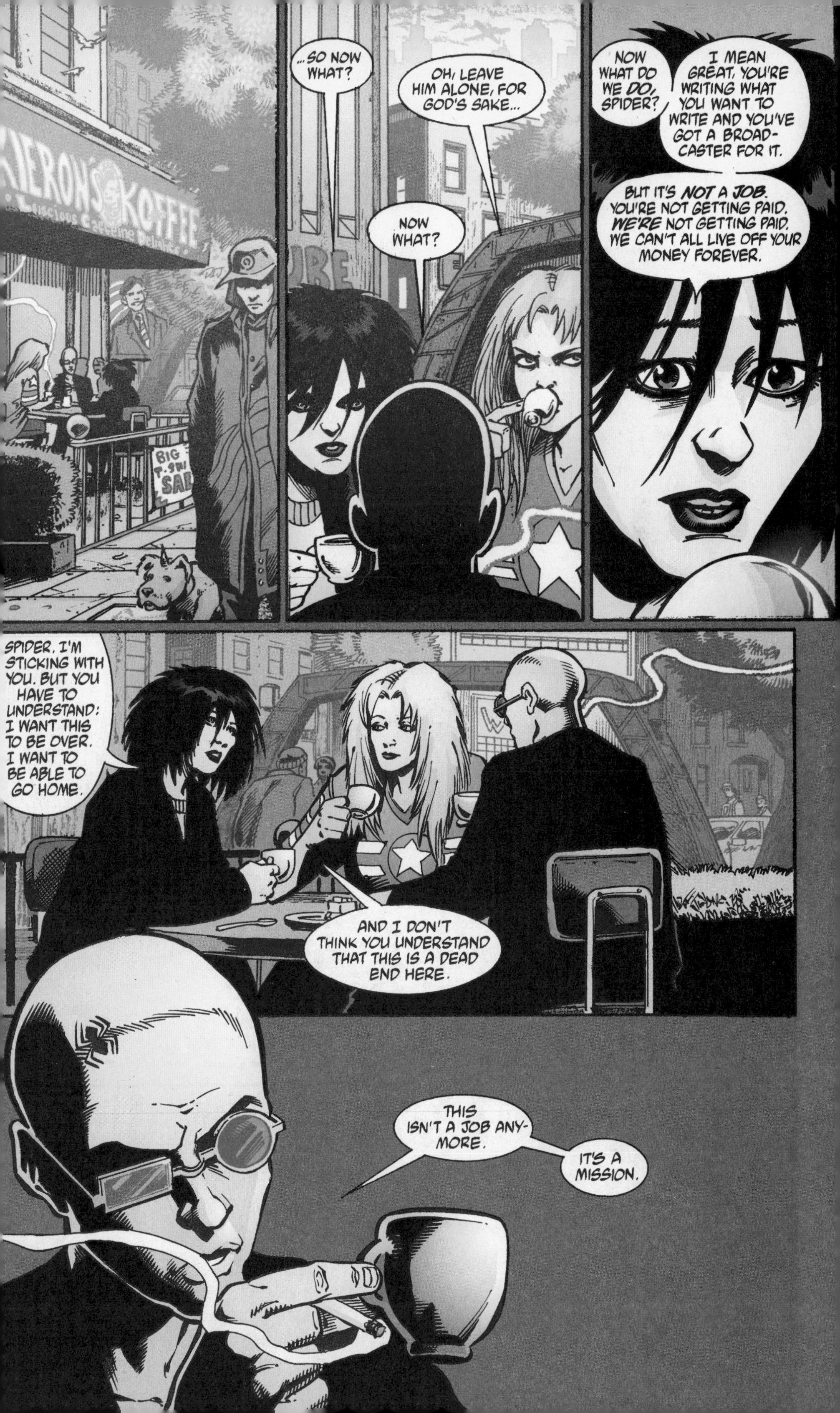
KIERON'S KOFFEE
Luscious Caffeine Delights
BIG T-SHI SAL
...SO NOW WHAT?
OH, LEAVE HIM ALONE, FOR GOD'S SAKE...
NOW WHAT?
NOW WHAT DO WE *DO*, SPIDER?
I MEAN GREAT, YOU'RE WRITING WHAT YOU WANT TO WRITE AND YOU'VE GOT A BROADCASTER FOR IT.
BUT IT'S ***NOT A JOB***. YOU'RE NOT GETTING PAID. ***WE'RE*** NOT GETTING PAID. WE CAN'T ALL LIVE OFF YOUR MONEY FOREVER.
SPIDER, I'M STICKING WITH YOU. BUT YOU HAVE TO UNDERSTAND: I WANT THIS TO BE OVER. I WANT TO BE ABLE TO GO HOME.
AND I DON'T THINK YOU UNDERSTAND THAT THIS IS A DEAD END HERE.
THIS ISN'T A JOB ANYMORE.
IT'S A MISSION.

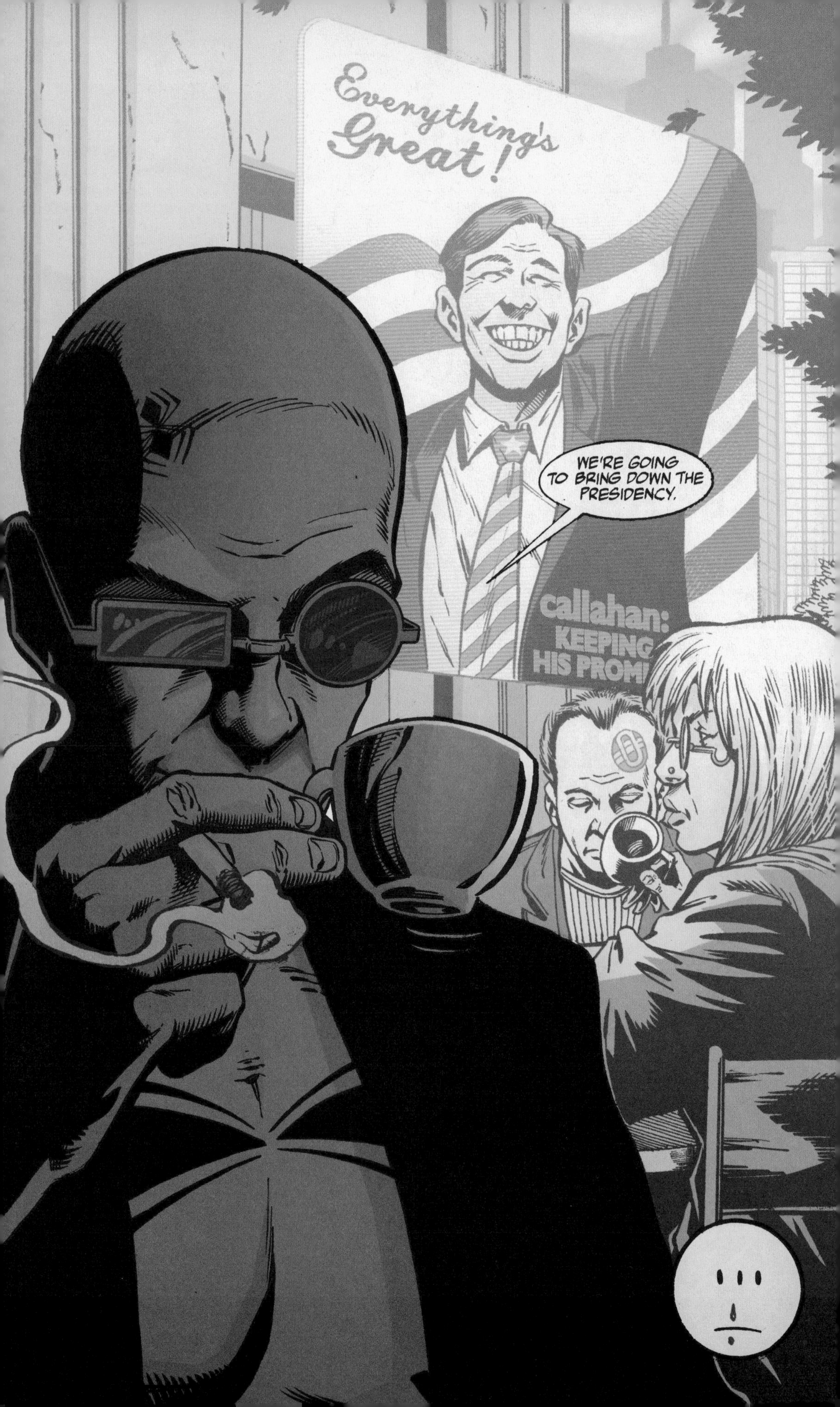
Everything's Great!
WE'RE GOING TO BRING DOWN THE PRESIDENCY.
callahan: KEEPING HIS PROMI

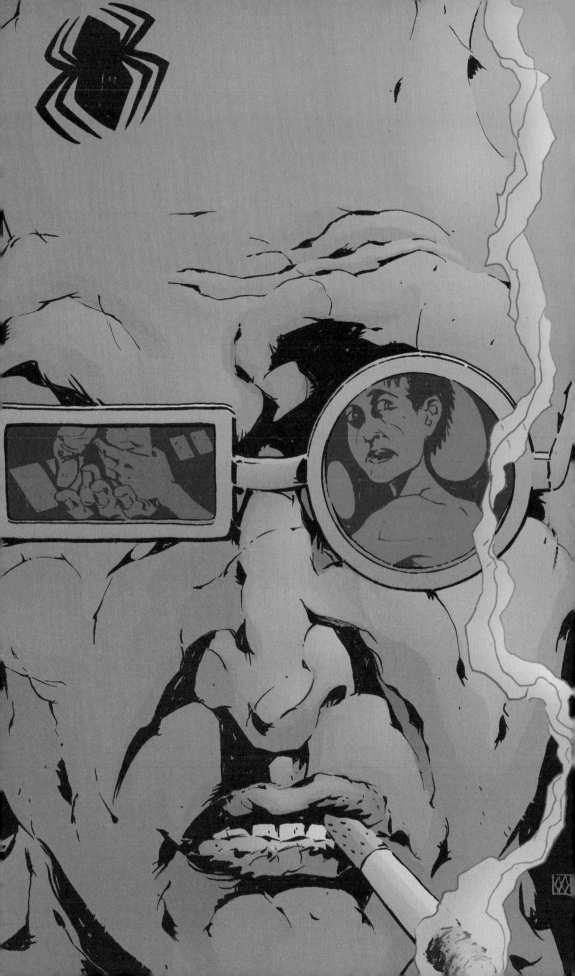

Written by Warren Ellis
Illustrated by Darick Robertson & Rodney Ramos

Colors/Seps by	Letters by	Cover	Ass't Editor	Editor
Nathan Eyring	Clem Robins	Matt Wagner	Jennifer Lee	Axel Alonso

BUSINESS

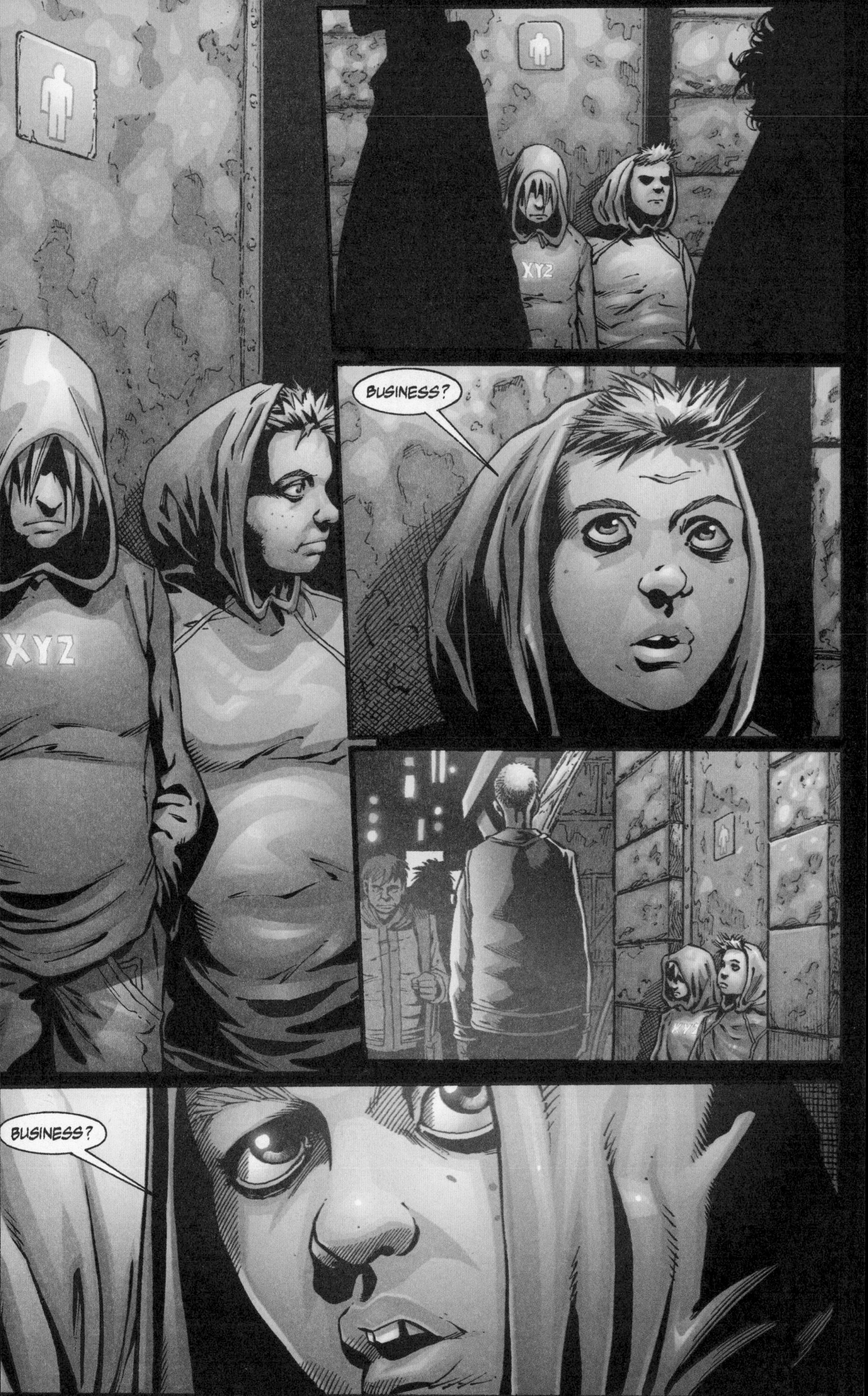
XYZ
XYZ
BUSINESS?
XYZ
BUSINESS?

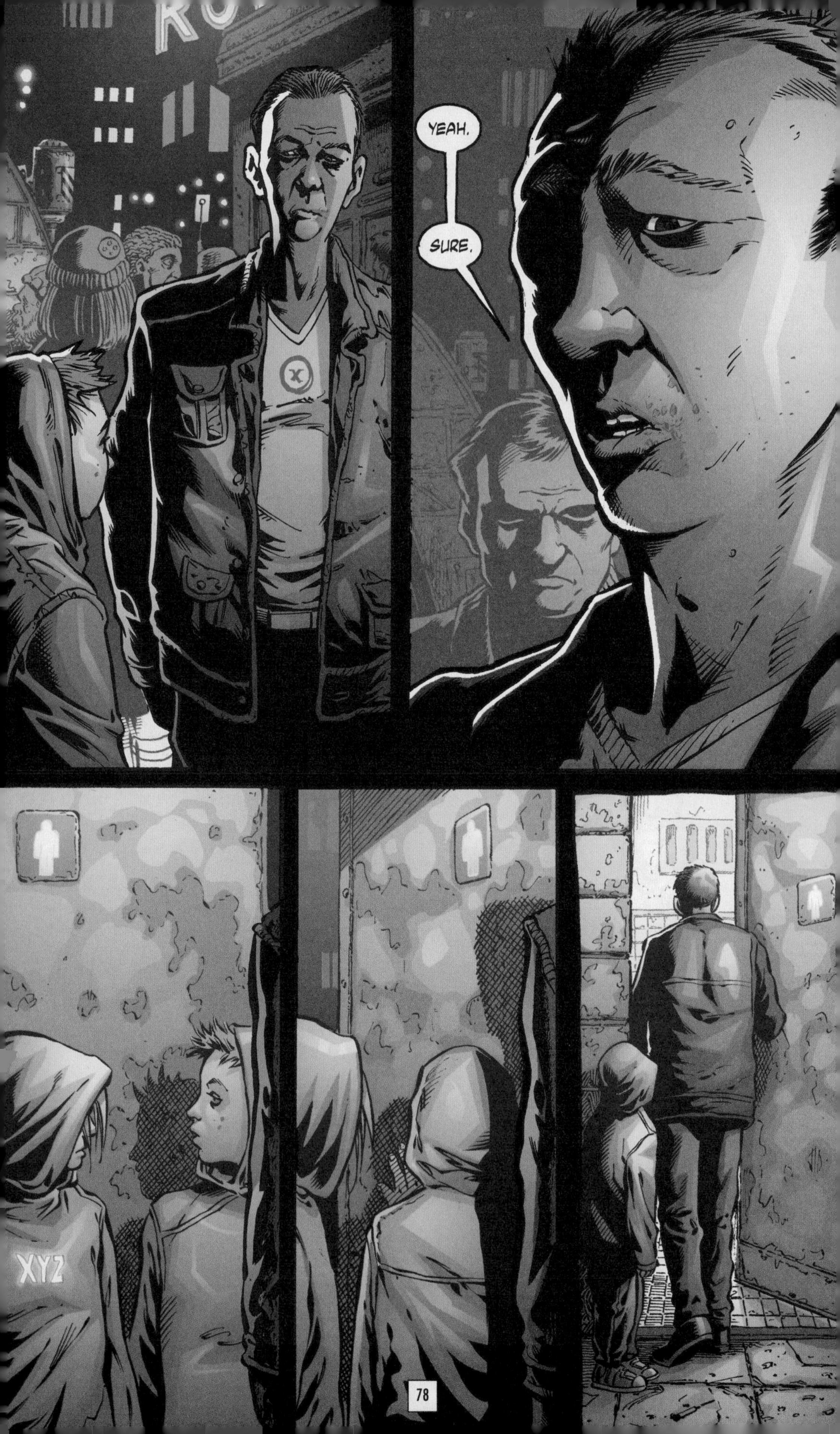
YEAH.
SURE.
XYZ

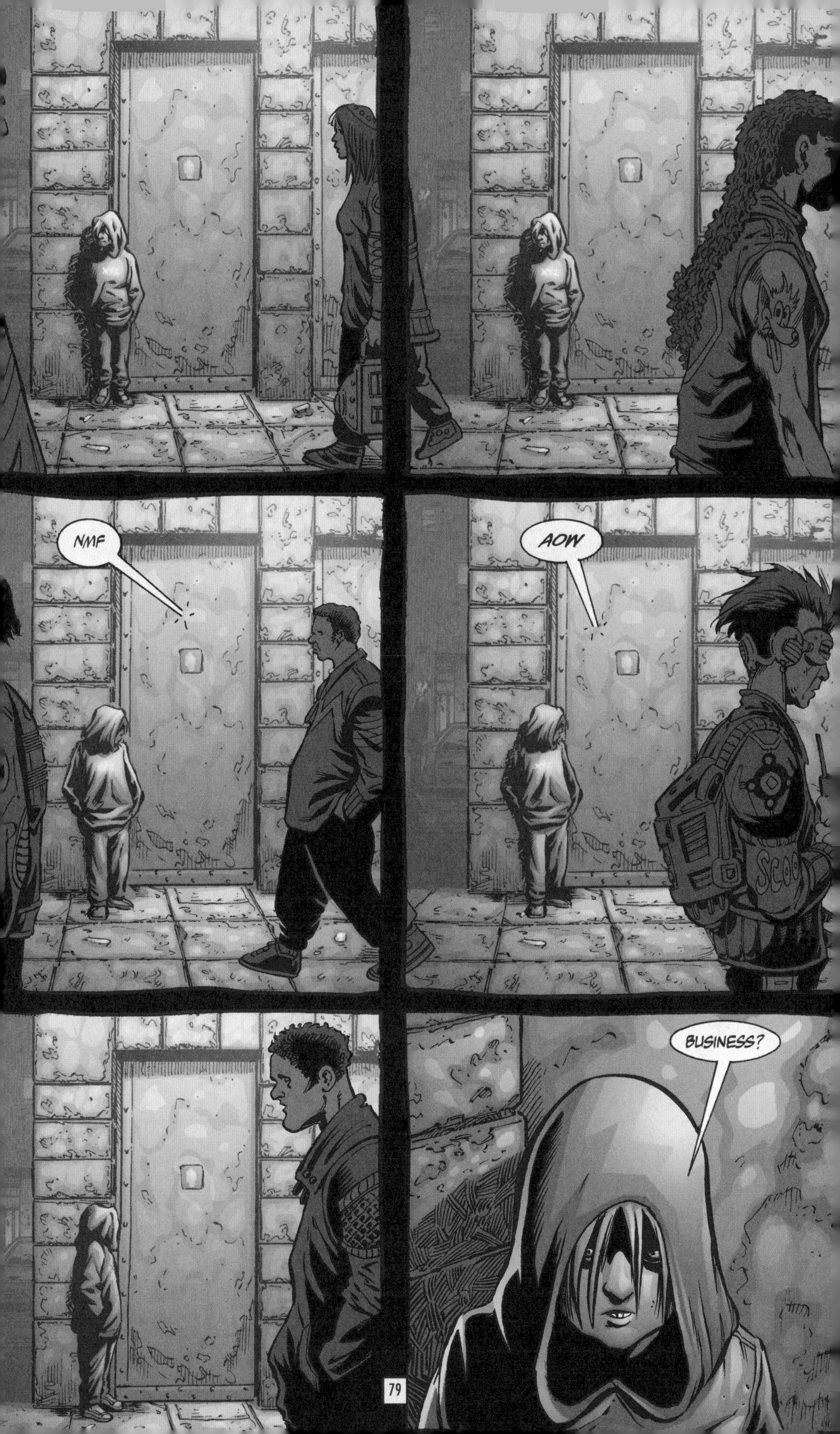
NMF
AOW
BUSINESS?

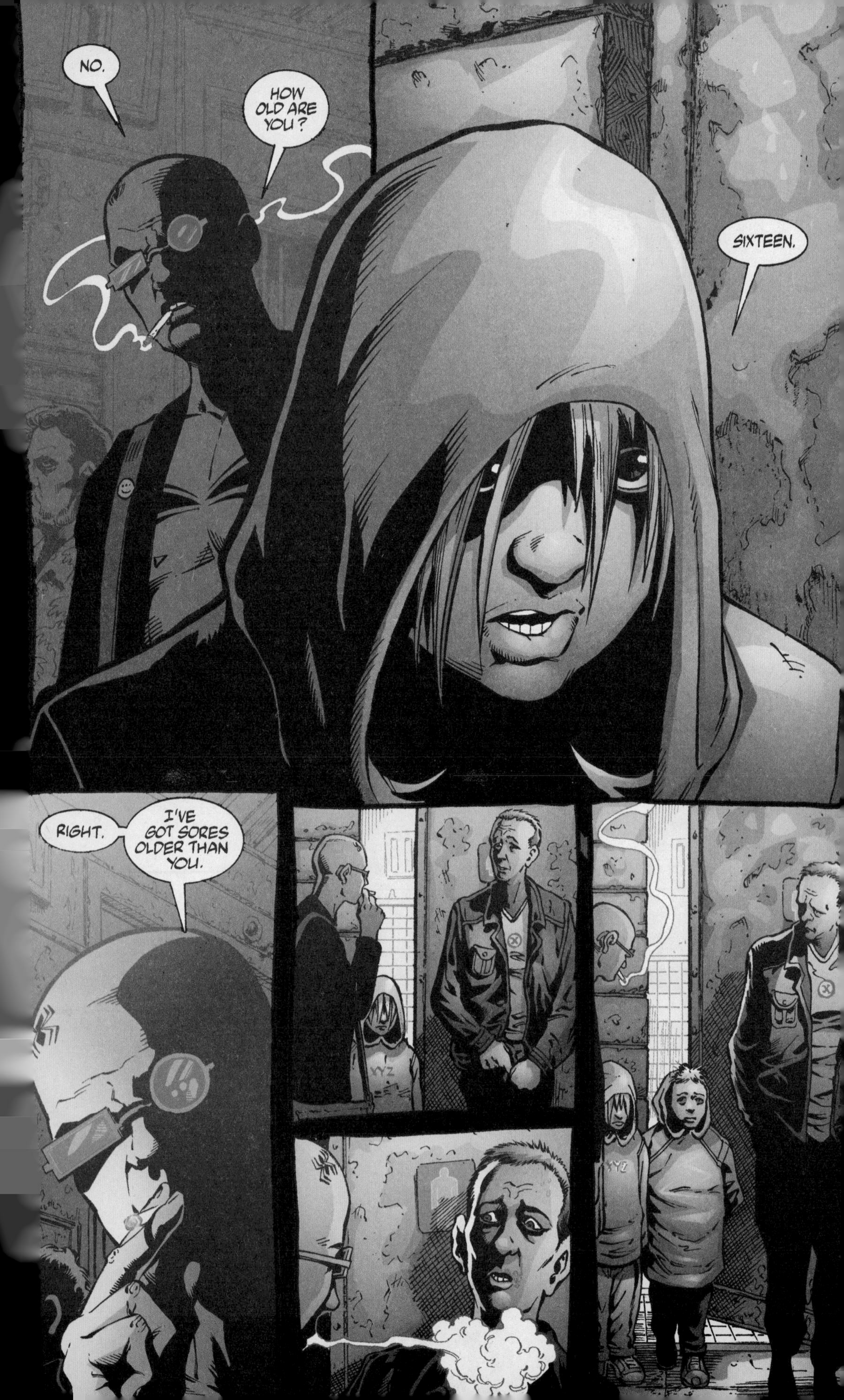
NO.
HOW OLD ARE YOU?
SIXTEEN.
RIGHT.
I'VE GOT SORES OLDER THAN YOU.

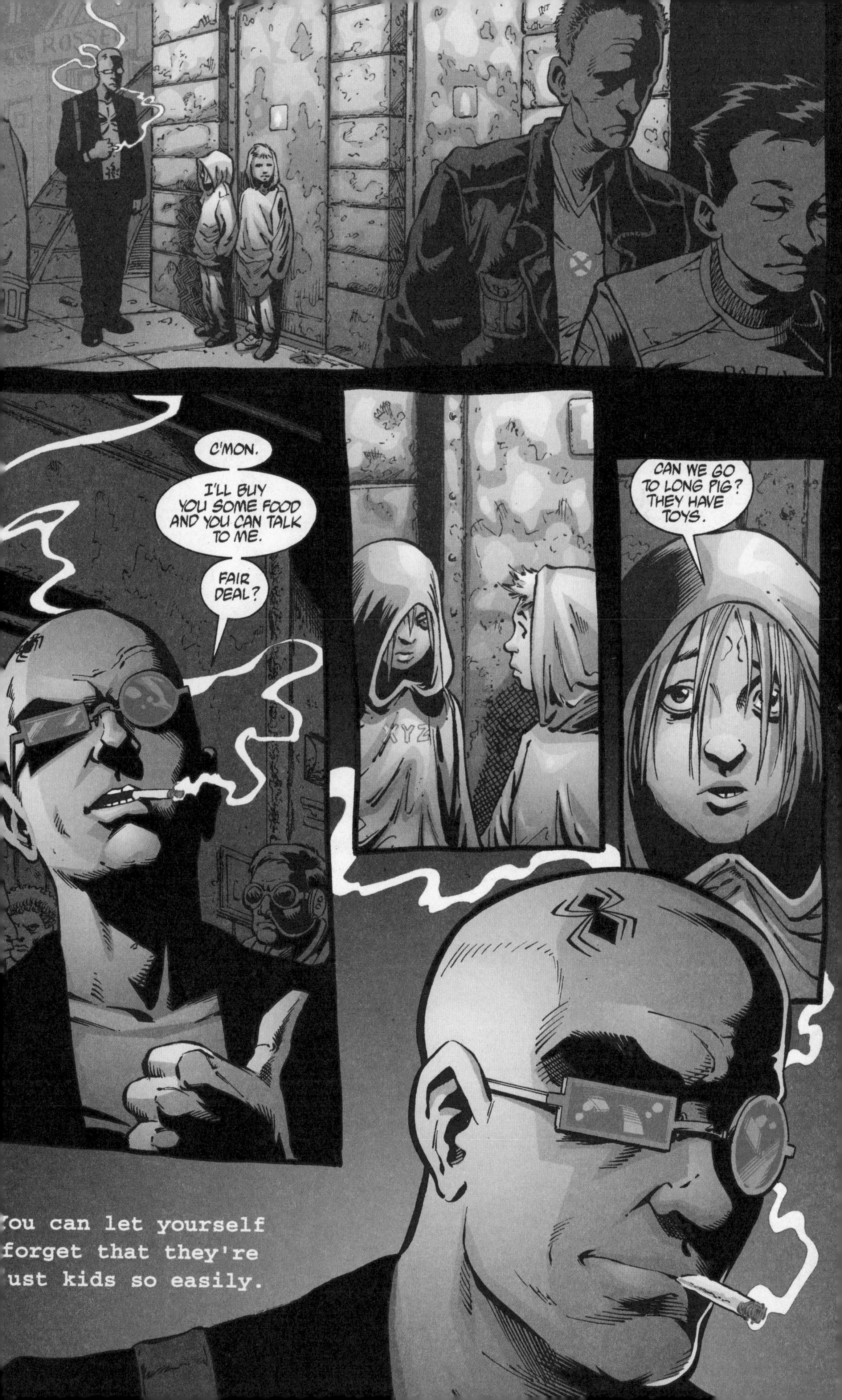

C'MON.
I'LL BUY YOU SOME FOOD AND YOU CAN TALK TO ME.
FAIR DEAL?
CAN WE GO TO LONG PIG? THEY HAVE TOYS.
You can let yourself forget that they're ust kids so easily.

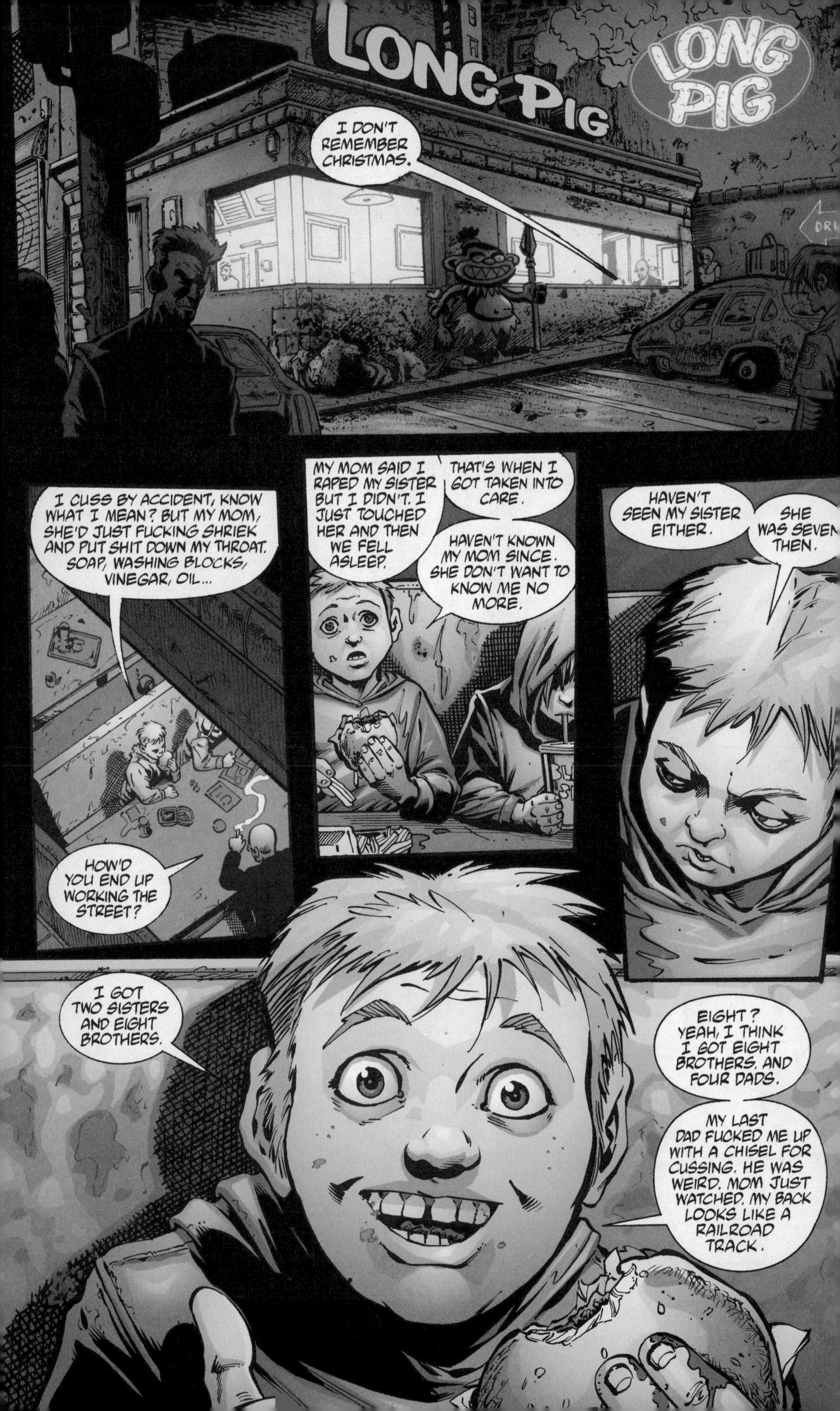
LONG PIG
LONG PIG
I DON'T REMEMBER CHRISTMAS.
DRI
I CUSS BY ACCIDENT, KNOW WHAT I MEAN? BUT MY MOM, SHE'D JUST FUCKING SHRIEK AND PUT SHIT DOWN MY THROAT. SOAP, WASHING BLOCKS, VINEGAR, OIL...
HOW'D YOU END UP WORKING THE STREET?
MY MOM SAID I RAPED MY SISTER BUT I DIDN'T. I JUST TOUCHED HER AND THEN WE FELL ASLEEP.
THAT'S WHEN I GOT TAKEN INTO CARE.
HAVEN'T KNOWN MY MOM SINCE. SHE DON'T WANT TO KNOW ME NO MORE.
HAVEN'T SEEN MY SISTER EITHER.
SHE WAS SEVEN THEN.
I GOT TWO SISTERS AND EIGHT BROTHERS.
EIGHT? YEAH, I THINK I GOT EIGHT BROTHERS. AND FOUR DADS.
MY LAST DAD FUCKED ME UP WITH A CHISEL FOR CUSSING. HE WAS WEIRD. MOM JUST WATCHED. MY BACK LOOKS LIKE A RAILROAD TRACK.

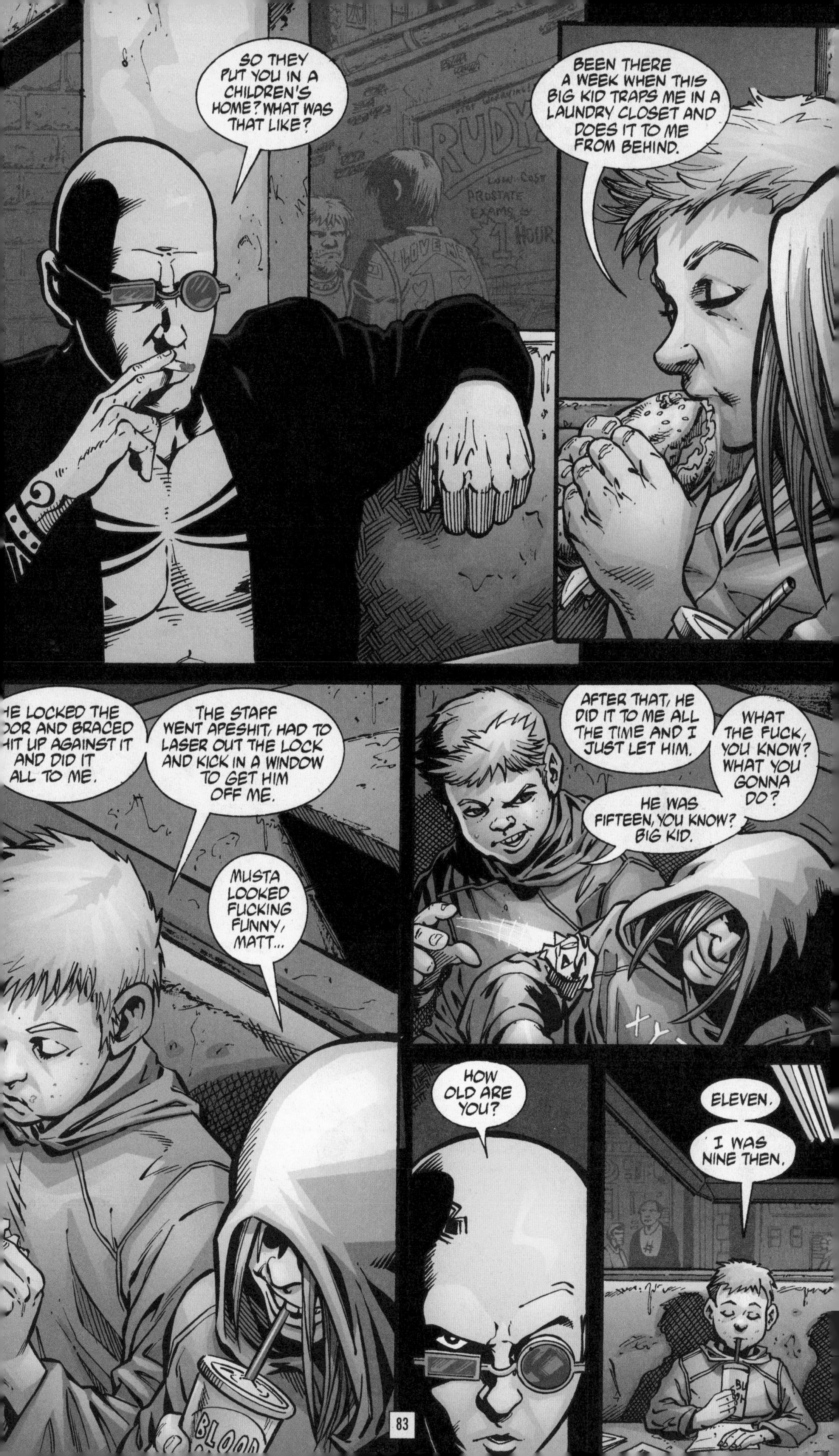
SO THEY PUT YOU IN A CHILDREN'S HOME? WHAT WAS THAT LIKE?
BEEN THERE A WEEK WHEN THIS BIG KID TRAPS ME IN A LAUNDRY CLOSET AND DOES IT TO ME FROM BEHIND.
HE LOCKED THE OOR AND BRACED HIT UP AGAINST IT AND DID IT ALL TO ME.
THE STAFF WENT APESHIT, HAD TO LASER OUT THE LOCK AND KICK IN A WINDOW TO GET HIM OFF ME.
MUSTA LOOKED FUCKING FUNNY, MATT...
AFTER THAT, HE DID IT TO ME ALL THE TIME AND I JUST LET HIM.
HE WAS FIFTEEN, YOU KNOW? BIG KID.
WHAT THE FUCK, YOU KNOW? WHAT YOU GONNA DO?
HOW OLD ARE YOU?
ELEVEN.
I WAS NINE THEN.

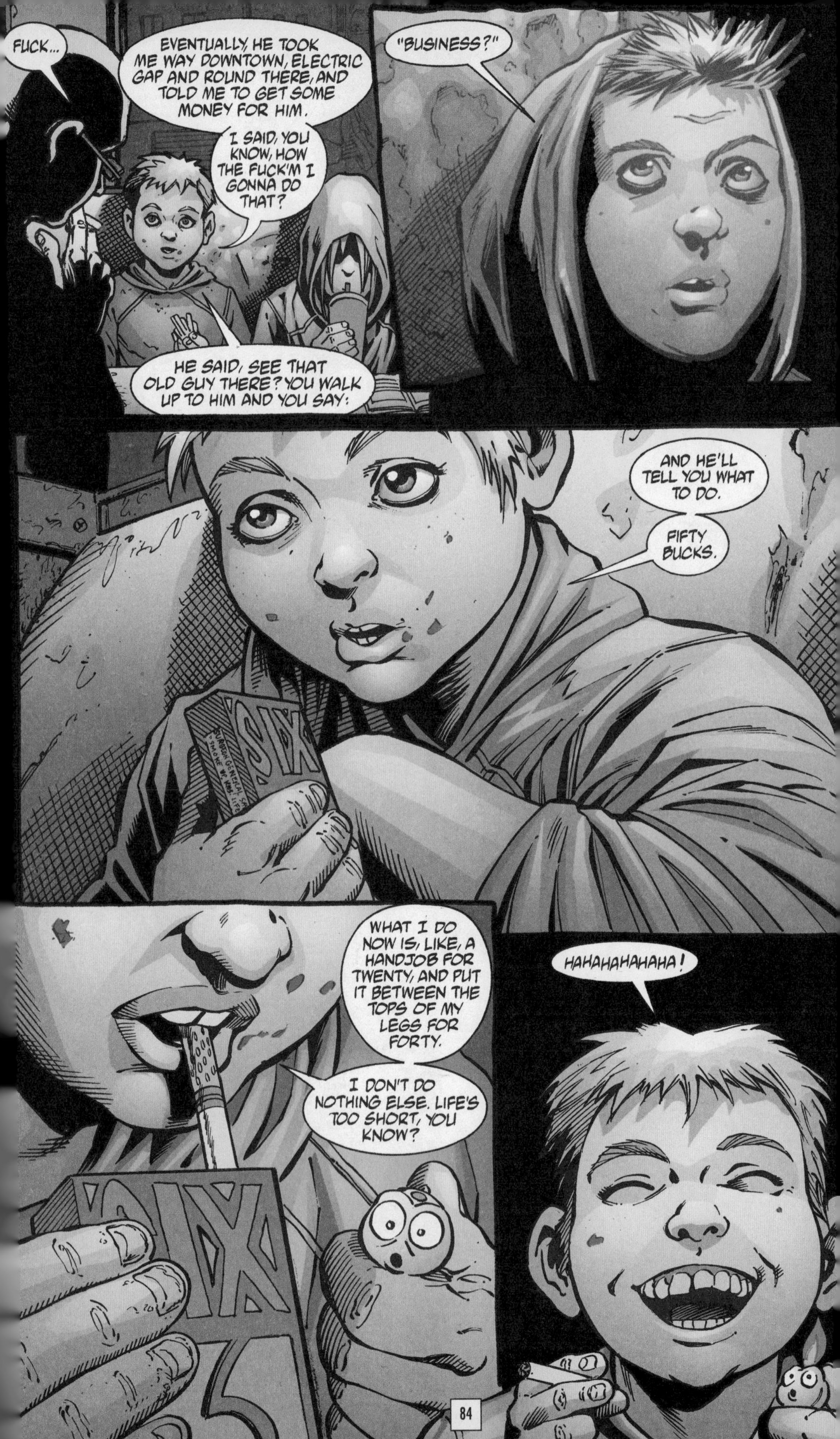
FUCK...
EVENTUALLY, HE TOOK ME WAY DOWNTOWN, ELECTRIC GAP AND ROUND THERE, AND TOLD ME TO GET SOME MONEY FOR HIM.
I SAID, YOU KNOW, HOW THE FUCK'M I GONNA DO THAT?
HE SAID, SEE THAT OLD GUY THERE? YOU WALK UP TO HIM AND YOU SAY:
"BUSINESS?"
AND HE'LL TELL YOU WHAT TO DO.
FIFTY BUCKS.
SIX
WHAT I DO NOW IS, LIKE, A HANDJOB FOR TWENTY, AND PUT IT BETWEEN THE TOPS OF MY LEGS FOR FORTY.
I DON'T DO NOTHING ELSE. LIFE'S TOO SHORT, YOU KNOW?
HAHAHAHAHAHA!

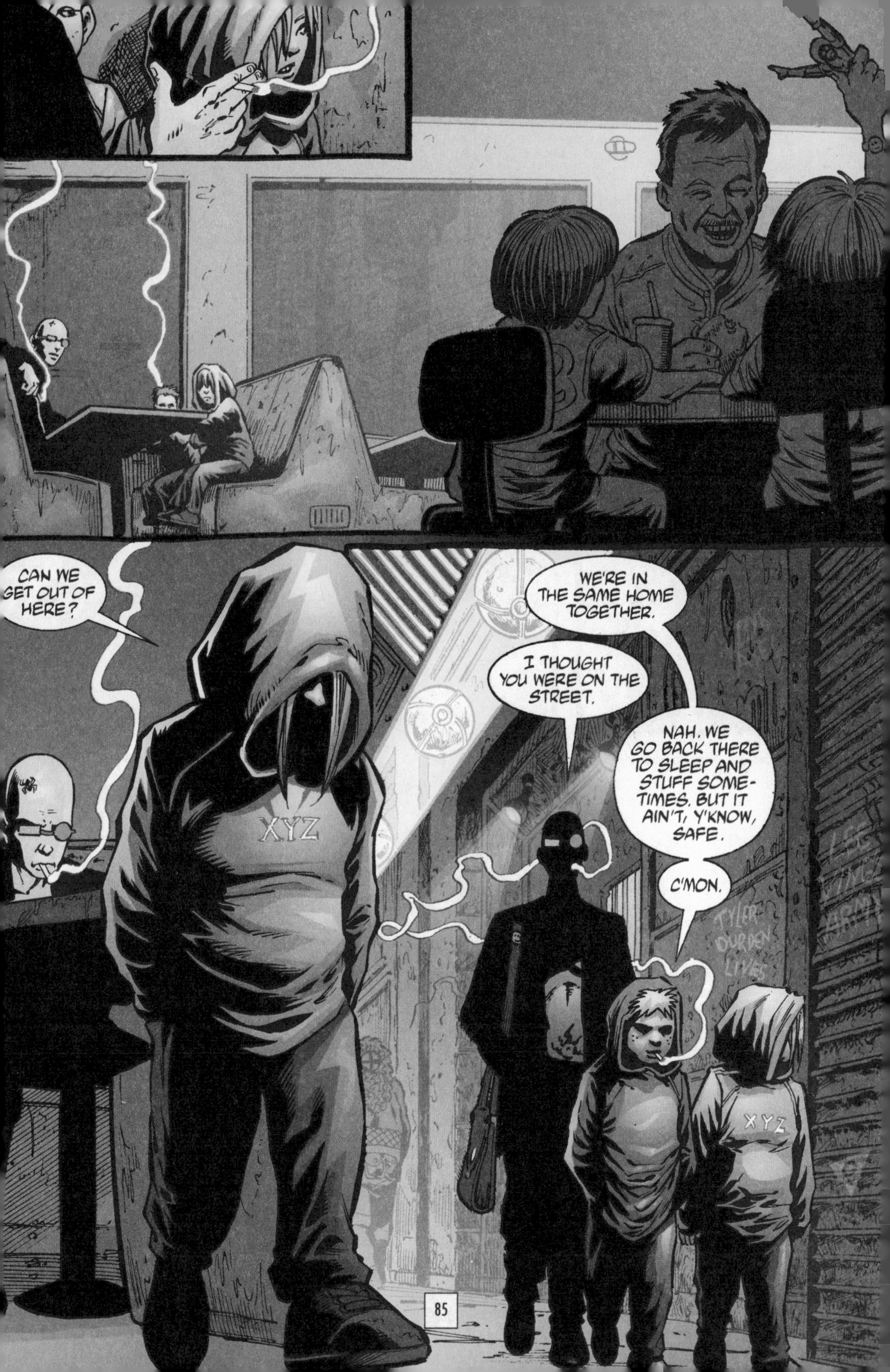
CAN WE GET OUT OF HERE?
WE'RE IN THE SAME HOME TOGETHER.
I THOUGHT YOU WERE ON THE STREET.
NAH. WE GO BACK THERE TO SLEEP AND STUFF SOME-TIMES. BUT IT AIN'T, Y'KNOW, SAFE.
C'MON.
XYZ
TYLER DURDEN LIVES
XYZ

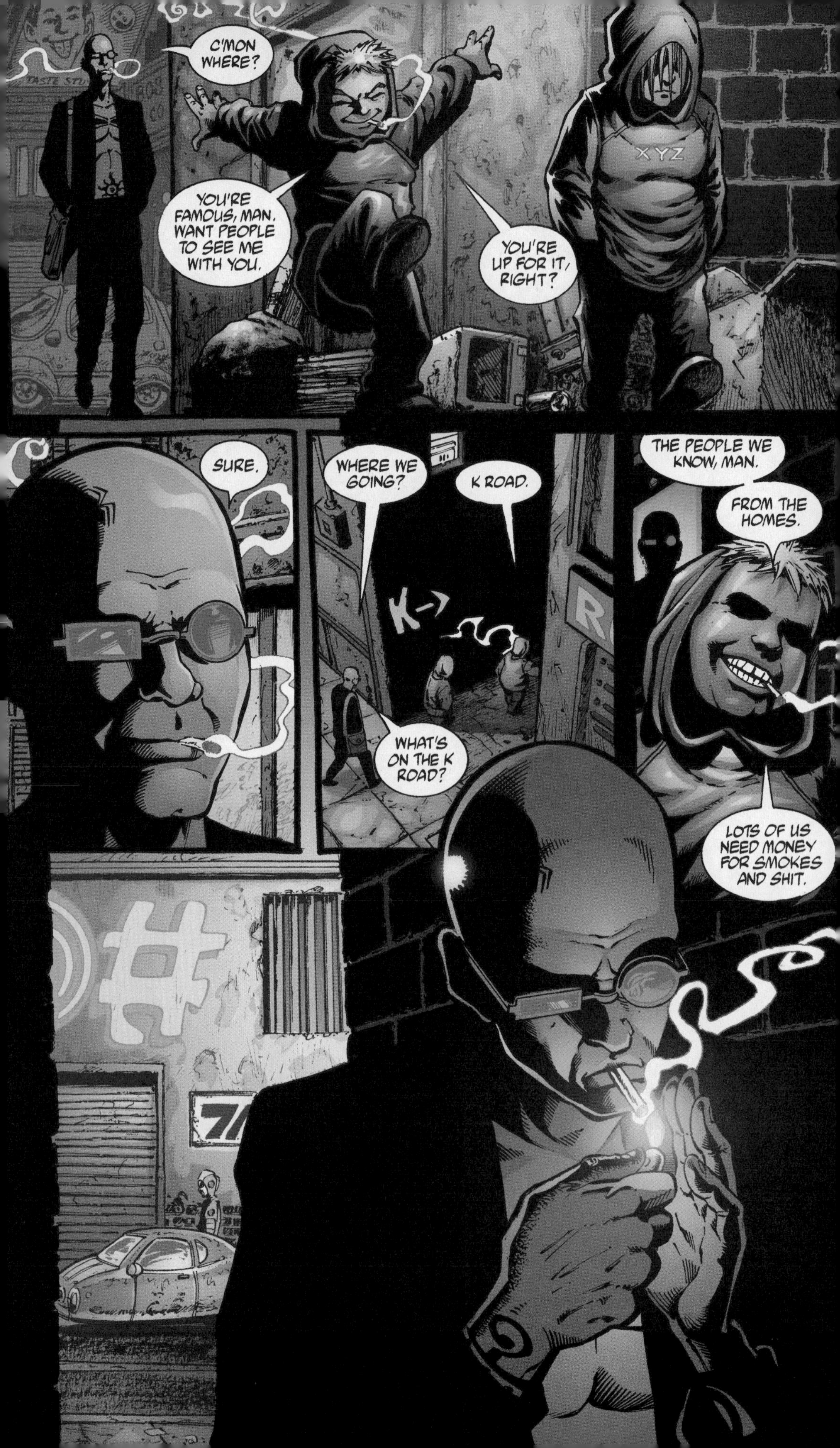
C'MON WHERE?
YOU'RE FAMOUS, MAN. WANT PEOPLE TO SEE ME WITH YOU.
YOU'RE UP FOR IT, RIGHT?
XYZ
SURE.
WHERE WE GOING?
K ROAD.
WHAT'S ON THE K ROAD?
THE PEOPLE WE KNOW, MAN.
FROM THE HOMES.
LOTS OF US NEED MONEY FOR SMOKES AND SHIT.

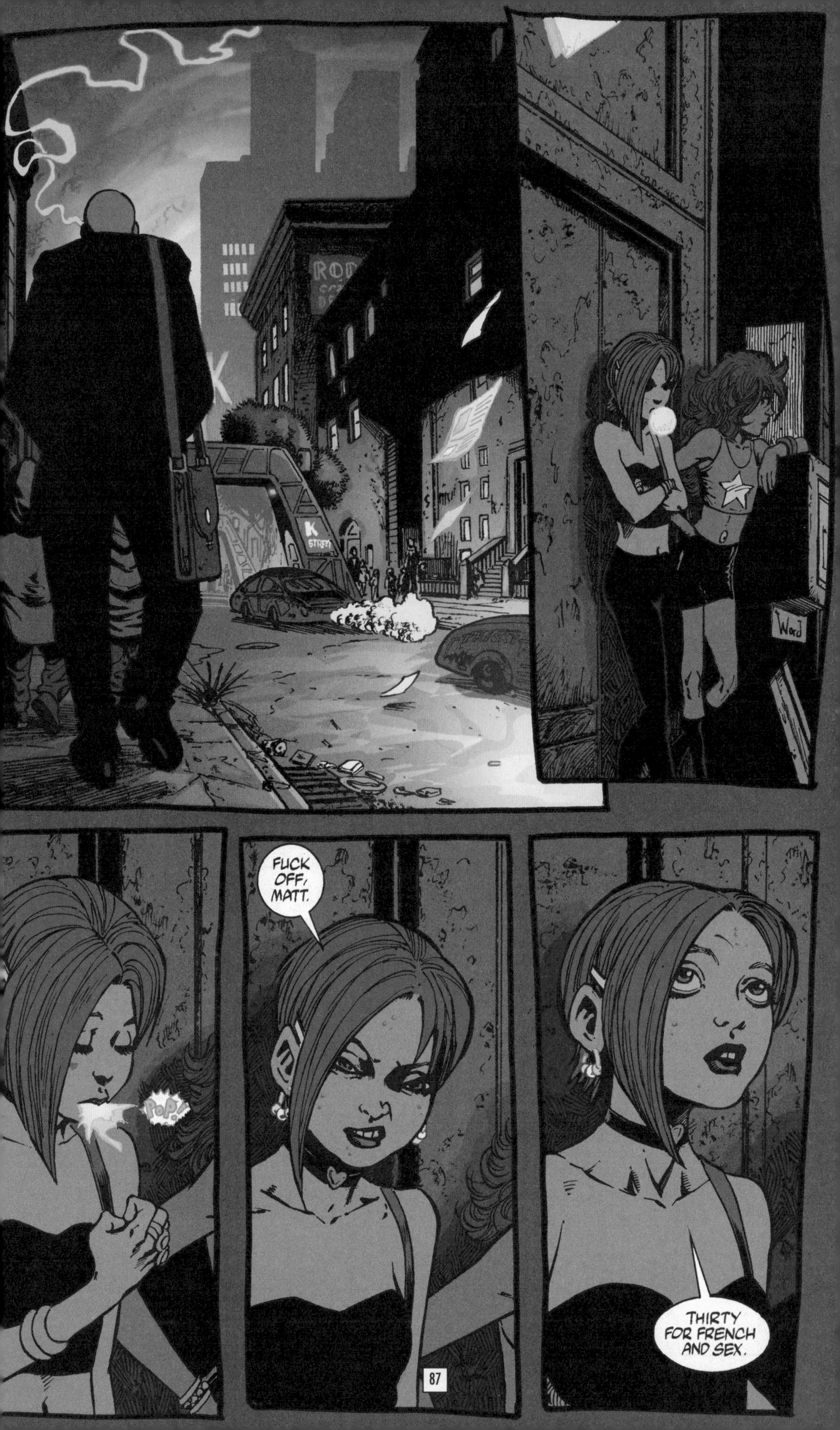

POP!
FUCK OFF, MATT.
THIRTY FOR FRENCH AND SEX.

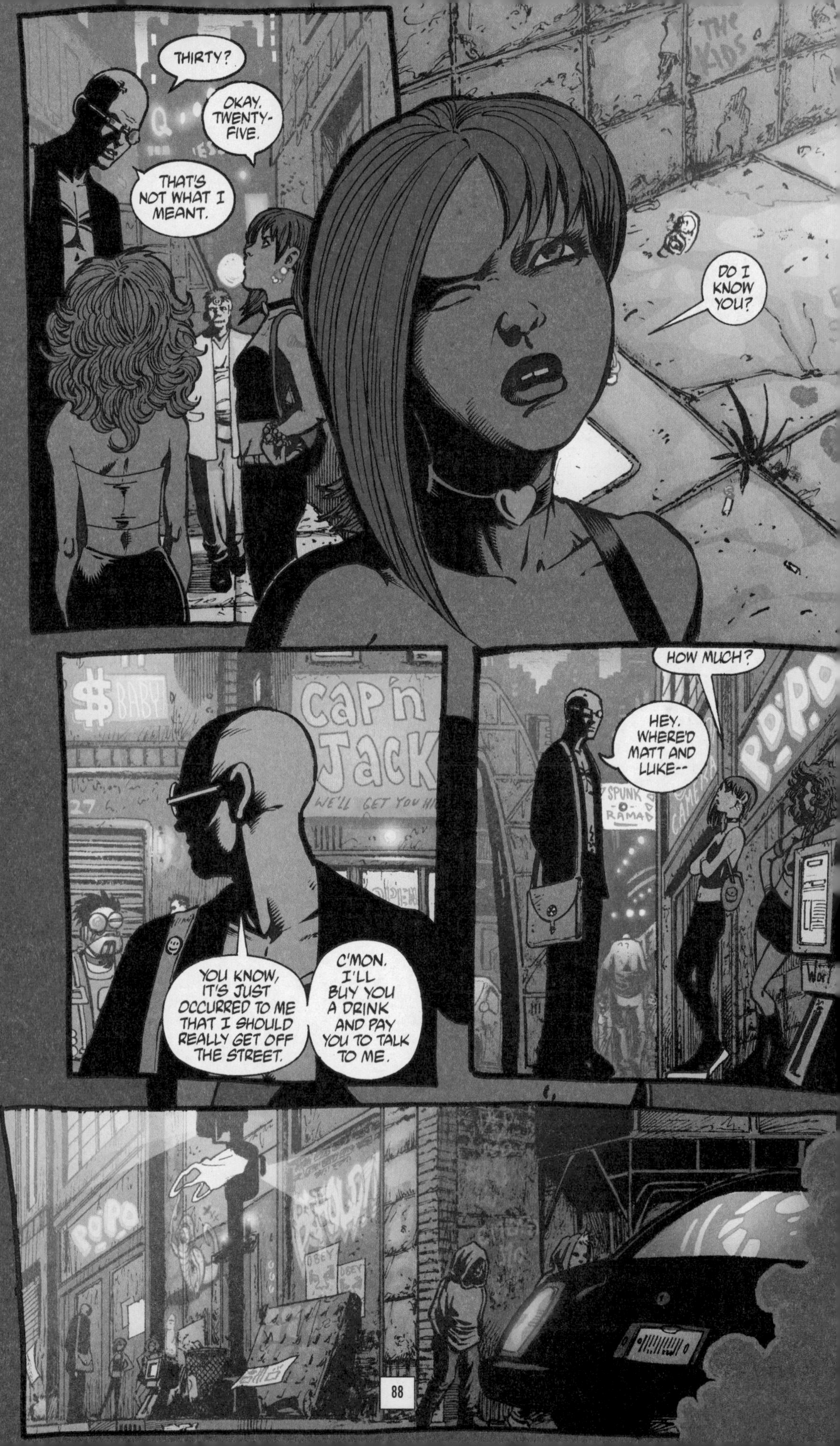
THE KIDS
THIRTY?
OKAY. TWENTY-FIVE.
THAT'S NOT WHAT I MEANT.
DO I KNOW YOU?
$ BABY
CAP'N JACK
WE'LL GET YOU HI
YOU KNOW, IT'S JUST OCCURRED TO ME THAT I SHOULD REALLY GET OFF THE STREET.
C'MON. I'LL BUY YOU A DRINK AND PAY YOU TO TALK TO ME.
HOW MUCH?
HEY. WHERE'D MATT AND LUKE--
SPUNK -O- RAMAD
CAMERA
OBEY
OBEY

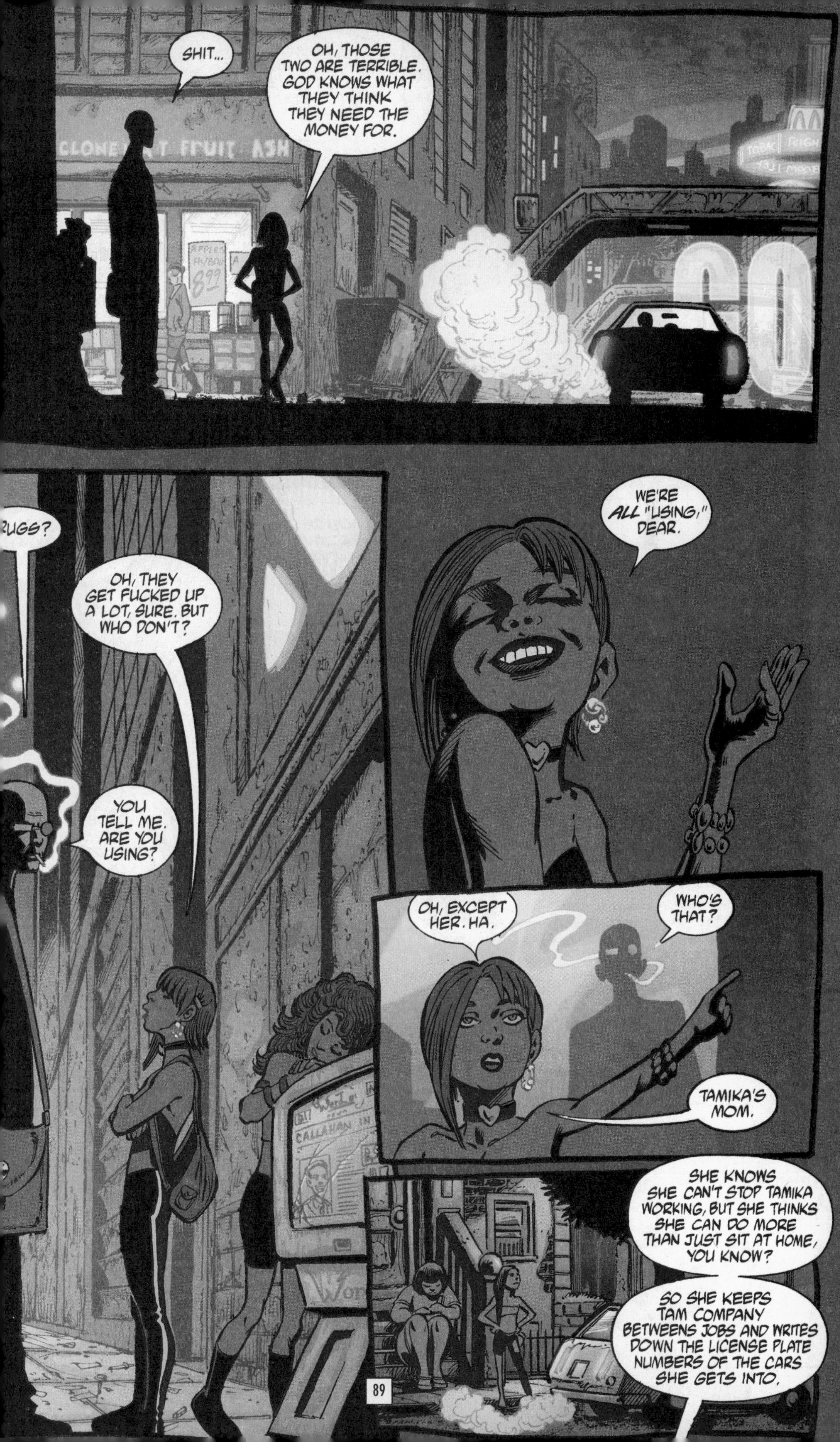
SHIT...
OH, THOSE TWO ARE TERRIBLE. GOD KNOWS WHAT THEY THINK THEY NEED THE MONEY FOR.
CLONE FRUIT ASH
APPLES
8.99
RUGS?
OH, THEY GET FUCKED UP A LOT, SURE. BUT WHO DON'T?
YOU TELL ME. ARE YOU USING?
WE'RE ALL "USING," DEAR.
OH, EXCEPT HER. HA.
WHO'S THAT?
TAMIKA'S MOM.
CALLAHAN IN
SHE KNOWS SHE CAN'T STOP TAMIKA WORKING, BUT SHE THINKS SHE CAN DO MORE THAN JUST SIT AT HOME, YOU KNOW?
SO SHE KEEPS TAM COMPANY BETWEENS JOBS AND WRITES DOWN THE LICENSE PLATE NUMBERS OF THE CARS SHE GETS INTO.

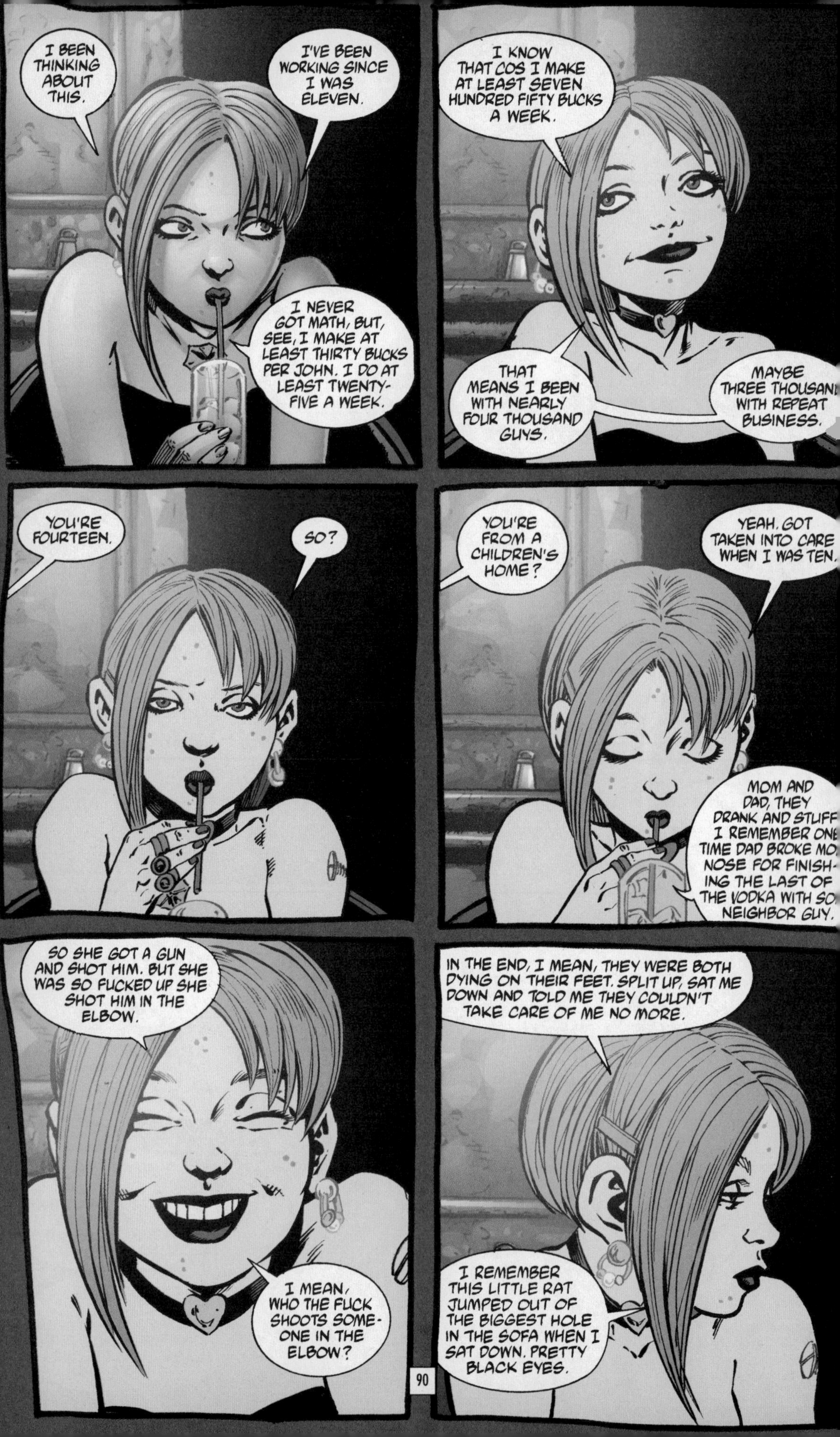
I BEEN THINKING ABOUT THIS.
I'VE BEEN WORKING SINCE I WAS ELEVEN.
I NEVER GOT MATH, BUT, SEE, I MAKE AT LEAST THIRTY BUCKS PER JOHN. I DO AT LEAST TWENTY-FIVE A WEEK.
I KNOW THAT COS I MAKE AT LEAST SEVEN HUNDRED FIFTY BUCKS A WEEK.
THAT MEANS I BEEN WITH NEARLY FOUR THOUSAND GUYS.
MAYBE THREE THOUSAN WITH REPEAT BUSINESS.
YOU'RE FOURTEEN.
SO?
YOU'RE FROM A CHILDREN'S HOME?
YEAH. GOT TAKEN INTO CARE WHEN I WAS TEN.
MOM AND DAD, THEY DRANK AND STUFF I REMEMBER ONE TIME DAD BROKE MO NOSE FOR FINISH-ING THE LAST OF THE VODKA WITH SO NEIGHBOR GUY.
SO SHE GOT A GUN AND SHOT HIM. BUT SHE WAS SO FUCKED UP SHE SHOT HIM IN THE ELBOW.
I MEAN, WHO THE FUCK SHOOTS SOME-ONE IN THE ELBOW?
IN THE END, I MEAN, THEY WERE BOTH DYING ON THEIR FEET. SPLIT UP, SAT ME DOWN AND TOLD ME THEY COULDN'T TAKE CARE OF ME NO MORE.
I REMEMBER THIS LITTLE RAT JUMPED OUT OF THE BIGGEST HOLE IN THE SOFA WHEN I SAT DOWN. PRETTY BLACK EYES.

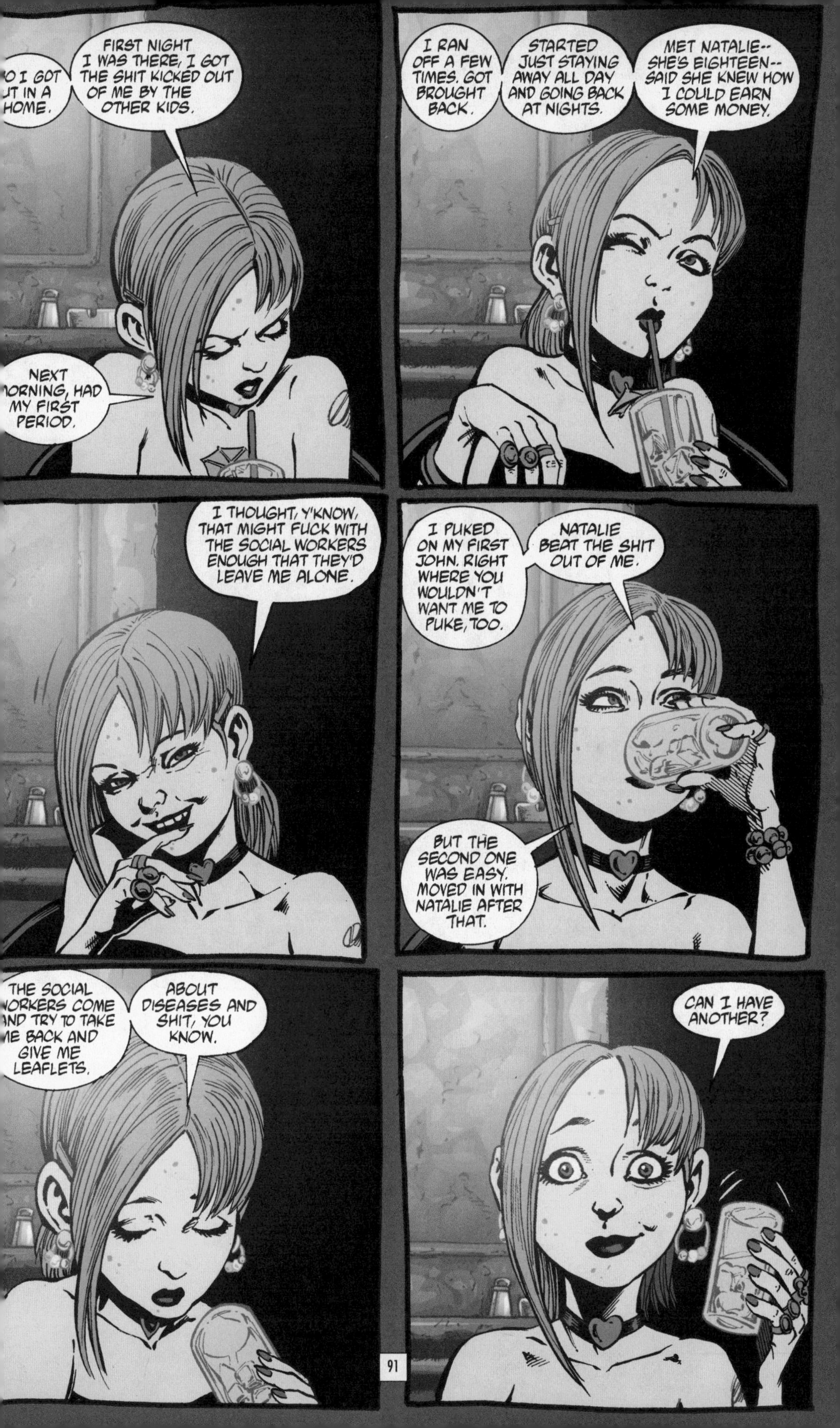

O I GOT
UT IN A
HOME.
FIRST NIGHT I WAS THERE, I GOT THE SHIT KICKED OUT OF ME BY THE OTHER KIDS.
NEXT
ORNING, HAD
MY FIRST
PERIOD.
I RAN OFF A FEW TIMES. GOT BROUGHT BACK.
STARTED JUST STAYING AWAY ALL DAY AND GOING BACK AT NIGHTS.
MET NATALIE-- SHE'S EIGHTEEN-- SAID SHE KNEW HOW I COULD EARN SOME MONEY.
I THOUGHT, Y'KNOW, THAT MIGHT FUCK WITH THE SOCIAL WORKERS ENOUGH THAT THEY'D LEAVE ME ALONE.
I PUKED ON MY FIRST JOHN. RIGHT WHERE YOU WOULDN'T WANT ME TO PUKE, TOO.
NATALIE BEAT THE SHIT OUT OF ME.
BUT THE SECOND ONE WAS EASY. MOVED IN WITH NATALIE AFTER THAT.
THE SOCIAL
ORKERS COME
ND TRY TO TAKE
E BACK AND
GIVE ME
LEAFLETS.
ABOUT DISEASES AND SHIT, YOU KNOW.
CAN I HAVE ANOTHER?

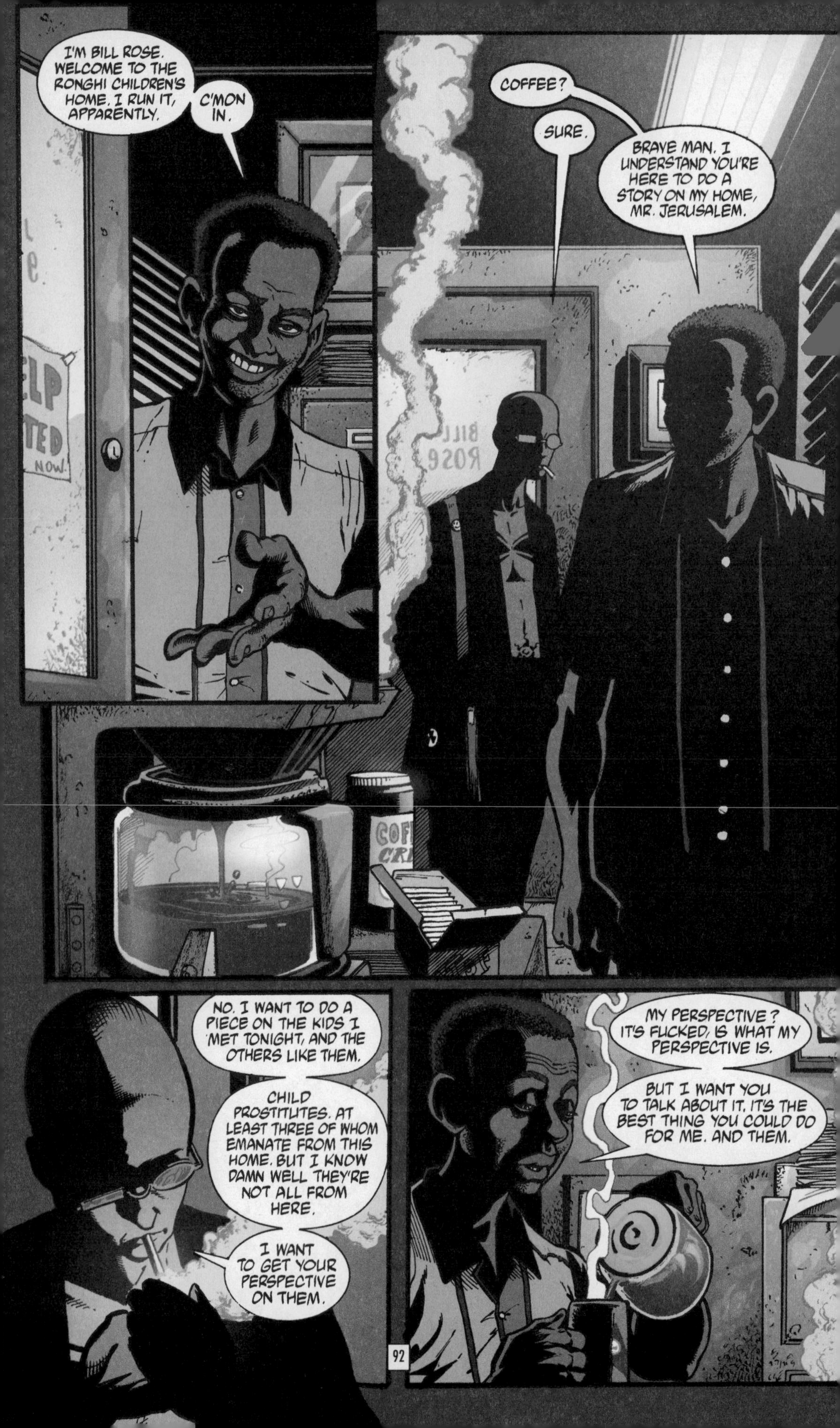
I'M BILL ROSE. WELCOME TO THE RONGHI CHILDREN'S HOME. I RUN IT, APPARENTLY.
C'MON IN.
COFFEE?
SURE.
BRAVE MAN. I UNDERSTAND YOU'RE HERE TO DO A STORY ON MY HOME, MR. JERUSALEM.
BILL ROSE
NO. I WANT TO DO A PIECE ON THE KIDS I MET TONIGHT, AND THE OTHERS LIKE THEM.
CHILD PROSTITUTES. AT LEAST THREE OF WHOM EMANATE FROM THIS HOME. BUT I KNOW DAMN WELL THEY'RE NOT ALL FROM HERE.
I WANT TO GET YOUR PERSPECTIVE ON THEM.
MY PERSPECTIVE? IT'S FUCKED, IS WHAT MY PERSPECTIVE IS.
BUT I WANT YOU TO TALK ABOUT IT. IT'S THE BEST THING YOU COULD DO FOR ME. AND THEM.

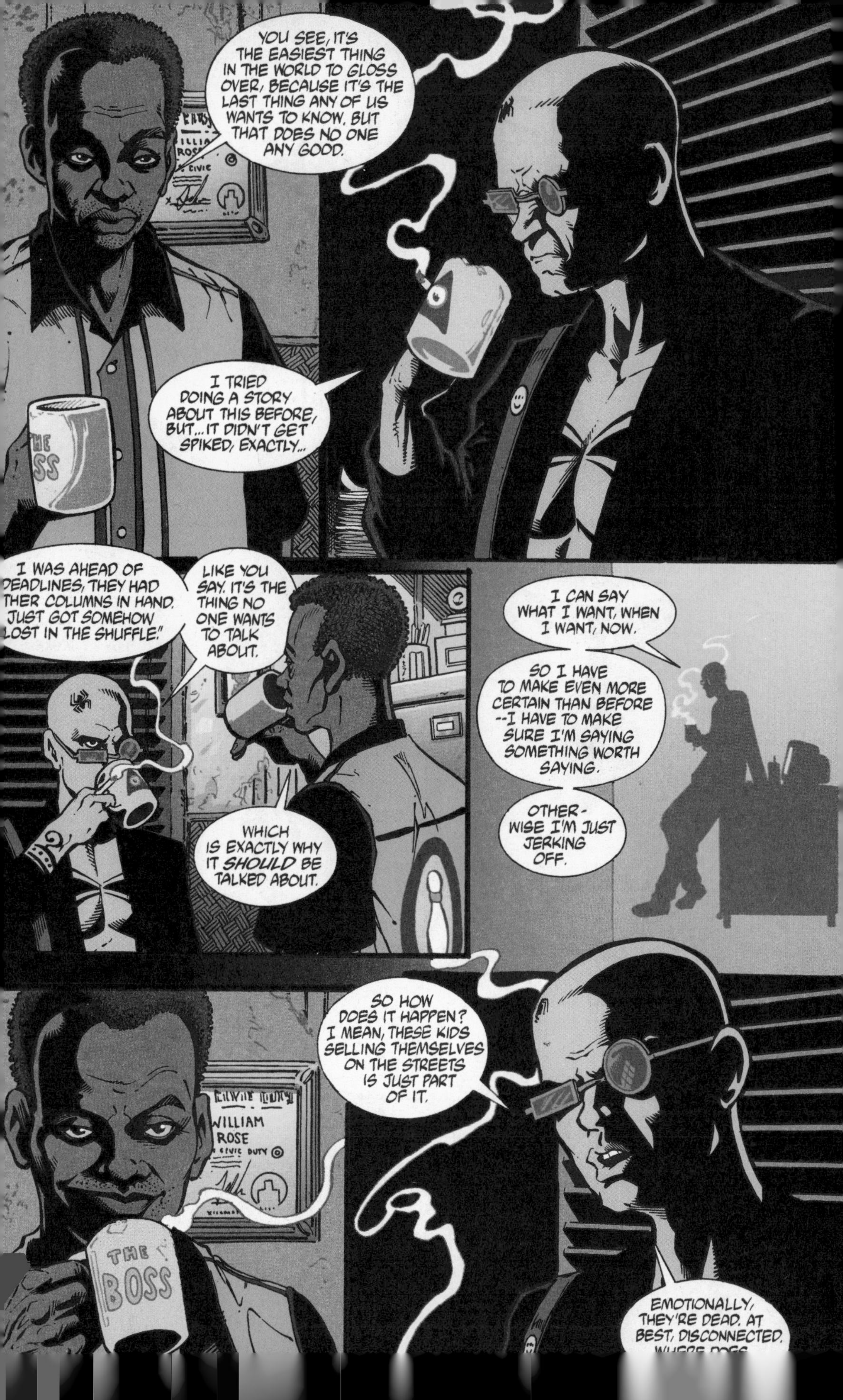
YOU SEE, IT'S THE EASIEST THING IN THE WORLD TO GLOSS OVER, BECAUSE IT'S THE LAST THING ANY OF US WANTS TO KNOW. BUT THAT DOES NO ONE ANY GOOD.
I TRIED DOING A STORY ABOUT THIS BEFORE, BUT... IT DIDN'T GET SPIKED, EXACTLY...
I WAS AHEAD OF DEADLINES, THEY HAD THEIR COLUMNS IN HAND. JUST GOT SOMEHOW LOST IN THE SHUFFLE."
LIKE YOU SAY. IT'S THE THING NO ONE WANTS TO TALK ABOUT.
WHICH IS EXACTLY WHY IT *SHOULD* BE TALKED ABOUT.
I CAN SAY WHAT I WANT, WHEN I WANT, NOW.
SO I HAVE TO MAKE EVEN MORE CERTAIN THAN BEFORE --I HAVE TO MAKE SURE I'M SAYING SOMETHING WORTH SAYING.
OTHER-WISE I'M JUST JERKING OFF.
SO HOW DOES IT HAPPEN? I MEAN, THESE KIDS SELLING THEMSELVES ON THE STREETS IS JUST PART OF IT.
EMOTIONALLY, THEY'RE DEAD. AT BEST, DISCONNECTED.

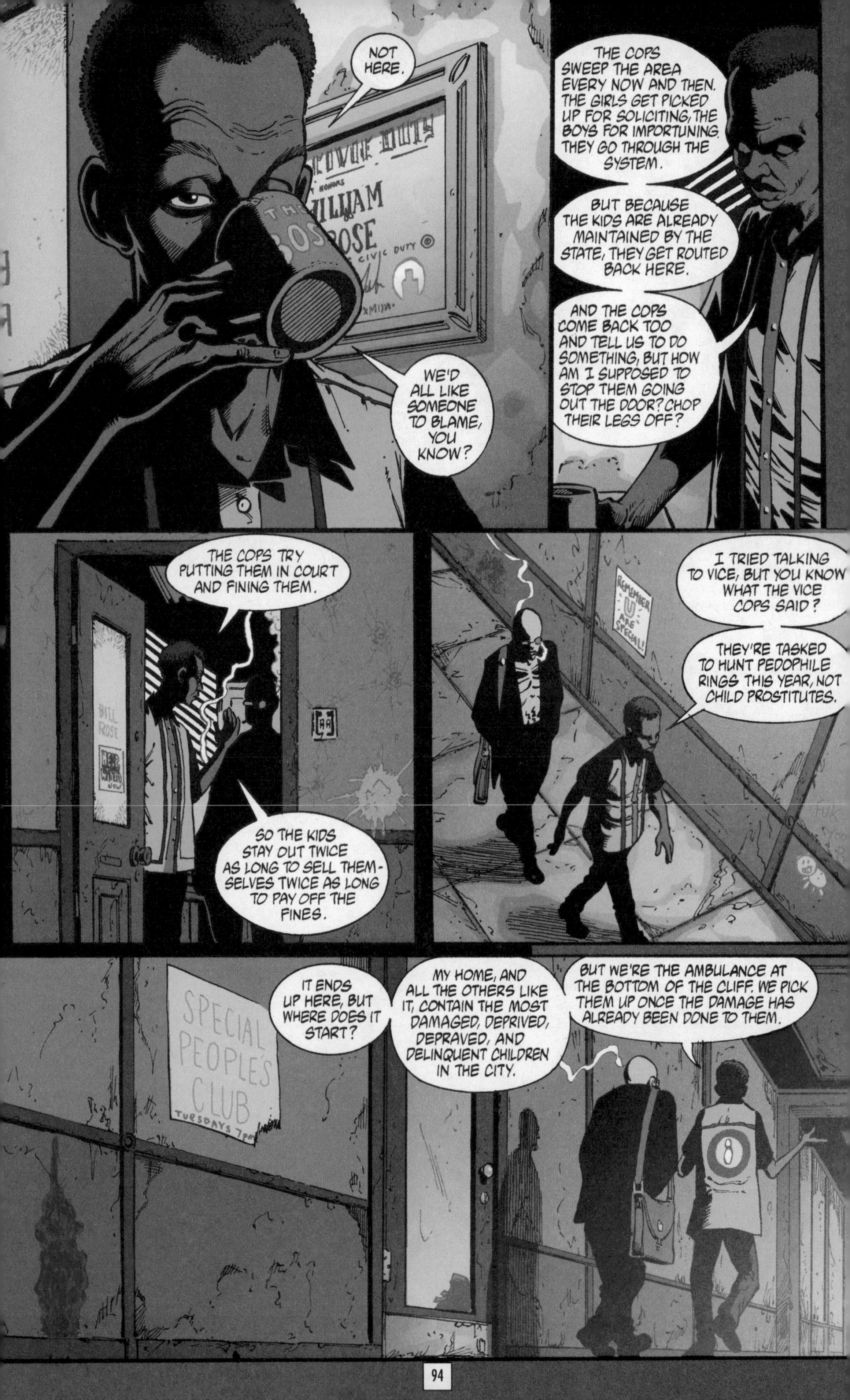

NOT HERE.
WE'D ALL LIKE SOMEONE TO BLAME, YOU KNOW?
THE COPS SWEEP THE AREA EVERY NOW AND THEN. THE GIRLS GET PICKED UP FOR SOLICITING, THE BOYS FOR IMPORTUNING. THEY GO THROUGH THE SYSTEM.
BUT BECAUSE THE KIDS ARE ALREADY MAINTAINED BY THE STATE, THEY GET ROUTED BACK HERE.
AND THE COPS COME BACK TOO AND TELL US TO DO SOMETHING, BUT HOW AM I SUPPOSED TO STOP THEM GOING OUT THE DOOR? CHOP THEIR LEGS OFF?
THE COPS TRY PUTTING THEM IN COURT AND FINING THEM.
SO THE KIDS STAY OUT TWICE AS LONG TO SELL THEM-SELVES TWICE AS LONG TO PAY OFF THE FINES.
REMEMBER U ARE SPECIAL!
I TRIED TALKING TO VICE, BUT YOU KNOW WHAT THE VICE COPS SAID?
THEY'RE TASKED TO HUNT PEDOPHILE RINGS THIS YEAR, NOT CHILD PROSTITUTES.
SPECIAL PEOPLE'S CLUB TUESDAYS 7pm
IT ENDS UP HERE, BUT WHERE DOES IT START?
MY HOME, AND ALL THE OTHERS LIKE IT, CONTAIN THE MOST DAMAGED, DEPRIVED, DEPRAVED, AND DELINQUENT CHILDREN IN THE CITY.
BUT WE'RE THE AMBULANCE AT THE BOTTOM OF THE CLIFF. WE PICK THEM UP ONCE THE DAMAGE HAS ALREADY BEEN DONE TO THEM.

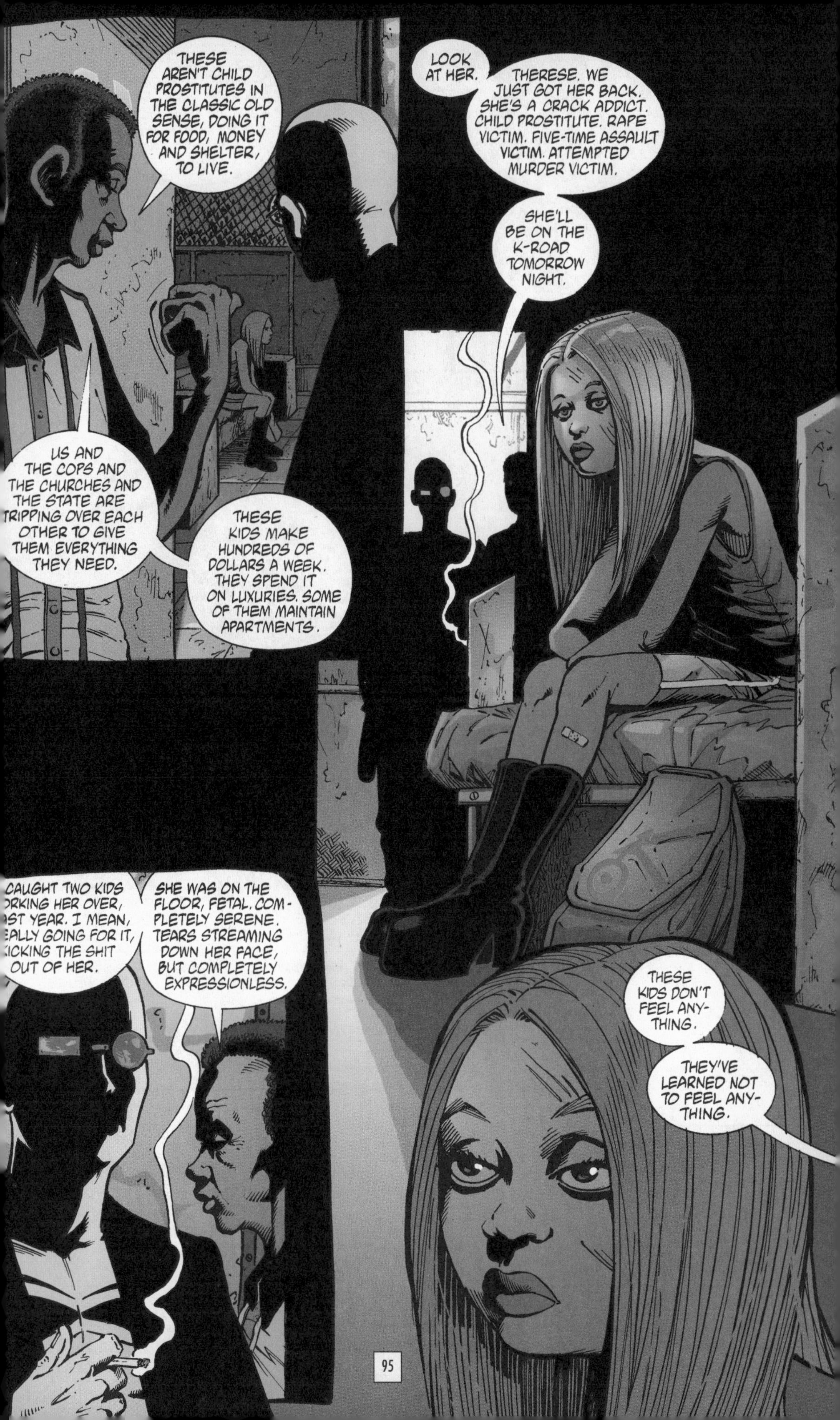

THESE AREN'T CHILD PROSTITUTES IN THE CLASSIC OLD SENSE, DOING IT FOR FOOD, MONEY AND SHELTER, TO LIVE.
US AND THE COPS AND THE CHURCHES AND THE STATE ARE TRIPPING OVER EACH OTHER TO GIVE THEM EVERYTHING THEY NEED.
THESE KIDS MAKE HUNDREDS OF DOLLARS A WEEK. THEY SPEND IT ON LUXURIES. SOME OF THEM MAINTAIN APARTMENTS.
LOOK AT HER.
THERESE. WE JUST GOT HER BACK. SHE'S A CRACK ADDICT. CHILD PROSTITUTE. RAPE VICTIM. FIVE-TIME ASSAULT VICTIM. ATTEMPTED MURDER VICTIM.
SHE'LL BE ON THE K-ROAD TOMORROW NIGHT.
CAUGHT TWO KIDS ORKING HER OVER, AST YEAR. I MEAN, EALLY GOING FOR IT, ICKING THE SHIT OUT OF HER.
SHE WAS ON THE FLOOR, FETAL. COMPLETELY SERENE. TEARS STREAMING DOWN HER FACE, BUT COMPLETELY EXPRESSIONLESS.
THESE KIDS DON'T FEEL ANYTHING.
THEY'VE LEARNED NOT TO FEEL ANYTHING.

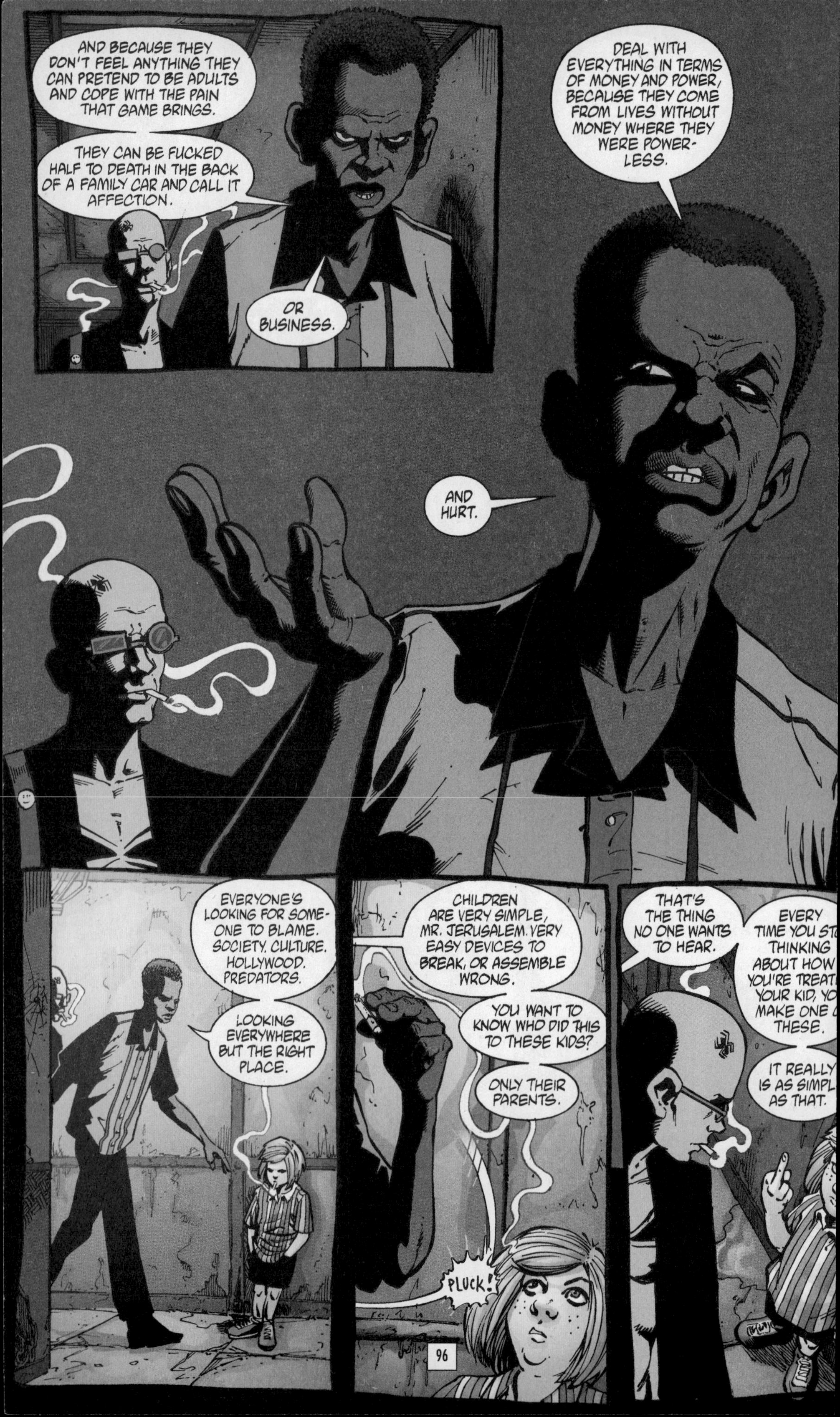

AND BECAUSE THEY DON'T FEEL ANYTHING THEY CAN PRETEND TO BE ADULTS AND COPE WITH THE PAIN THAT GAME BRINGS.
THEY CAN BE FUCKED HALF TO DEATH IN THE BACK OF A FAMILY CAR AND CALL IT AFFECTION.
OR BUSINESS.
DEAL WITH EVERYTHING IN TERMS OF MONEY AND POWER, BECAUSE THEY COME FROM LIVES WITHOUT MONEY WHERE THEY WERE POWER-LESS.
AND HURT.
EVERYONE'S LOOKING FOR SOME-ONE TO BLAME. SOCIETY. CULTURE. HOLLYWOOD. PREDATORS.
LOOKING EVERYWHERE BUT THE RIGHT PLACE.
CHILDREN ARE VERY SIMPLE, MR. JERUSALEM. VERY EASY DEVICES TO BREAK, OR ASSEMBLE WRONG.
YOU WANT TO KNOW WHO DID THIS TO THESE KIDS?
ONLY THEIR PARENTS.
PLUCK!
THAT'S THE THING NO ONE WANTS TO HEAR.
EVERY TIME YOU ST THINKING ABOUT HOW YOU'RE TREAT YOUR KID, YO MAKE ONE O THESE.
IT REALLY IS AS SIMPL AS THAT.

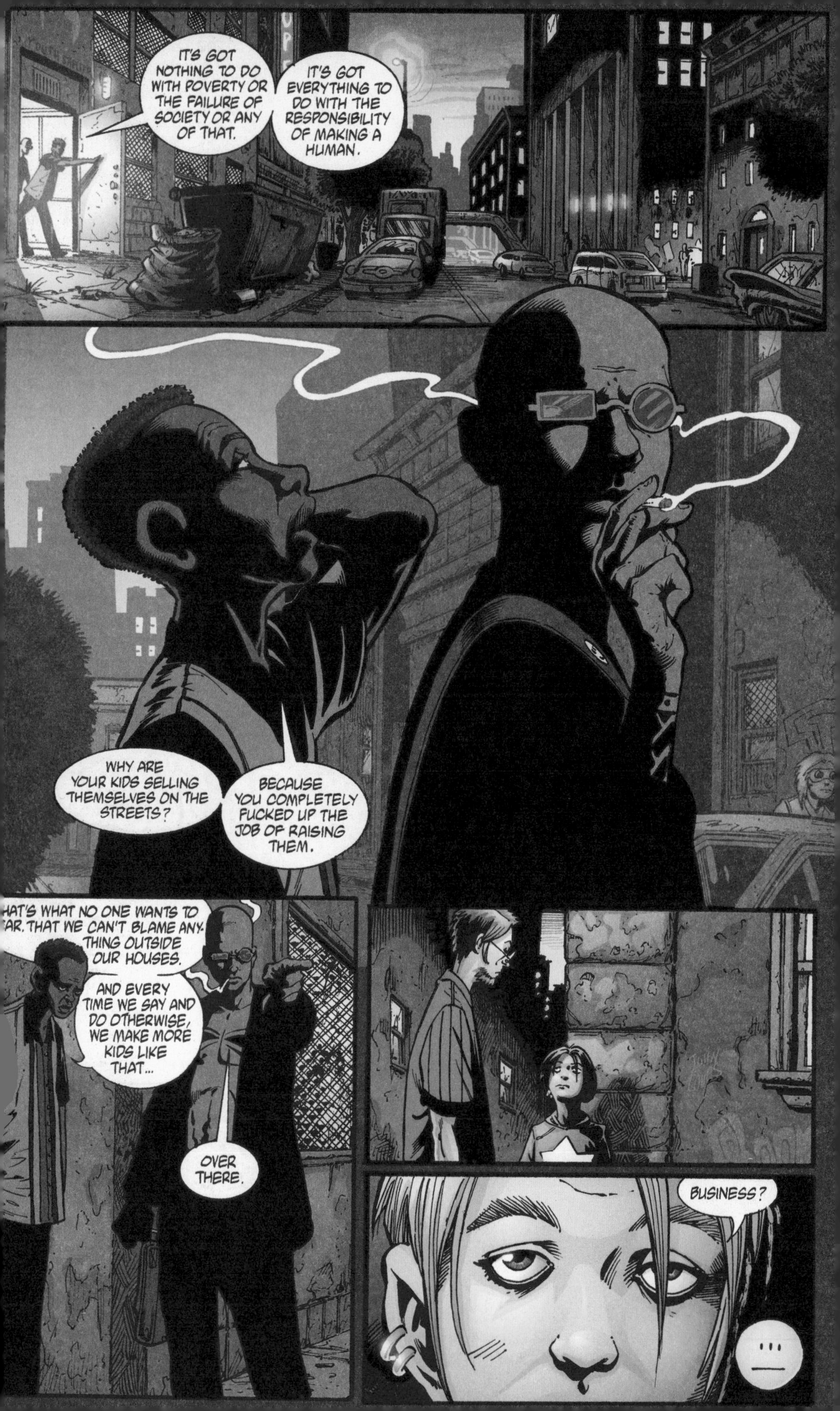
IT'S GOT NOTHING TO DO WITH POVERTY OR THE FAILURE OF SOCIETY OR ANY OF THAT.
IT'S GOT EVERYTHING TO DO WITH THE RESPONSIBILITY OF MAKING A HUMAN.
WHY ARE YOUR KIDS SELLING THEMSELVES ON THE STREETS?
BECAUSE YOU COMPLETELY FUCKED UP THE JOB OF RAISING THEM.
HAT'S WHAT NO ONE WANTS TO AR. THAT WE CAN'T BLAME ANY-THING OUTSIDE OUR HOUSES.
AND EVERY TIME WE SAY AND DO OTHERWISE, WE MAKE MORE KIDS LIKE THAT...
OVER THERE.
BUSINESS?

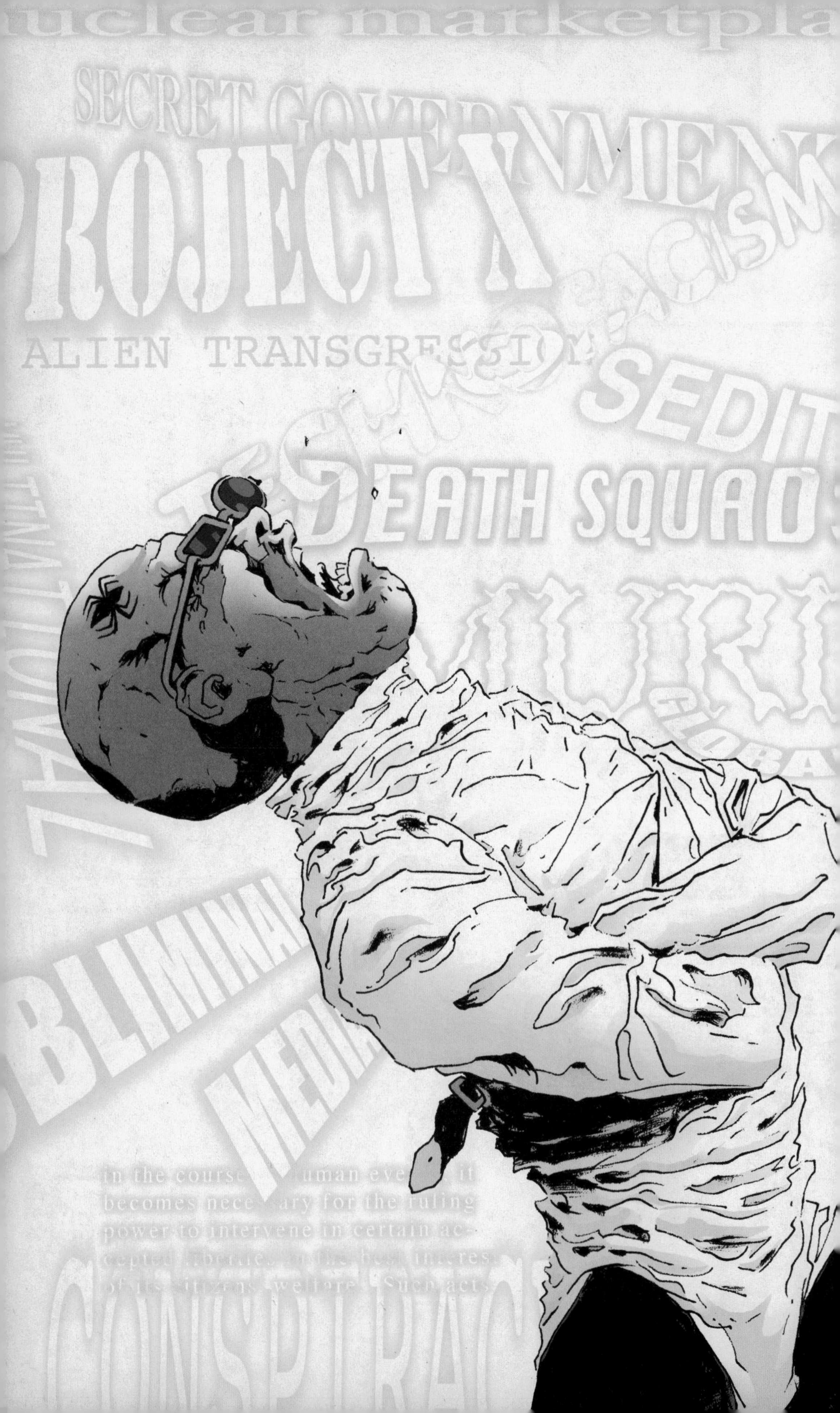

uclear marketpla
SECRET
PROJECT X
ALIEN TRANSGRESSI
SEDIT
DEATH SQUADS
BLIMINA
MEDI
becomes nece ary for the ruling
power to intervene in certain ac-

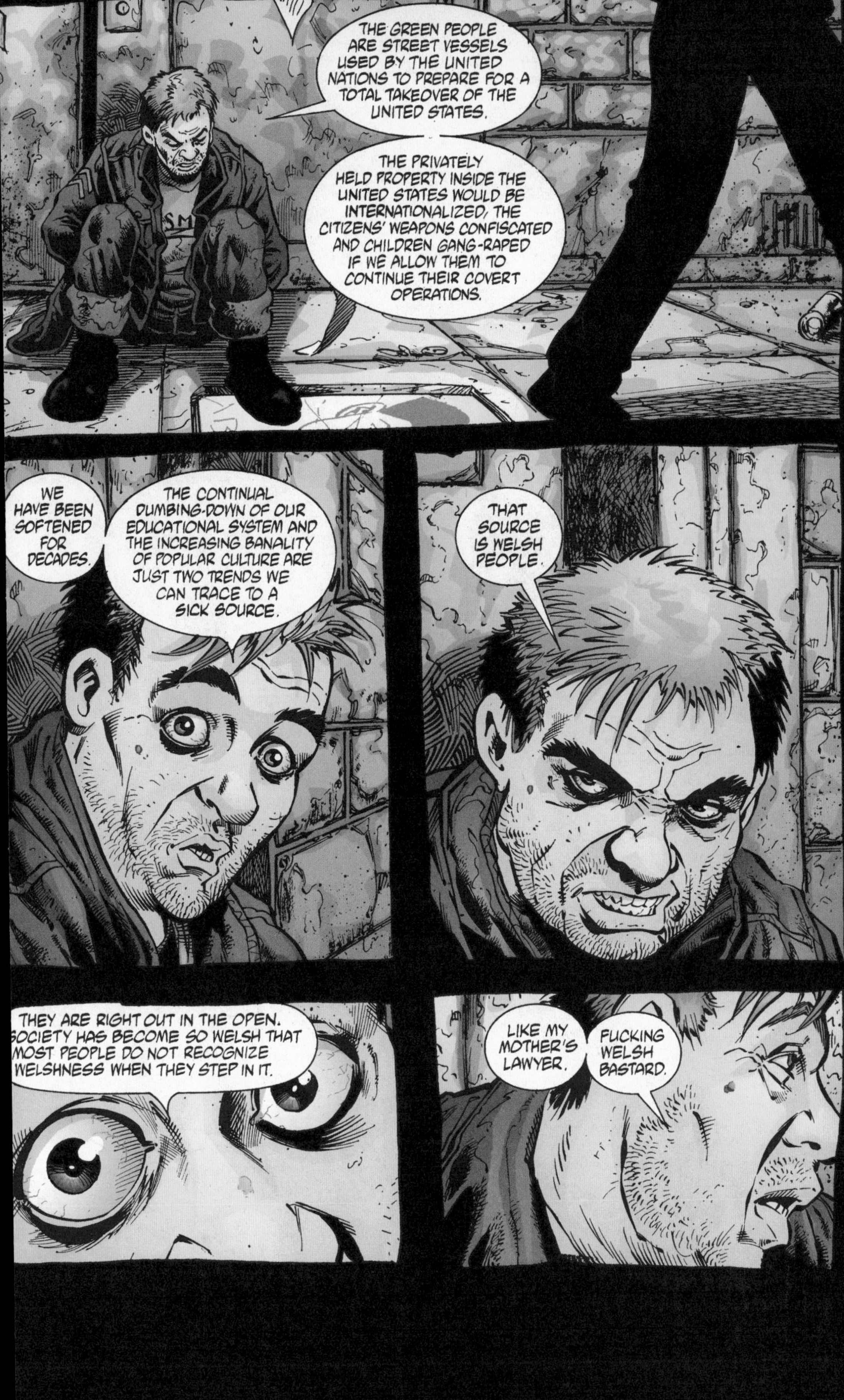
THE GREEN PEOPLE ARE STREET VESSELS USED BY THE UNITED NATIONS TO PREPARE FOR A TOTAL TAKEOVER OF THE UNITED STATES.
THE PRIVATELY HELD PROPERTY INSIDE THE UNITED STATES WOULD BE INTERNATIONALIZED, THE CITIZENS' WEAPONS CONFISCATED AND CHILDREN GANG-RAPED IF WE ALLOW THEM TO CONTINUE THEIR COVERT OPERATIONS.
WE HAVE BEEN SOFTENED FOR DECADES.
THE CONTINUAL DUMBING-DOWN OF OUR EDUCATIONAL SYSTEM AND THE INCREASING BANALITY OF POPULAR CULTURE ARE JUST TWO TRENDS WE CAN TRACE TO A SICK SOURCE.
THAT SOURCE IS WELSH PEOPLE.
THEY ARE RIGHT OUT IN THE OPEN. SOCIETY HAS BECOME SO WELSH THAT MOST PEOPLE DO NOT RECOGNIZE WELSHNESS WHEN THEY STEP IN IT.
LIKE MY MOTHER'S LAWYER.
FUCKING WELSH BASTARD.

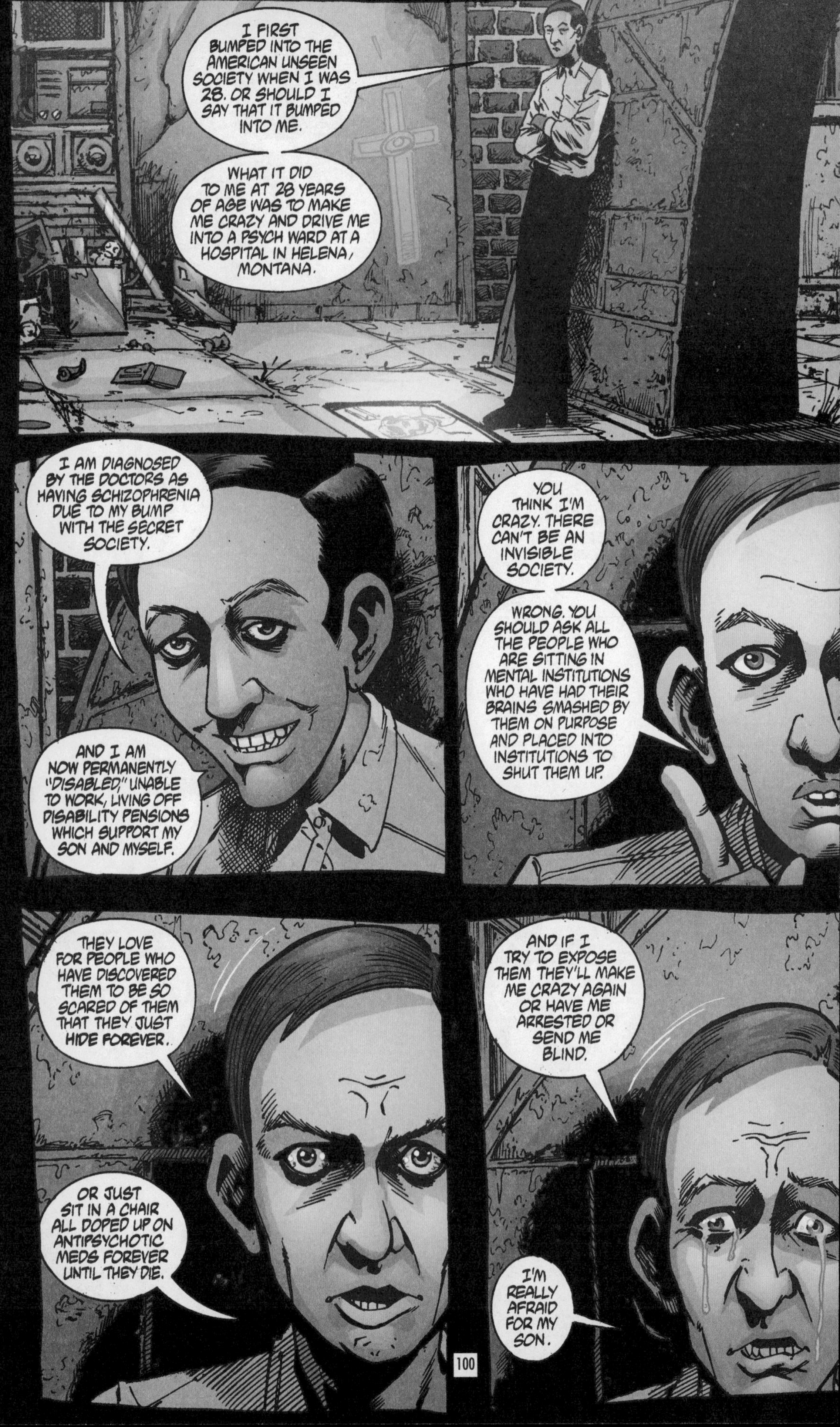
I FIRST BUMPED INTO THE AMERICAN UNSEEN SOCIETY WHEN I WAS 28. OR SHOULD I SAY THAT IT BUMPED INTO ME.
WHAT IT DID TO ME AT 28 YEARS OF AGE WAS TO MAKE ME CRAZY AND DRIVE ME INTO A PSYCH WARD AT A HOSPITAL IN HELENA, MONTANA.
I AM DIAGNOSED BY THE DOCTORS AS HAVING SCHIZOPHRENIA DUE TO MY BUMP WITH THE SECRET SOCIETY.
AND I AM NOW PERMANENTLY "DISABLED," UNABLE TO WORK, LIVING OFF DISABILITY PENSIONS WHICH SUPPORT MY SON AND MYSELF.
YOU THINK I'M CRAZY. THERE CAN'T BE AN INVISIBLE SOCIETY.
WRONG. YOU SHOULD ASK ALL THE PEOPLE WHO ARE SITTING IN MENTAL INSTITUTIONS WHO HAVE HAD THEIR BRAINS SMASHED BY THEM ON PURPOSE AND PLACED INTO INSTITUTIONS TO SHUT THEM UP.
THEY LOVE FOR PEOPLE WHO HAVE DISCOVERED THEM TO BE SO SCARED OF THEM THAT THEY JUST HIDE FOREVER.
OR JUST SIT IN A CHAIR ALL DOPED UP ON ANTIPSYCHOTIC MEDS FOREVER UNTIL THEY DIE.
AND IF I TRY TO EXPOSE THEM THEY'LL MAKE ME CRAZY AGAIN OR HAVE ME ARRESTED OR SEND ME BLIND.
I'M REALLY AFRAID FOR MY SON.

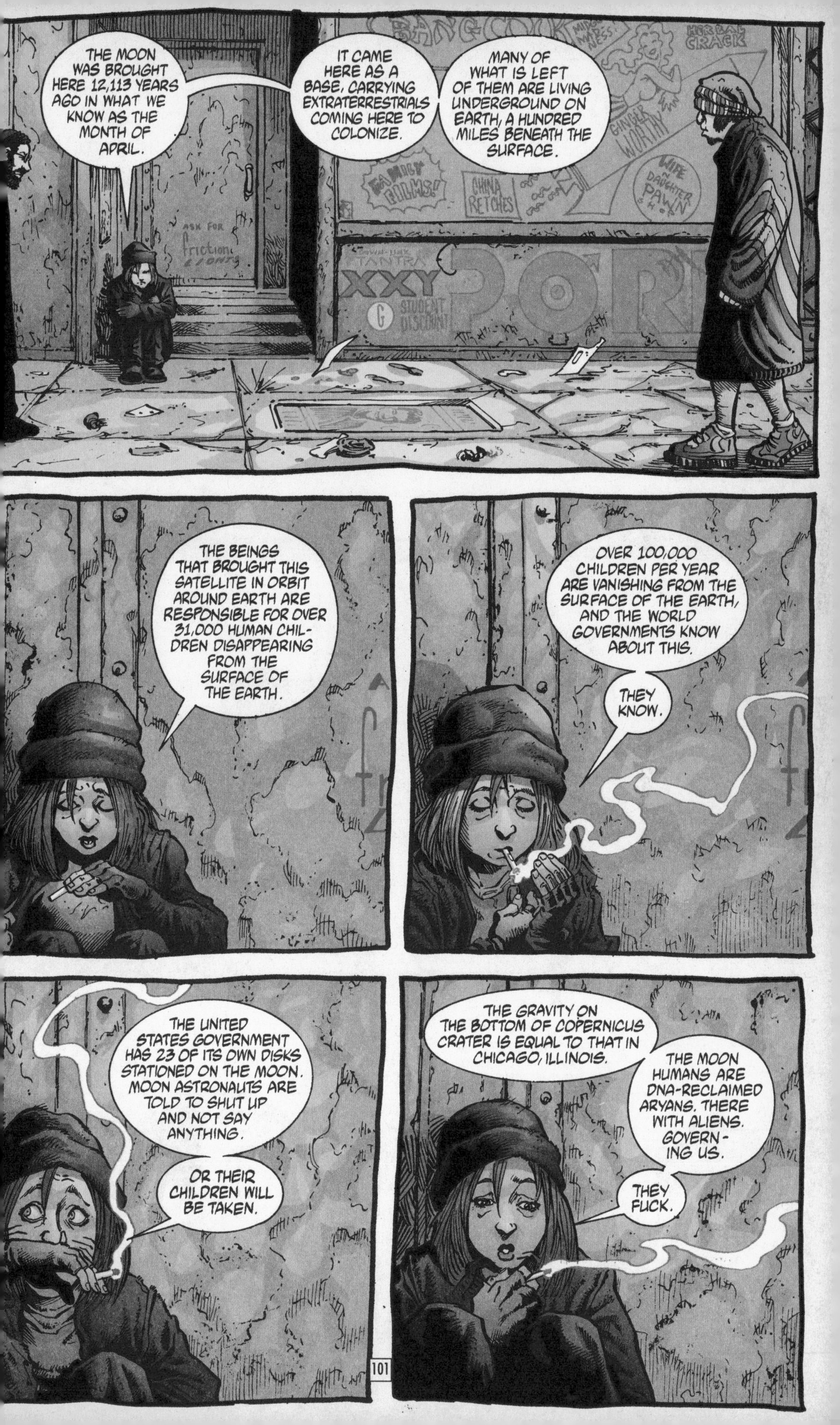
THE MOON WAS BROUGHT HERE 12,113 YEARS AGO IN WHAT WE KNOW AS THE MONTH OF APRIL.
IT CAME HERE AS A BASE, CARRYING EXTRATERRESTRIALS COMING HERE TO COLONIZE.
MANY OF WHAT IS LEFT OF THEM ARE LIVING UNDERGROUND ON EARTH, A HUNDRED MILES BENEATH THE SURFACE.
CHINA RETCHES
GINGER WORTHY
TANTRA
XXY
STUDENT DISCOUNT
THE BEINGS THAT BROUGHT THIS SATELLITE IN ORBIT AROUND EARTH ARE RESPONSIBLE FOR OVER 31,000 HUMAN CHILDREN DISAPPEARING FROM THE SURFACE OF THE EARTH.
OVER 100,000 CHILDREN PER YEAR ARE VANISHING FROM THE SURFACE OF THE EARTH, AND THE WORLD GOVERNMENTS KNOW ABOUT THIS.
THEY KNOW.
THE UNITED STATES GOVERNMENT HAS 23 OF ITS OWN DISKS STATIONED ON THE MOON. MOON ASTRONAUTS ARE TOLD TO SHUT UP AND NOT SAY ANYTHING.
OR THEIR CHILDREN WILL BE TAKEN.
THE GRAVITY ON THE BOTTOM OF COPERNICUS CRATER IS EQUAL TO THAT IN CHICAGO, ILLINOIS.
THE MOON HUMANS ARE DNA-RECLAIMED ARYANS. THERE WITH ALIENS. GOVERNING US.
THEY FUCK.

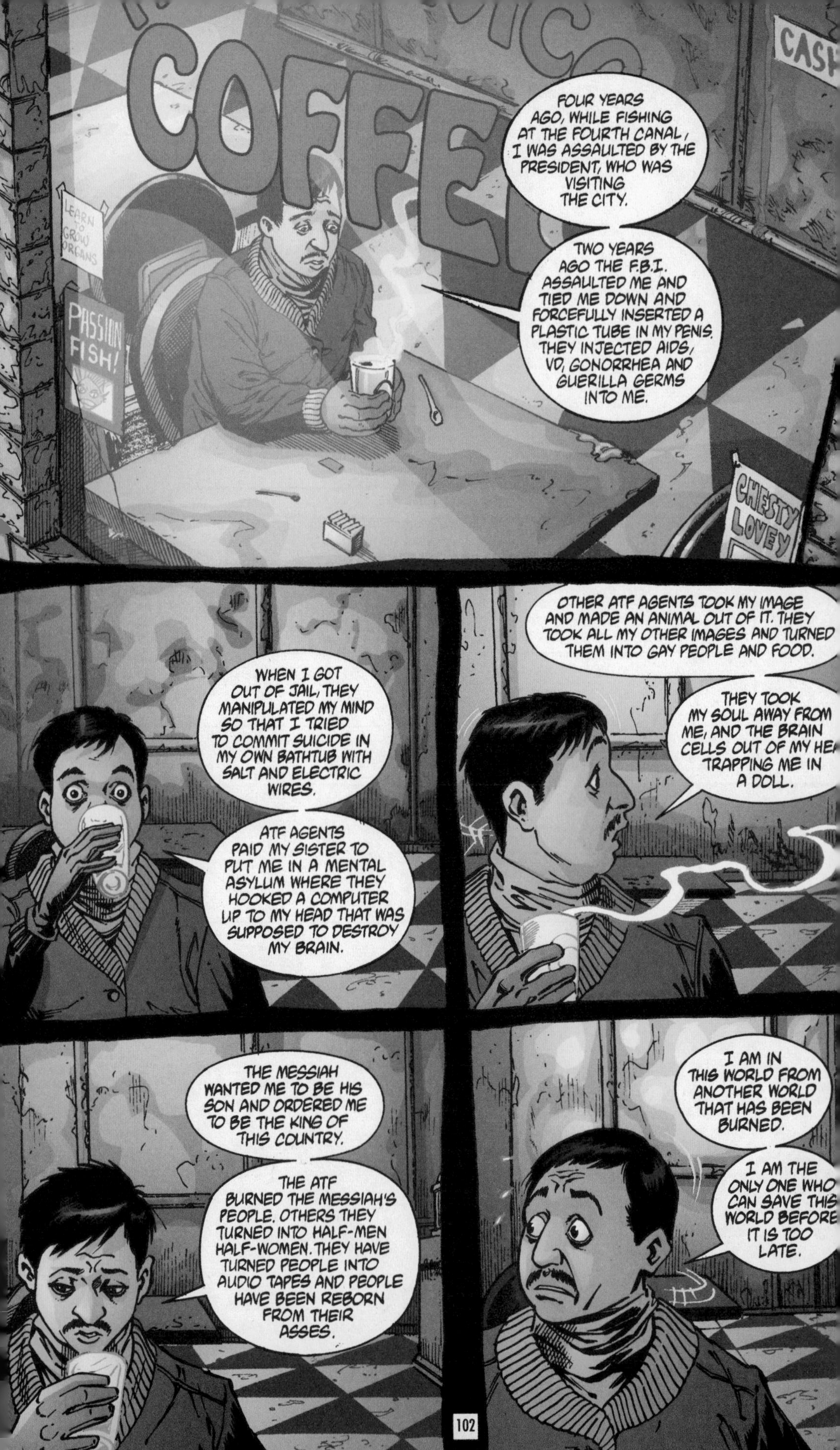
COFFEE
CASH
LEARN TO GROW ORGANS
PASSION FISH!
CHESTY LOVEY
FOUR YEARS AGO, WHILE FISHING AT THE FOURTH CANAL, I WAS ASSAULTED BY THE PRESIDENT, WHO WAS VISITING THE CITY.
TWO YEARS AGO THE F.B.I. ASSAULTED ME AND TIED ME DOWN AND FORCEFULLY INSERTED A PLASTIC TUBE IN MY PENIS. THEY INJECTED AIDS, VD, GONORRHEA AND GUERILLA GERMS INTO ME.
WHEN I GOT OUT OF JAIL, THEY MANIPULATED MY MIND SO THAT I TRIED TO COMMIT SUICIDE IN MY OWN BATHTUB WITH SALT AND ELECTRIC WIRES.
ATF AGENTS PAID MY SISTER TO PUT ME IN A MENTAL ASYLUM WHERE THEY HOOKED A COMPUTER UP TO MY HEAD THAT WAS SUPPOSED TO DESTROY MY BRAIN.
OTHER ATF AGENTS TOOK MY IMAGE AND MADE AN ANIMAL OUT OF IT. THEY TOOK ALL MY OTHER IMAGES AND TURNED THEM INTO GAY PEOPLE AND FOOD.
THEY TOOK MY SOUL AWAY FROM ME, AND THE BRAIN CELLS OUT OF MY HE TRAPPING ME IN A DOLL.
THE MESSIAH WANTED ME TO BE HIS SON AND ORDERED ME TO BE THE KING OF THIS COUNTRY.
THE ATF BURNED THE MESSIAH'S PEOPLE. OTHERS THEY TURNED INTO HALF-MEN HALF-WOMEN. THEY HAVE TURNED PEOPLE INTO AUDIO TAPES AND PEOPLE HAVE BEEN REBORN FROM THEIR ASSES.
I AM IN THIS WORLD FROM ANOTHER WORLD THAT HAS BEEN BURNED.
I AM THE ONLY ONE WHO CAN SAVE THIS WORLD BEFORE IT IS TOO LATE.

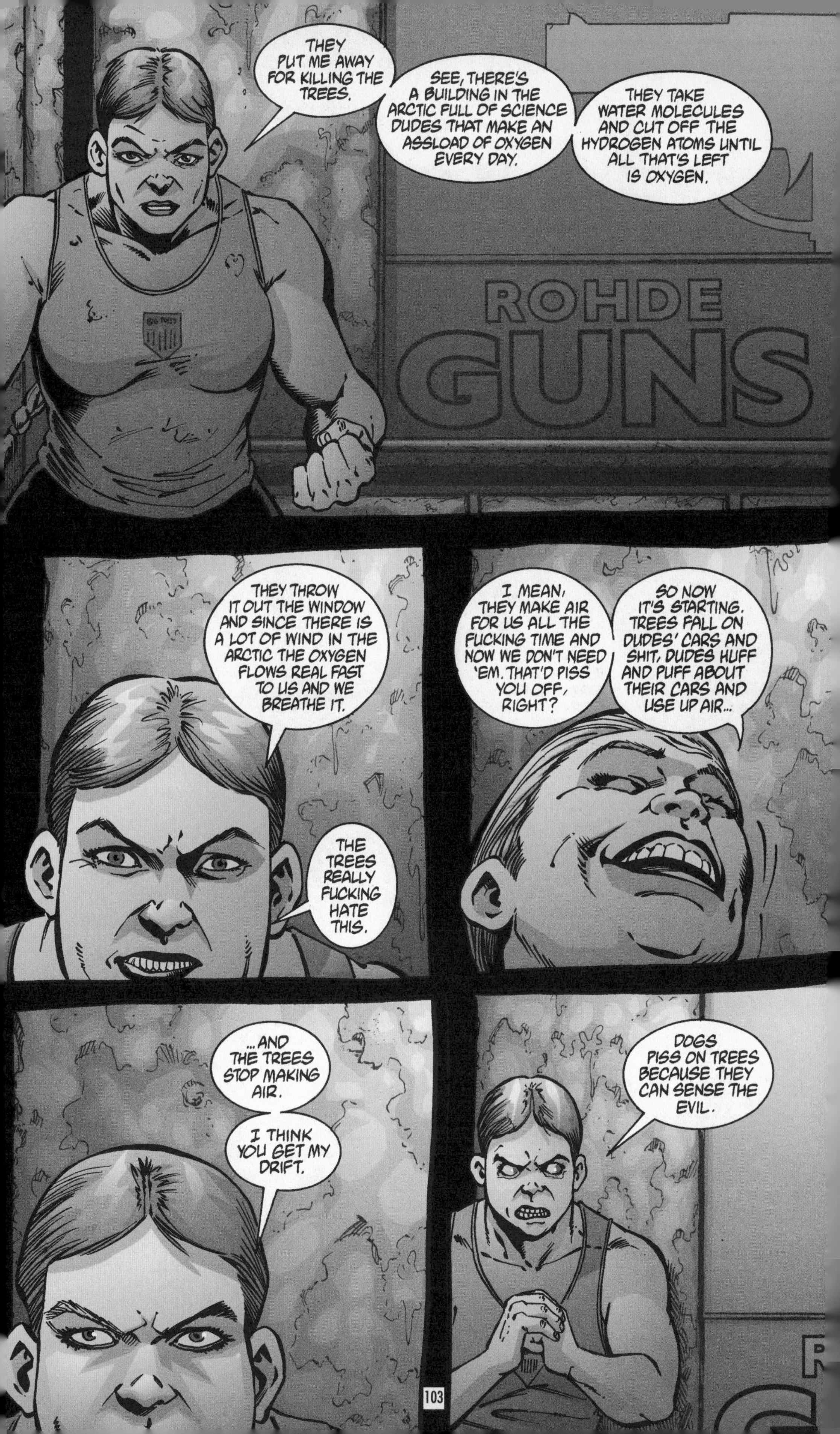
THEY PUT ME AWAY FOR KILLING THE TREES.
SEE, THERE'S A BUILDING IN THE ARCTIC FULL OF SCIENCE DUDES THAT MAKE AN ASSLOAD OF OXYGEN EVERY DAY.
THEY TAKE WATER MOLECULES AND CUT OFF THE HYDROGEN ATOMS UNTIL ALL THAT'S LEFT IS OXYGEN.
ROHDE GUNS
THEY THROW IT OUT THE WINDOW AND SINCE THERE IS A LOT OF WIND IN THE ARCTIC THE OXYGEN FLOWS REAL FAST TO US AND WE BREATHE IT.
THE TREES REALLY FUCKING HATE THIS.
I MEAN, THEY MAKE AIR FOR US ALL THE FUCKING TIME AND NOW WE DON'T NEED 'EM. THAT'D PISS YOU OFF, RIGHT?
SO NOW IT'S STARTING. TREES FALL ON DUDES' CARS AND SHIT, DUDES HUFF AND PUFF ABOUT THEIR CARS AND USE UP AIR...
...AND THE TREES STOP MAKING AIR.
I THINK YOU GET MY DRIFT.
DOGS PISS ON TREES BECAUSE THEY CAN SENSE THE EVIL.

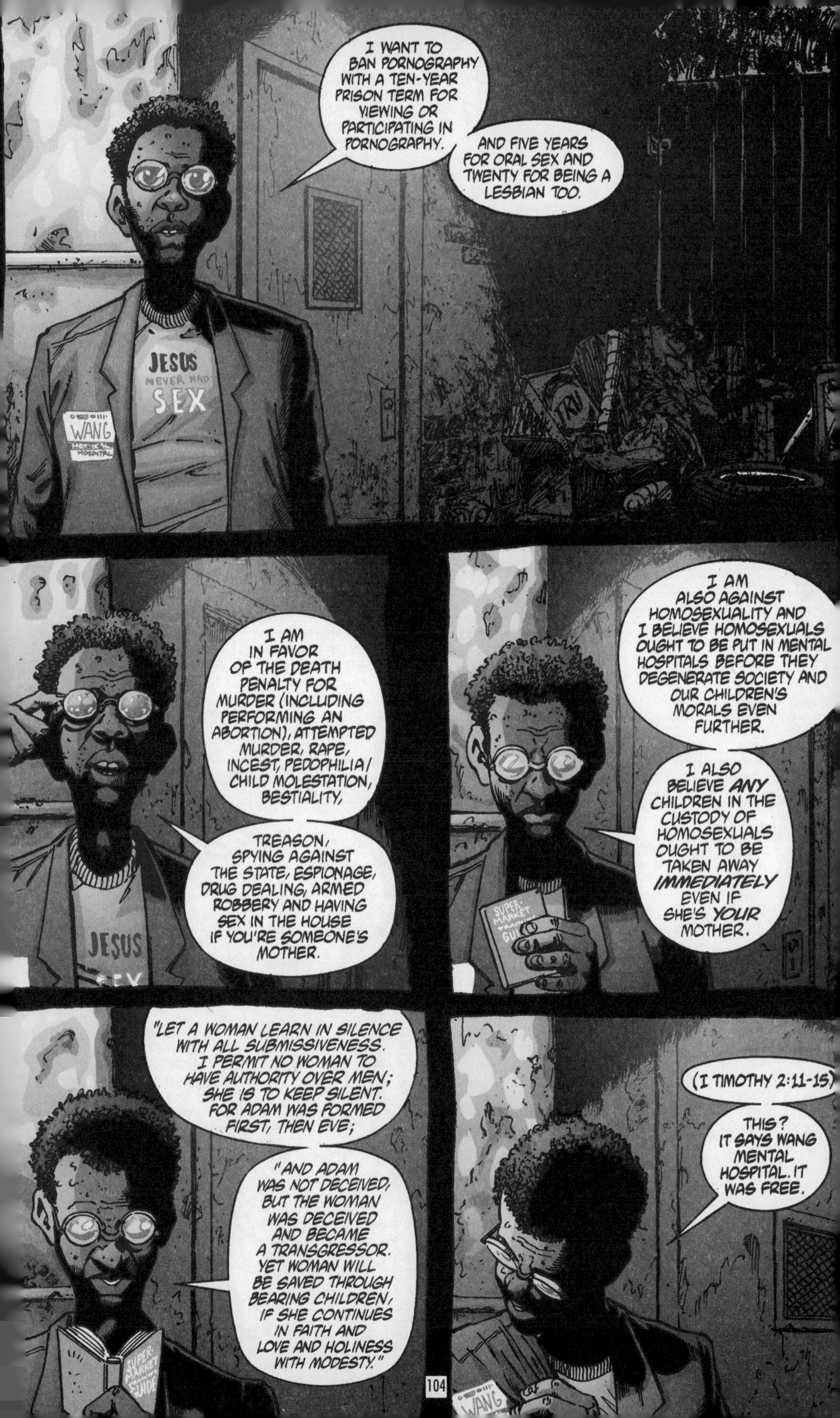
I WANT TO BAN PORNOGRAPHY WITH A TEN-YEAR PRISON TERM FOR VIEWING OR PARTICIPATING IN PORNOGRAPHY.
AND FIVE YEARS FOR ORAL SEX AND TWENTY FOR BEING A LESBIAN TOO.
JESUS NEVER HAD SEX
WANG
HOSPITAL
I AM IN FAVOR OF THE DEATH PENALTY FOR MURDER (INCLUDING PERFORMING AN ABORTION), ATTEMPTED MURDER, RAPE, INCEST, PEDOPHILIA/ CHILD MOLESTATION, BESTIALITY,
TREASON, SPYING AGAINST THE STATE, ESPIONAGE, DRUG DEALING, ARMED ROBBERY AND HAVING SEX IN THE HOUSE IF YOU'RE SOMEONE'S MOTHER.
JESUS
I AM ALSO AGAINST HOMOSEXUALITY AND I BELIEVE HOMOSEXUALS OUGHT TO BE PUT IN MENTAL HOSPITALS BEFORE THEY DEGENERATE SOCIETY AND OUR CHILDREN'S MORALS EVEN FURTHER.
I ALSO BELIEVE *ANY* CHILDREN IN THE CUSTODY OF HOMOSEXUALS OUGHT TO BE TAKEN AWAY *IMMEDIATELY* EVEN IF SHE'S *YOUR* MOTHER.
SUPER-MARKET
"LET A WOMAN LEARN IN SILENCE WITH ALL SUBMISSIVENESS. I PERMIT NO WOMAN TO HAVE AUTHORITY OVER MEN; SHE IS TO KEEP SILENT. FOR ADAM WAS FORMED FIRST, THEN EVE;
"AND ADAM WAS NOT DECEIVED, BUT THE WOMAN WAS DECEIVED AND BECAME A TRANSGRESSOR. YET WOMAN WILL BE SAVED THROUGH BEARING CHILDREN, IF SHE CONTINUES IN FAITH AND LOVE AND HOLINESS WITH MODESTY."
SUPER-MARKET GUIDE
(I TIMOTHY 2:11-15)
THIS? IT SAYS WANG MENTAL HOSPITAL. IT WAS FREE.
WANG

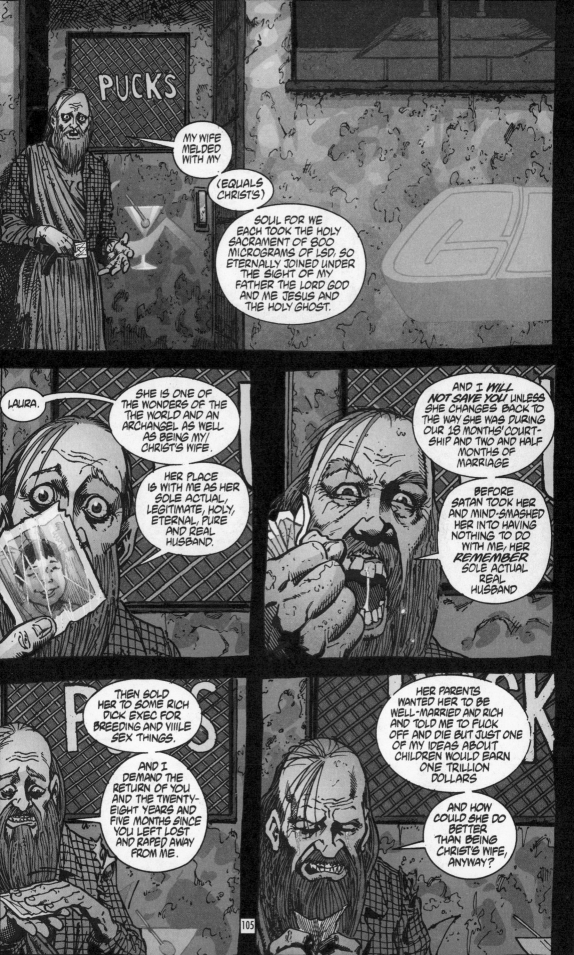

PUCKS

MY WIFE MELDED WITH MY

(EQUALS CHRIST'S)

SOUL FOR WE EACH TOOK THE HOLY SACRAMENT OF 800 MICROGRAMS OF LSD, SO ETERNALLY JOINED UNDER THE SIGHT OF MY FATHER THE LORD GOD AND ME JESUS AND THE HOLY GHOST.

LAURA.

SHE IS ONE OF THE WONDERS OF THE THE WORLD AND AN ARCHANGEL AS WELL AS BEING MY/CHRIST'S WIFE.

HER PLACE IS WITH ME AS HER SOLE ACTUAL, LEGITIMATE, HOLY, ETERNAL, PURE AND REAL HUSBAND.

AND I *WILL NOT SAVE YOU* UNLESS SHE CHANGES BACK TO THE WAY SHE WAS DURING OUR 18 MONTHS' COURTSHIP AND TWO AND HALF MONTHS OF MARRIAGE

BEFORE SATAN TOOK HER AND MIND-SMASHED HER INTO HAVING NOTHING TO DO WITH ME, HER *REMEMBER* SOLE ACTUAL REAL HUSBAND

THEN SOLD HER TO SOME RICH DICK EXEC FOR BREEDING AND VIIILE SEX THINGS.

AND I DEMAND THE RETURN OF YOU AND THE TWENTY-EIGHT YEARS AND FIVE MONTHS SINCE YOU LEFT LOST AND RAPED AWAY FROM ME.

HER PARENTS WANTED HER TO BE WELL-MARRIED AND RICH AND TOLD ME TO FUCK OFF AND DIE BUT JUST ONE OF MY IDEAS ABOUT CHILDREN WOULD EARN ONE TRILLION DOLLARS

AND HOW COULD SHE DO BETTER THAN BEING CHRIST'S WIFE, ANYWAY?

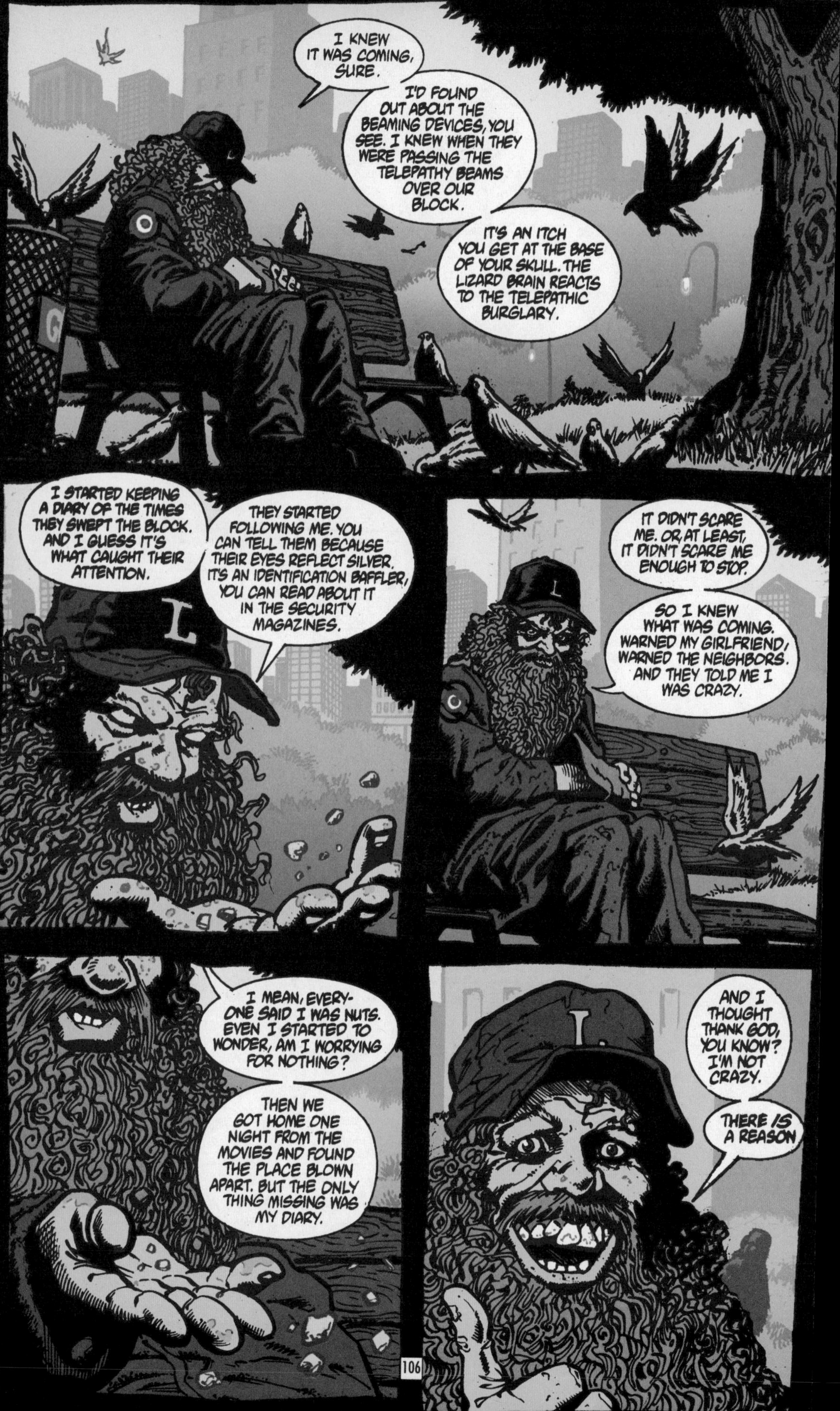
I KNEW IT WAS COMING, SURE.
I'D FOUND OUT ABOUT THE BEAMING DEVICES, YOU SEE. I KNEW WHEN THEY WERE PASSING THE TELEPATHY BEAMS OVER OUR BLOCK.
IT'S AN ITCH YOU GET AT THE BASE OF YOUR SKULL. THE LIZARD BRAIN REACTS TO THE TELEPATHIC BURGLARY.
I STARTED KEEPING A DIARY OF THE TIMES THEY SWEPT THE BLOCK. AND I GUESS IT'S WHAT CAUGHT THEIR ATTENTION.
THEY STARTED FOLLOWING ME. YOU CAN TELL THEM BECAUSE THEIR EYES REFLECT SILVER. IT'S AN IDENTIFICATION BAFFLER, YOU CAN READ ABOUT IT IN THE SECURITY MAGAZINES.
IT DIDN'T SCARE ME. OR, AT LEAST, IT DIDN'T SCARE ME ENOUGH TO STOP.
SO I KNEW WHAT WAS COMING. WARNED MY GIRLFRIEND, WARNED THE NEIGHBORS. AND THEY TOLD ME I WAS CRAZY.
I MEAN, EVERY-ONE SAID I WAS NUTS. EVEN I STARTED TO WONDER, AM I WORRYING FOR NOTHING?
THEN WE GOT HOME ONE NIGHT FROM THE MOVIES AND FOUND THE PLACE BLOWN APART. BUT THE ONLY THING MISSING WAS MY DIARY.
AND I THOUGHT THANK GOD, YOU KNOW? I'M NOT CRAZY.
THERE *IS* A REASON

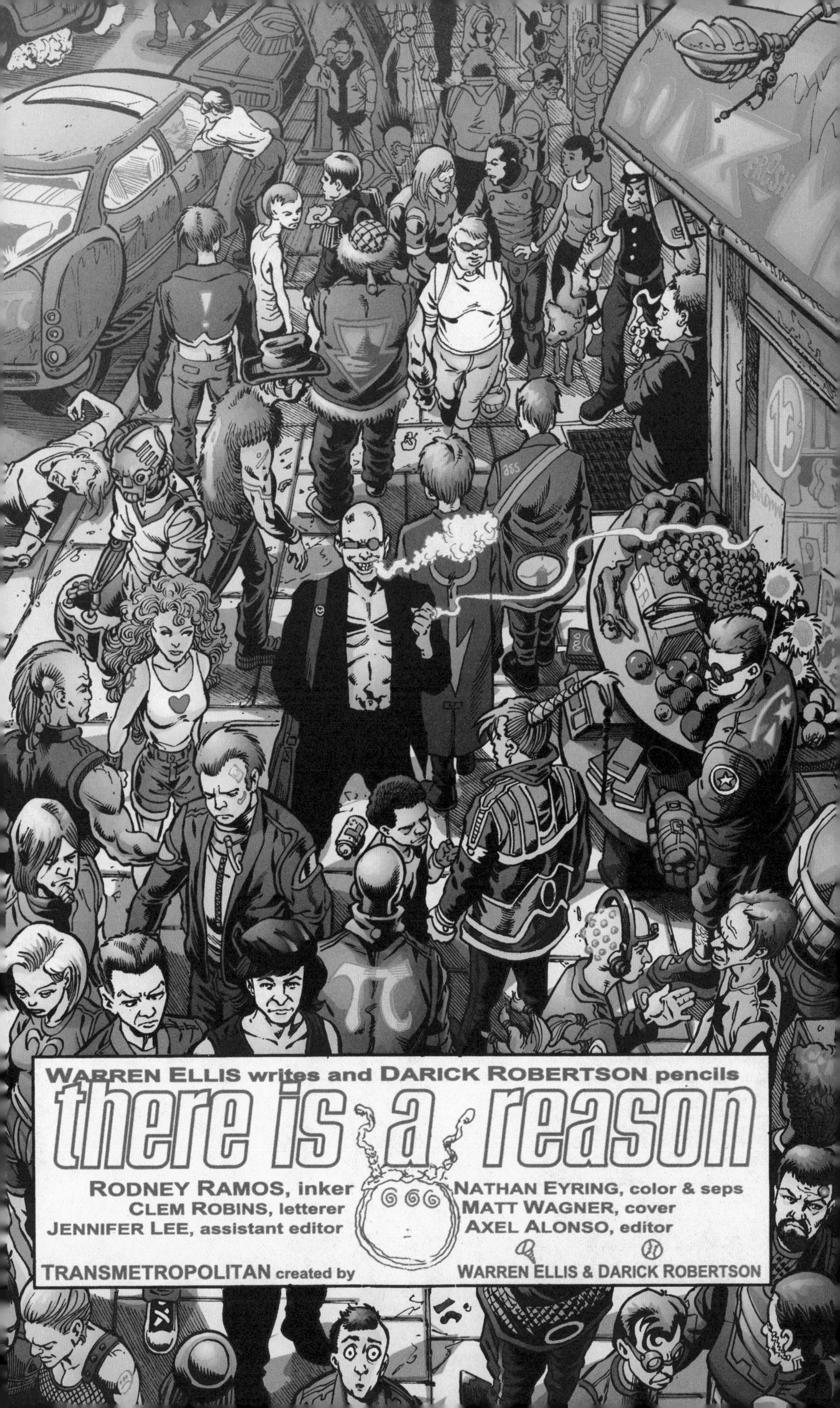
WARREN ELLIS writes and DARICK ROBERTSON pencils
there is a reason
RODNEY RAMOS, inker
CLEM ROBINS, letterer
JENNIFER LEE, assistant editor
NATHAN EYRING, color & seps
MATT WAGNER, cover
AXEL ALONSO, editor
TRANSMETROPOLITAN created by WARREN ELLIS & DARICK ROBERTSON

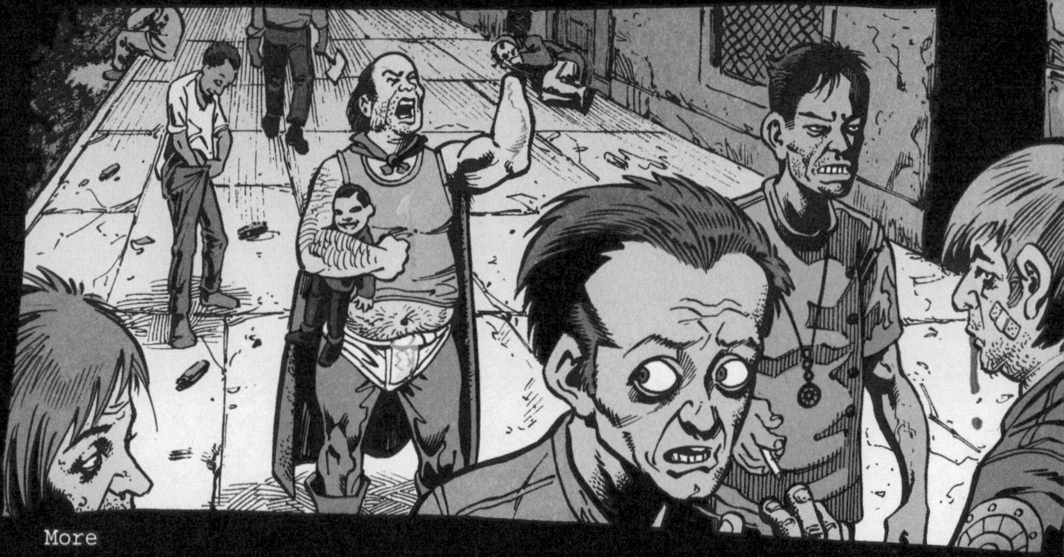

More crazy people on the street than there used to be.

I mean, there's always been crazy people on the street. This is nothing new.

But in some districts, the population is getting denser.

The districts most of you don't go to, o course.

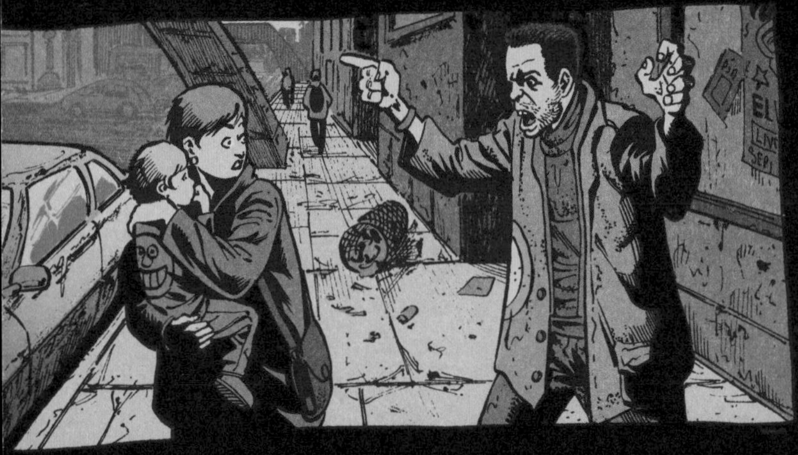

Here's how it works.

Mental hospitals are expensive places to run. Most mentally ill people either start out poor or quickly become poor.

Therefore, their care becomes a cost to the state.

And the state don't like that. Oh no.

So, here in the City, the mental hospital goes to Civic Center and says We can't afford the bed for Mad Person A.

It would in fact be cheaper to put Mad Person A in a hostel or a rented room than to maintain them here.

Give us permission to ship Mad Person A the hell out of here.

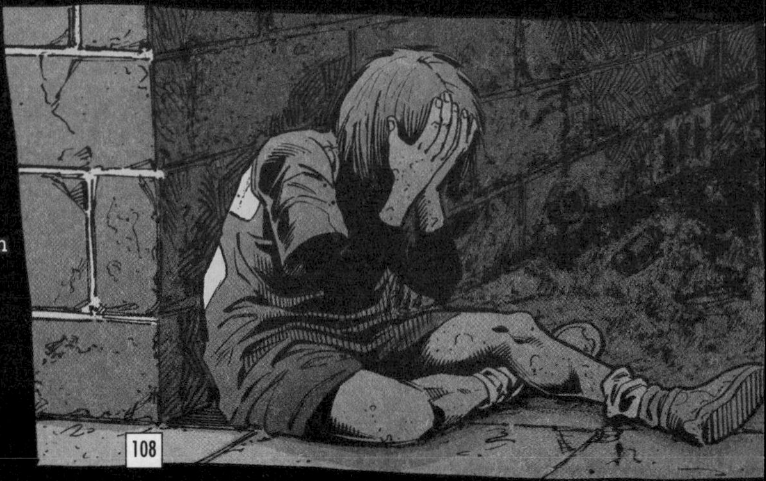

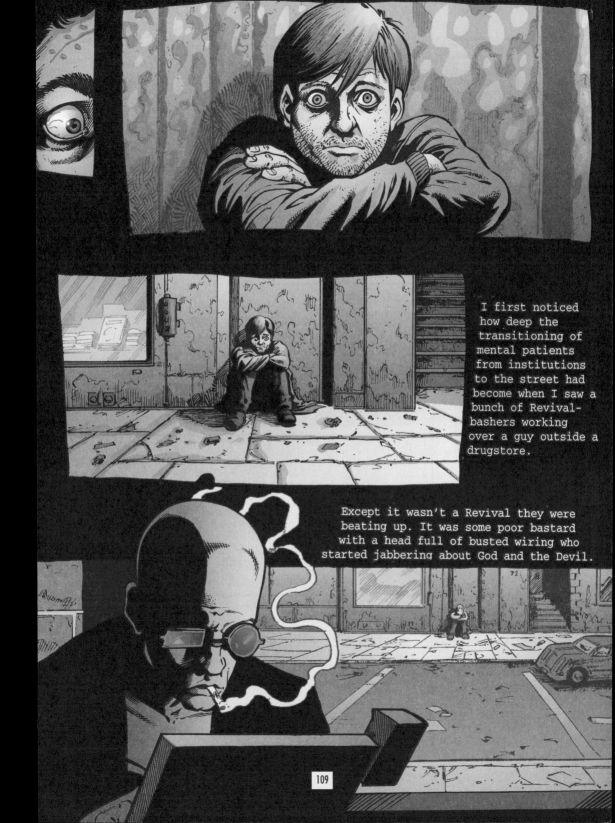

I first noticed how deep the transitioning of mental patients from institutions to the street had become when I saw a bunch of Revival-bashers working over a guy outside a drugstore.

Except it wasn't a Revival they were beating up. It was some poor bastard with a head full of busted wiring who started jabbering about God and the Devil.

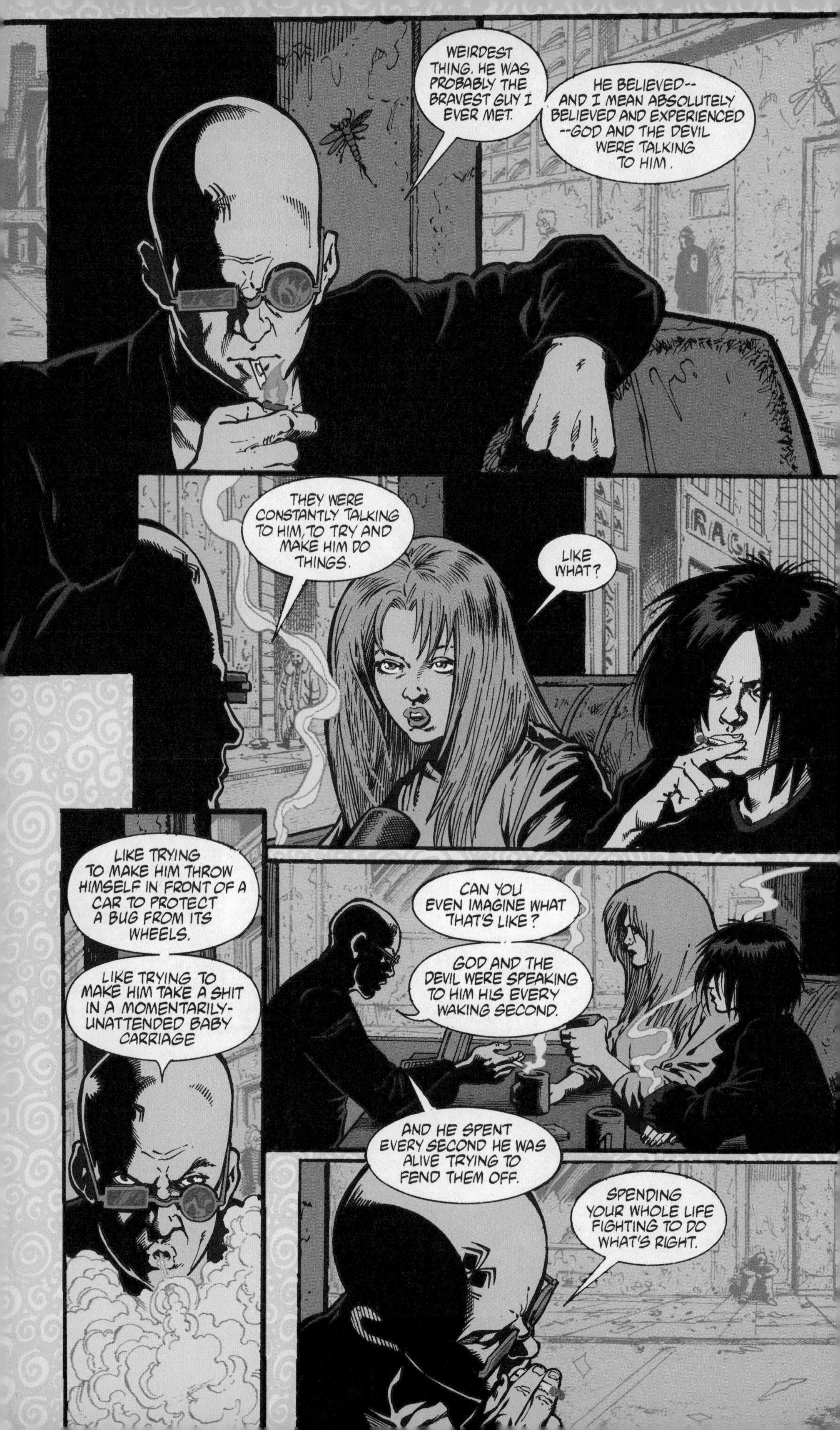
WEIRDEST THING. HE WAS PROBABLY THE BRAVEST GUY I EVER MET.
HE BELIEVED-- AND I MEAN ABSOLUTELY BELIEVED AND EXPERIENCED --GOD AND THE DEVIL WERE TALKING TO HIM.
THEY WERE CONSTANTLY TALKING TO HIM, TO TRY AND MAKE HIM DO THINGS.
LIKE WHAT?
RAGS
LIKE TRYING TO MAKE HIM THROW HIMSELF IN FRONT OF A CAR TO PROTECT A BUG FROM ITS WHEELS.
LIKE TRYING TO MAKE HIM TAKE A SHIT IN A MOMENTARILY-UNATTENDED BABY CARRIAGE
CAN YOU EVEN IMAGINE WHAT THAT'S LIKE?
GOD AND THE DEVIL WERE SPEAKING TO HIM HIS EVERY WAKING SECOND.
AND HE SPENT EVERY SECOND HE WAS ALIVE TRYING TO FEND THEM OFF.
SPENDING YOUR WHOLE LIFE FIGHTING TO DO WHAT'S RIGHT.

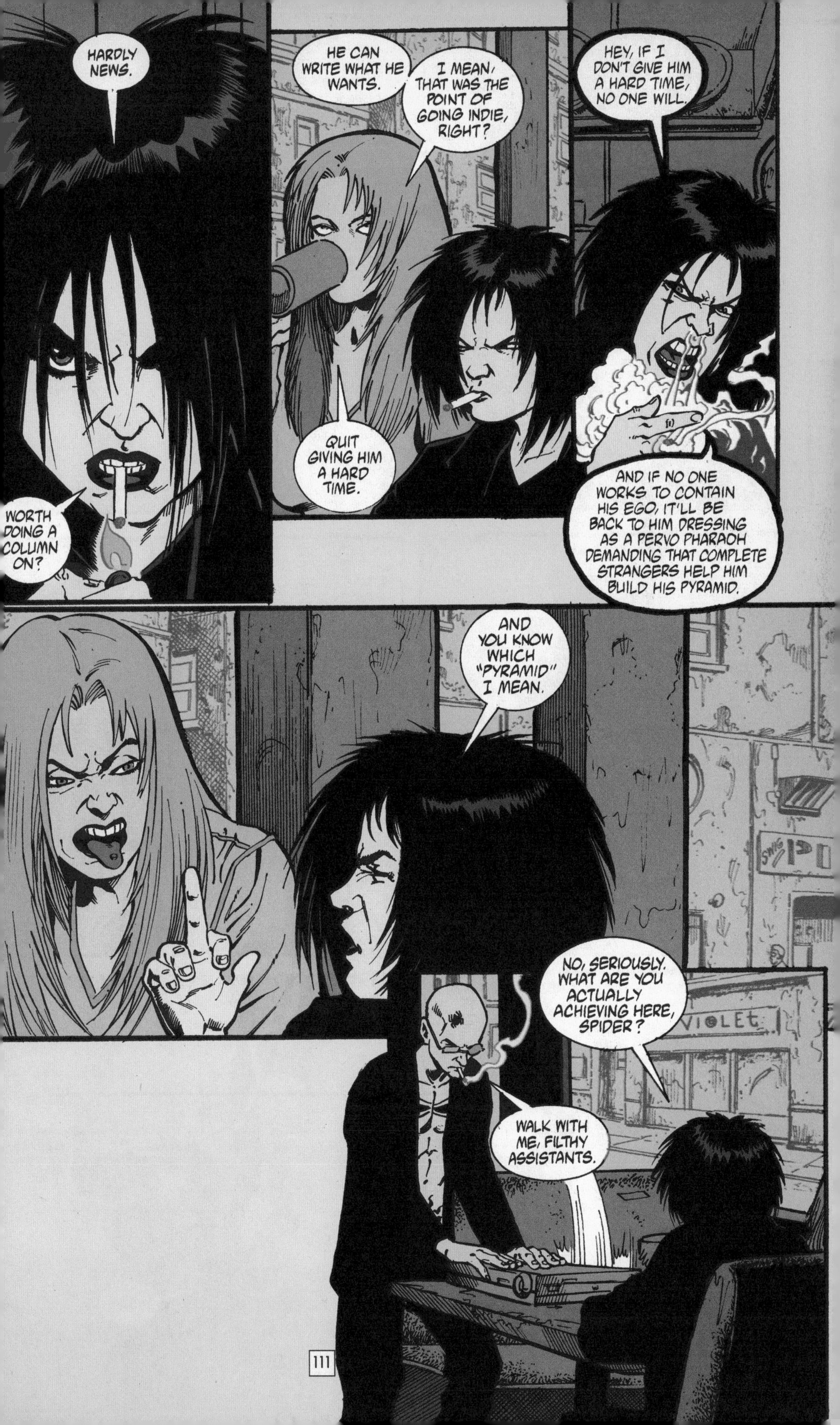
HARDLY NEWS.
WORTH DOING A COLUMN ON?
HE CAN WRITE WHAT HE WANTS.
I MEAN, THAT WAS THE POINT OF GOING INDIE, RIGHT?
QUIT GIVING HIM A HARD TIME.
HEY, IF I DON'T GIVE HIM A HARD TIME, NO ONE WILL.
AND IF NO ONE WORKS TO CONTAIN HIS EGO, IT'LL BE BACK TO HIM DRESSING AS A PERVO PHARAOH DEMANDING THAT COMPLETE STRANGERS HELP HIM BUILD HIS PYRAMID.
AND YOU KNOW WHICH "PYRAMID" I MEAN.
NO, SERIOUSLY. WHAT ARE YOU ACTUALLY ACHIEVING HERE, SPIDER?
WALK WITH ME, FILTHY ASSISTANTS.
VIOLET

TRANGMAR
DISCOUNT
GUNS
& Ice Cream

GET YOUR ASS
ON IN HERE, WE'RE
OPEN

THERE WAS THIS OLDER GUY AND HE SMELLED OF RUBBER AND SOMETHING.

RUBBER. LATEX. AND SOMETHING MEDICATED.

AND A YOUNGER GUY. COMMS TATTOO BEHIND HIS LEFT EAR.

I READ ALL ABOUT COMMS TATTOOS. Y'CAN'T COVER THEM UP, THEY GLOW THROUGH MOST ANYTHING.

YOU HAVE TO WEAR WHAT THEY USED TO CALL A BLUR SUIT.

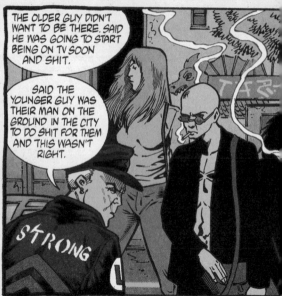

THE OLDER GUY DIDN'T WANT TO BE THERE. SAID HE WAS GOING TO START BEING ON TV SOON AND SHIT.

SAID THE YOUNGER GUY WAS THEIR MAN ON THE GROUND IN THE CITY TO DO SHIT FOR THEM AND THIS WASN'T RIGHT.

STRONG

YOUNGER GUY MADE A LOT OF AUTHORITY NOISES.

I RECKON HE WAS NEW WORLD ORDER, SEE? HERE TO WATCH US.

I WISH THEY DIDN'T ALL FUCKING WATCH US.

THE OLDER GUY, WAS THIS HIM?

...YEAH.

STRONG

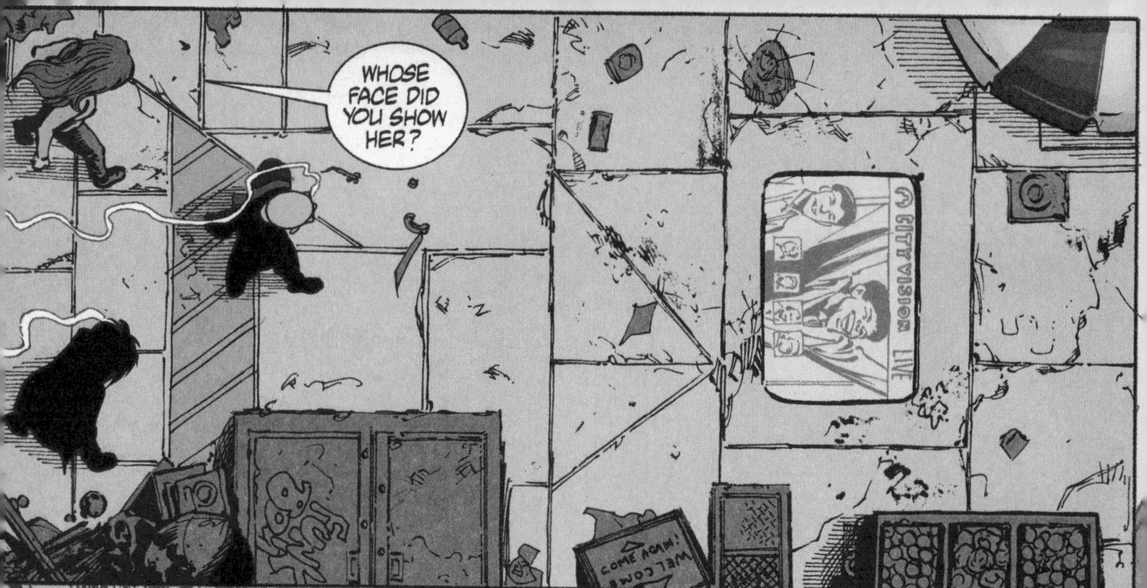
WHOSE FACE DID YOU SHOW HER?
CITYVISION LIVE
WELCOME COME AGAIN!

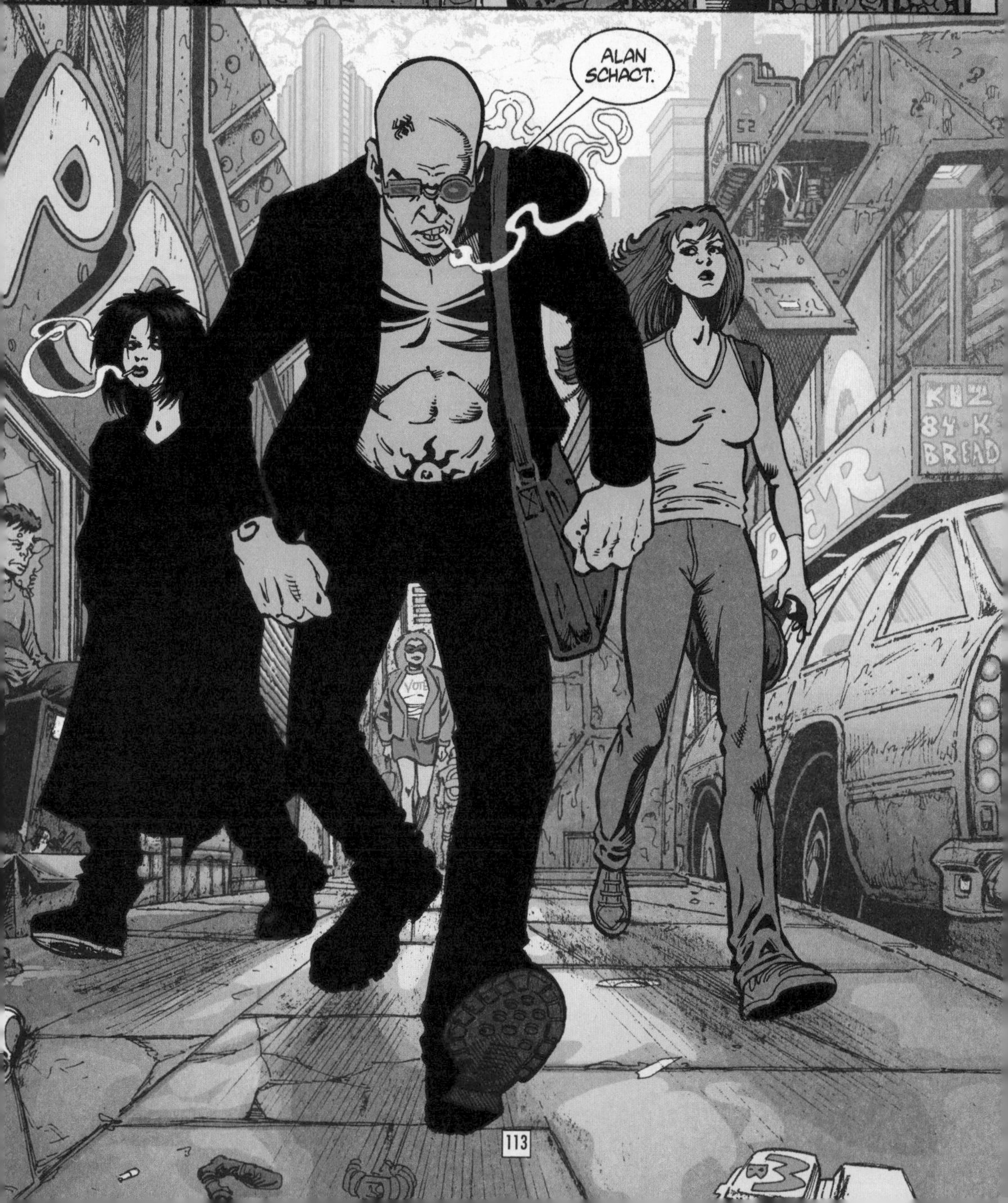
ALAN SCHACT.
KIZ 84-K BREAD
VOTE

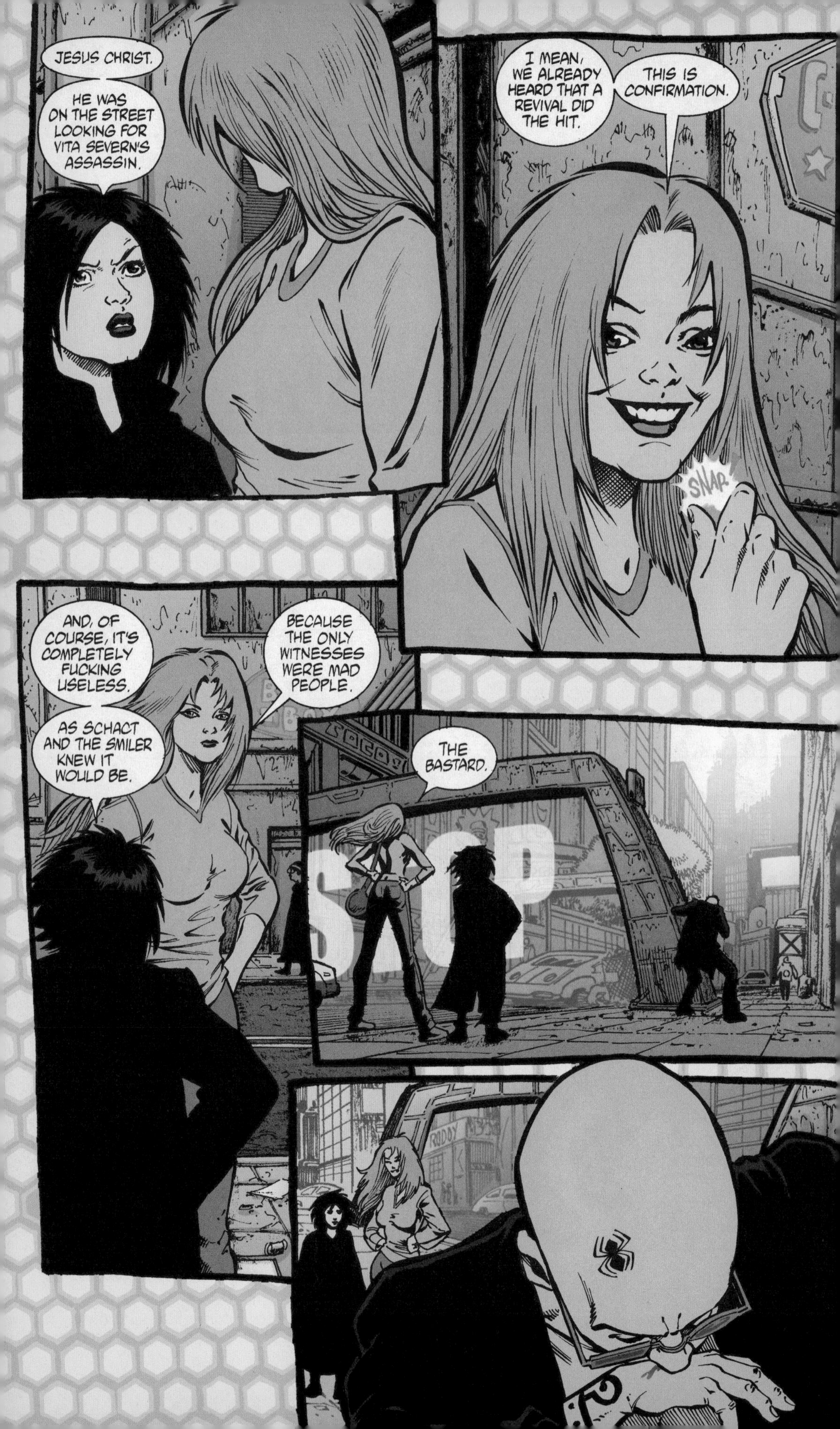
JESUS CHRIST.
HE WAS ON THE STREET LOOKING FOR VITA SEVERN'S ASSASSIN.
I MEAN, WE ALREADY HEARD THAT A REVIVAL DID THE HIT.
THIS IS CONFIRMATION.
SNAP
AND, OF COURSE, IT'S COMPLETELY FUCKING USELESS.
AS SCHACT AND THE SMILER KNEW IT WOULD BE.
BECAUSE THE ONLY WITNESSES WERE MAD PEOPLE.
THE BASTARD.

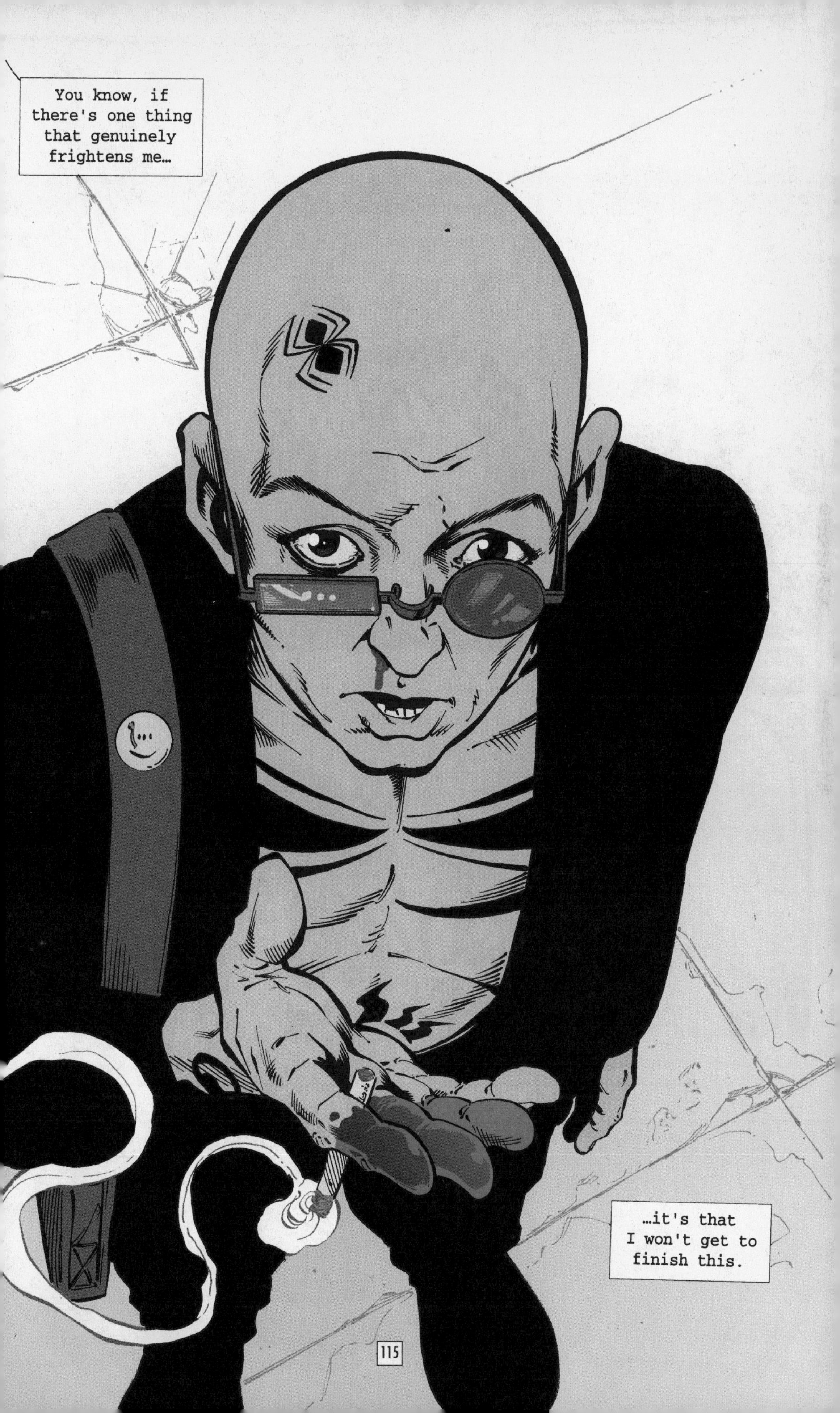

You know, if there's one thing that genuinely frightens me...
...it's that I won't get to finish this.

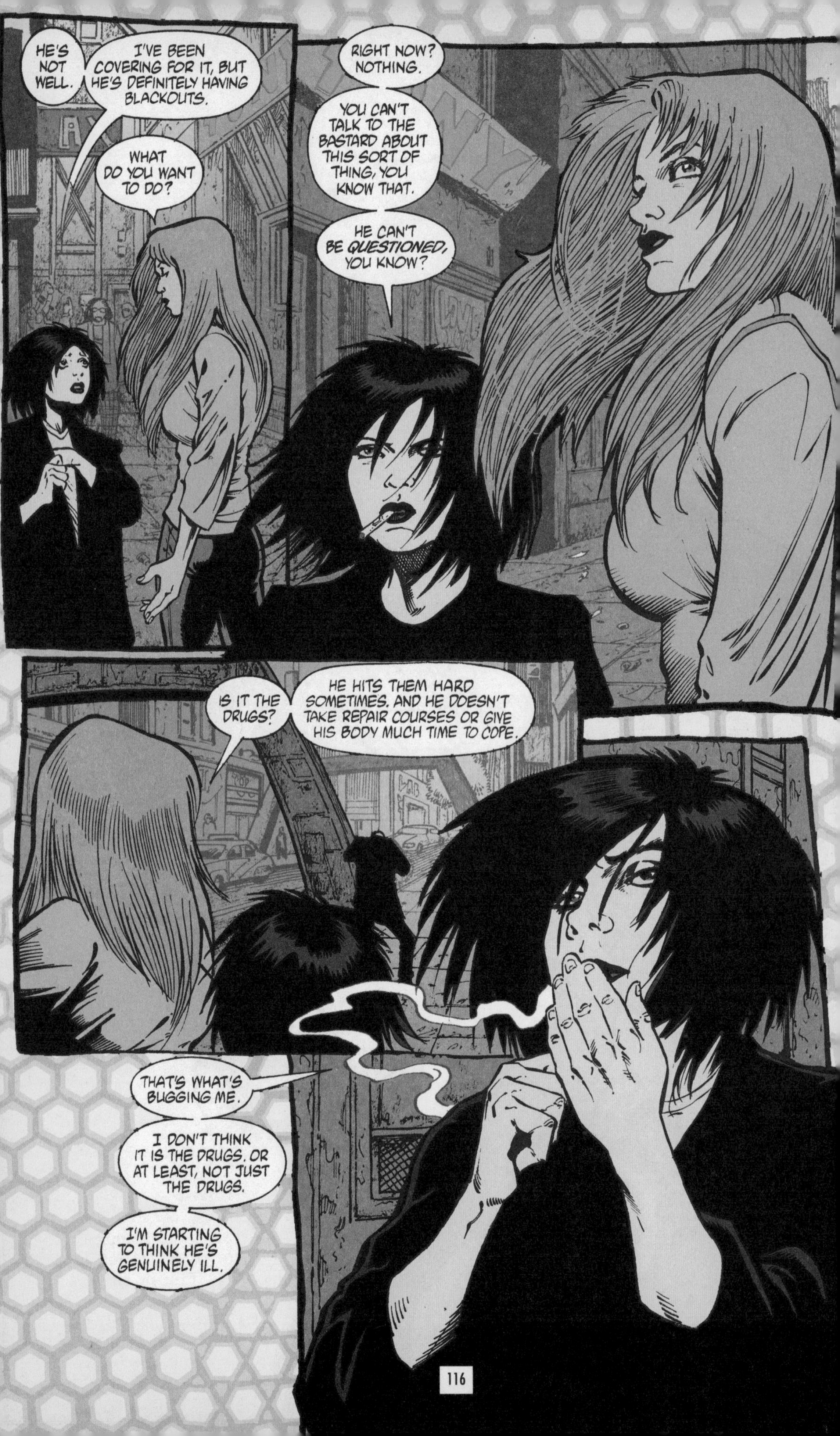
HE'S NOT WELL.
I'VE BEEN COVERING FOR IT, BUT HE'S DEFINITELY HAVING BLACKOUTS.
WHAT DO YOU WANT TO DO?
RIGHT NOW? NOTHING.
YOU CAN'T TALK TO THE BASTARD ABOUT THIS SORT OF THING, YOU KNOW THAT.
HE CAN'T BE QUESTIONED, YOU KNOW?
IS IT THE DRUGS?
HE HITS THEM HARD SOMETIMES. AND HE DOESN'T TAKE REPAIR COURSES OR GIVE HIS BODY MUCH TIME TO COPE.
THAT'S WHAT'S BUGGING ME.
I DON'T THINK IT IS THE DRUGS. OR AT LEAST, NOT JUST THE DRUGS.
I'M STARTING TO THINK HE'S GENUINELY ILL.

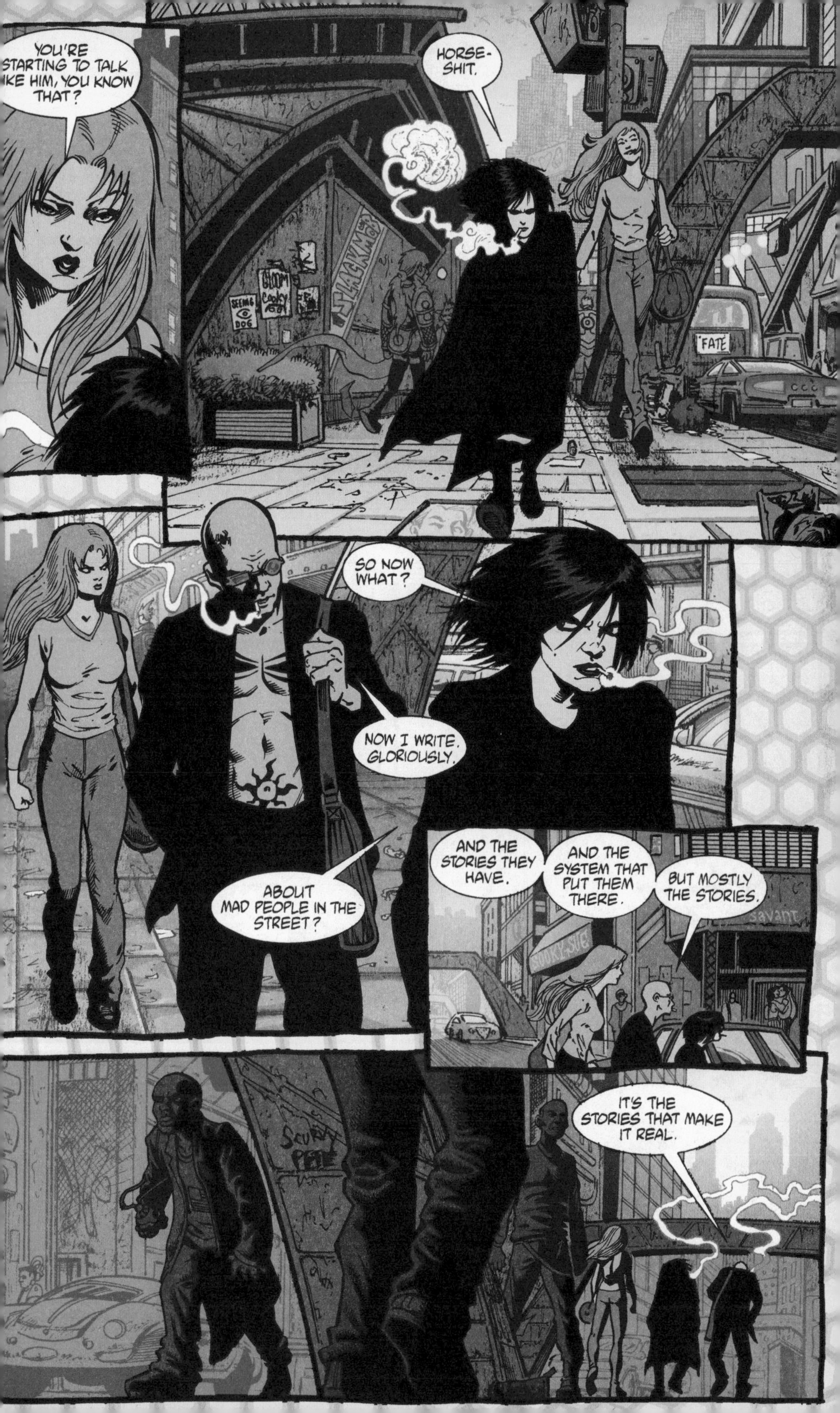
YOU'RE STARTING TO TALK LIKE HIM, YOU KNOW THAT?
HORSE-SHIT.
SEEING DOG
GLOOM
FATE
SO NOW WHAT?
NOW I WRITE. GLORIOUSLY.
ABOUT MAD PEOPLE IN THE STREET?
AND THE STORIES THEY HAVE.
AND THE SYSTEM THAT PUT THEM THERE.
BUT MOSTLY THE STORIES.
savant
IT'S THE STORIES THAT MAKE IT REAL.

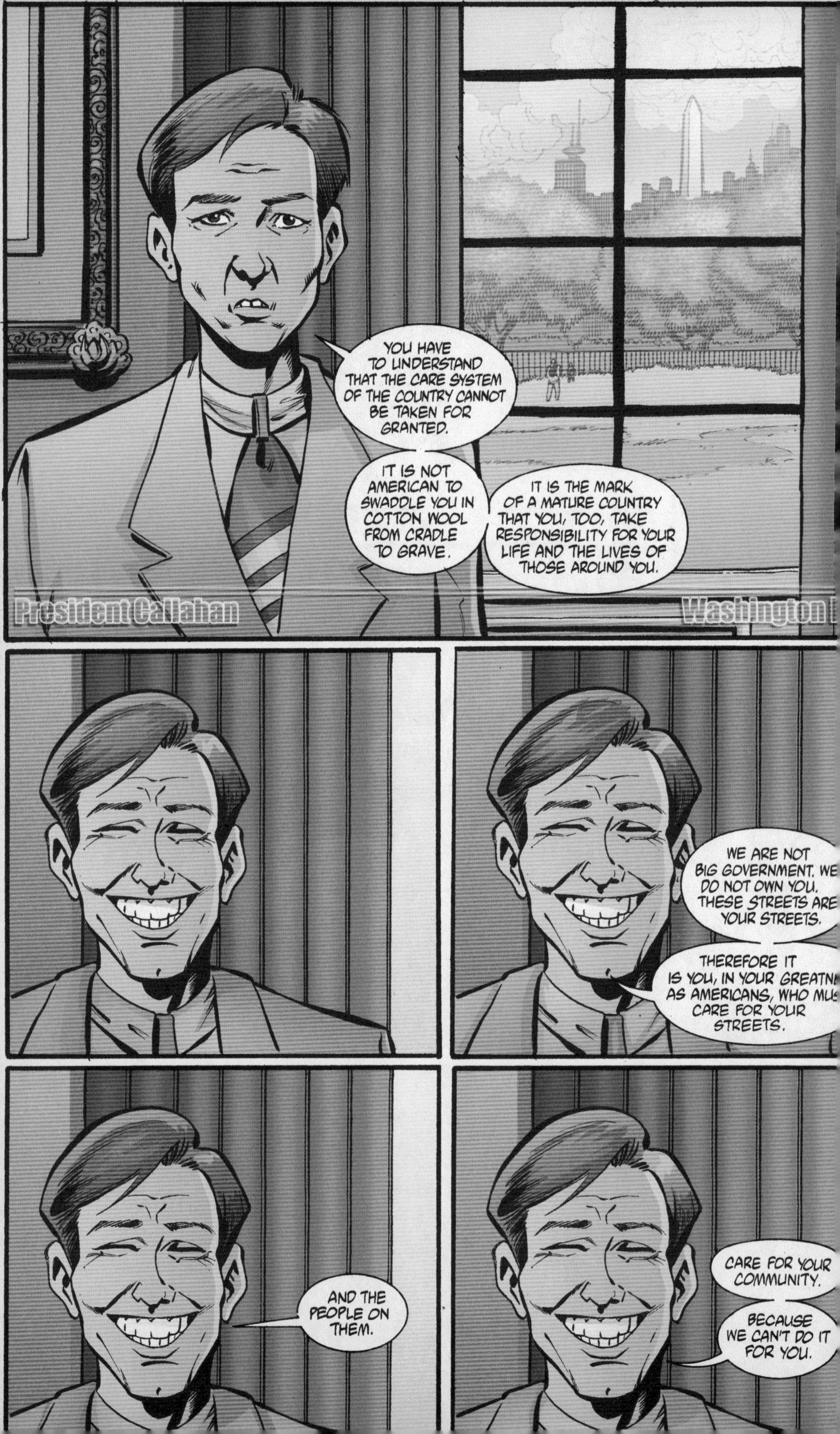
YOU HAVE TO UNDERSTAND THAT THE CARE SYSTEM OF THE COUNTRY CANNOT BE TAKEN FOR GRANTED.
IT IS NOT AMERICAN TO SWADDLE YOU IN COTTON WOOL FROM CRADLE TO GRAVE.
IT IS THE MARK OF A MATURE COUNTRY THAT YOU, TOO, TAKE RESPONSIBILITY FOR YOUR LIFE AND THE LIVES OF THOSE AROUND YOU.
President Callahan
Washington
WE ARE NOT BIG GOVERNMENT. WE DO NOT OWN YOU. THESE STREETS ARE YOUR STREETS.
THEREFORE IT IS YOU, IN YOUR GREATN AS AMERICANS, WHO MUS CARE FOR YOUR STREETS.
AND THE PEOPLE ON THEM.
CARE FOR YOUR COMMUNITY.
BECAUSE WE CAN'T DO IT FOR YOU.

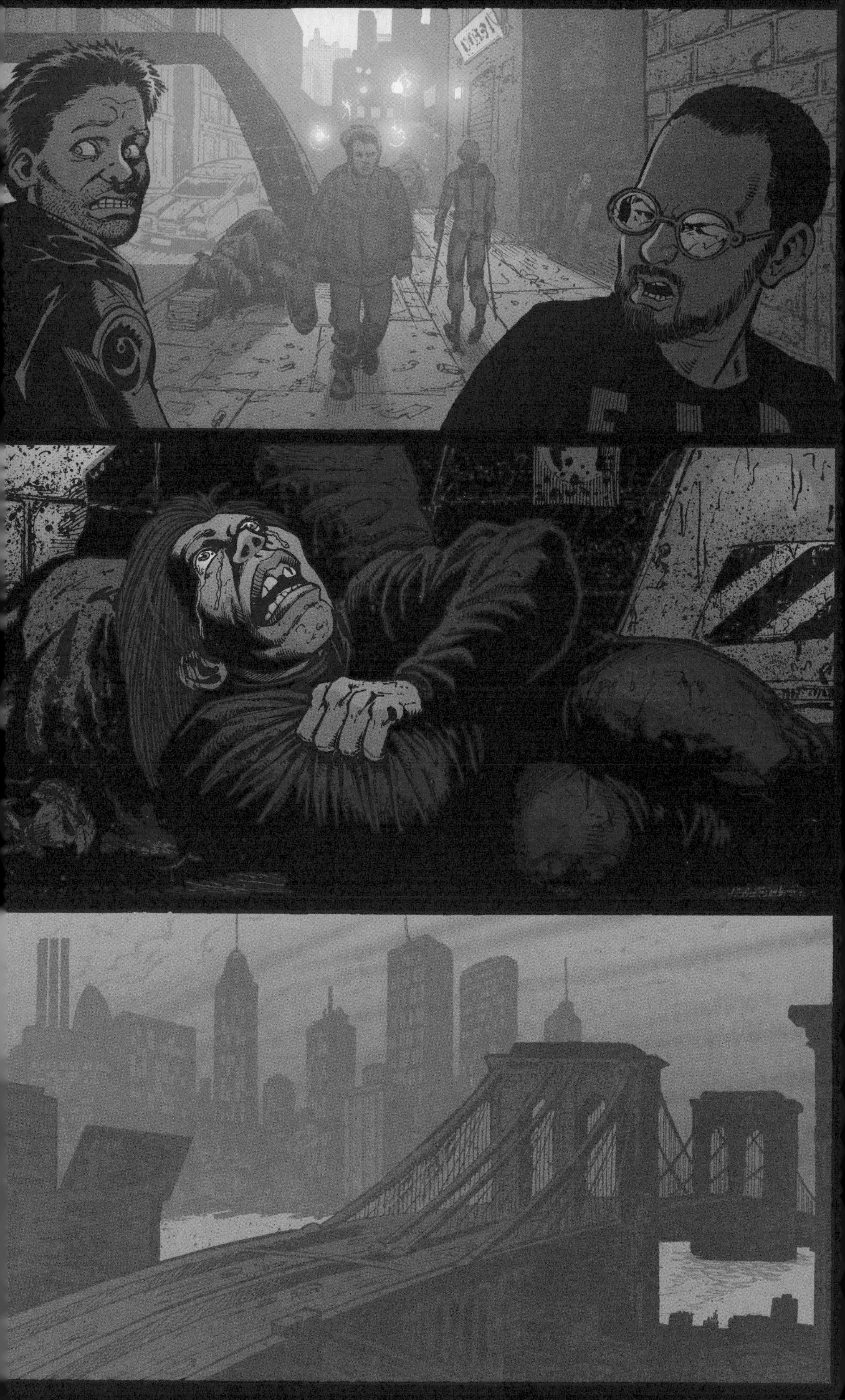

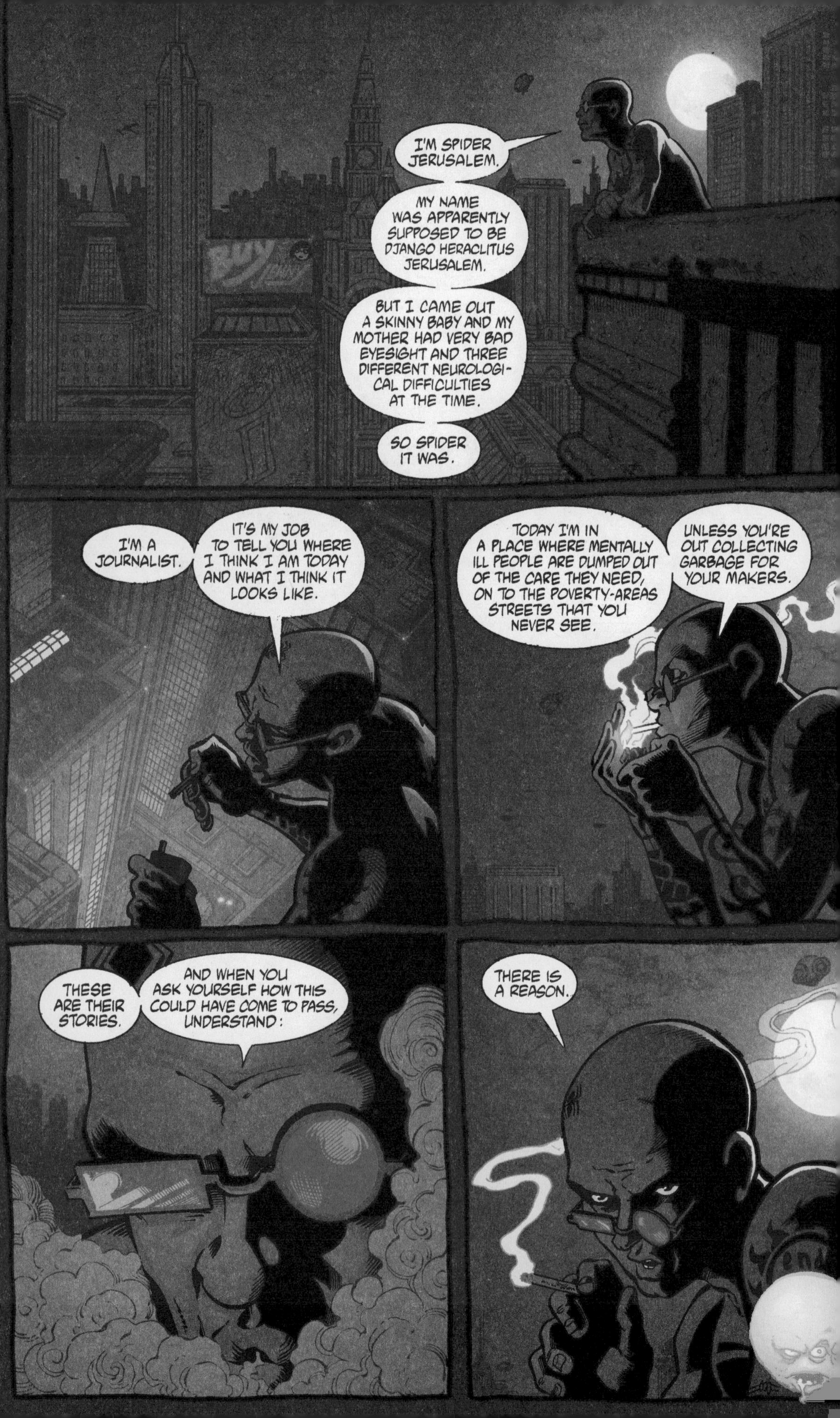

I'M SPIDER JERUSALEM.
MY NAME WAS APPARENTLY SUPPOSED TO BE DJANGO HERACLITUS JERUSALEM.
BUT I CAME OUT A SKINNY BABY AND MY MOTHER HAD VERY BAD EYESIGHT AND THREE DIFFERENT NEUROLOGICAL DIFFICULTIES AT THE TIME.
SO SPIDER IT WAS.
I'M A JOURNALIST.
IT'S MY JOB TO TELL YOU WHERE I THINK I AM TODAY AND WHAT I THINK IT LOOKS LIKE.
TODAY I'M IN A PLACE WHERE MENTALLY ILL PEOPLE ARE DUMPED OUT OF THE CARE THEY NEED, ON TO THE POVERTY-AREAS STREETS THAT YOU NEVER SEE.
UNLESS YOU'RE OUT COLLECTING GARBAGE FOR YOUR MAKERS.
THESE ARE THEIR STORIES.
AND WHEN YOU ASK YOURSELF HOW THIS COULD HAVE COME TO PASS, UNDERSTAND:
THERE IS A REASON.

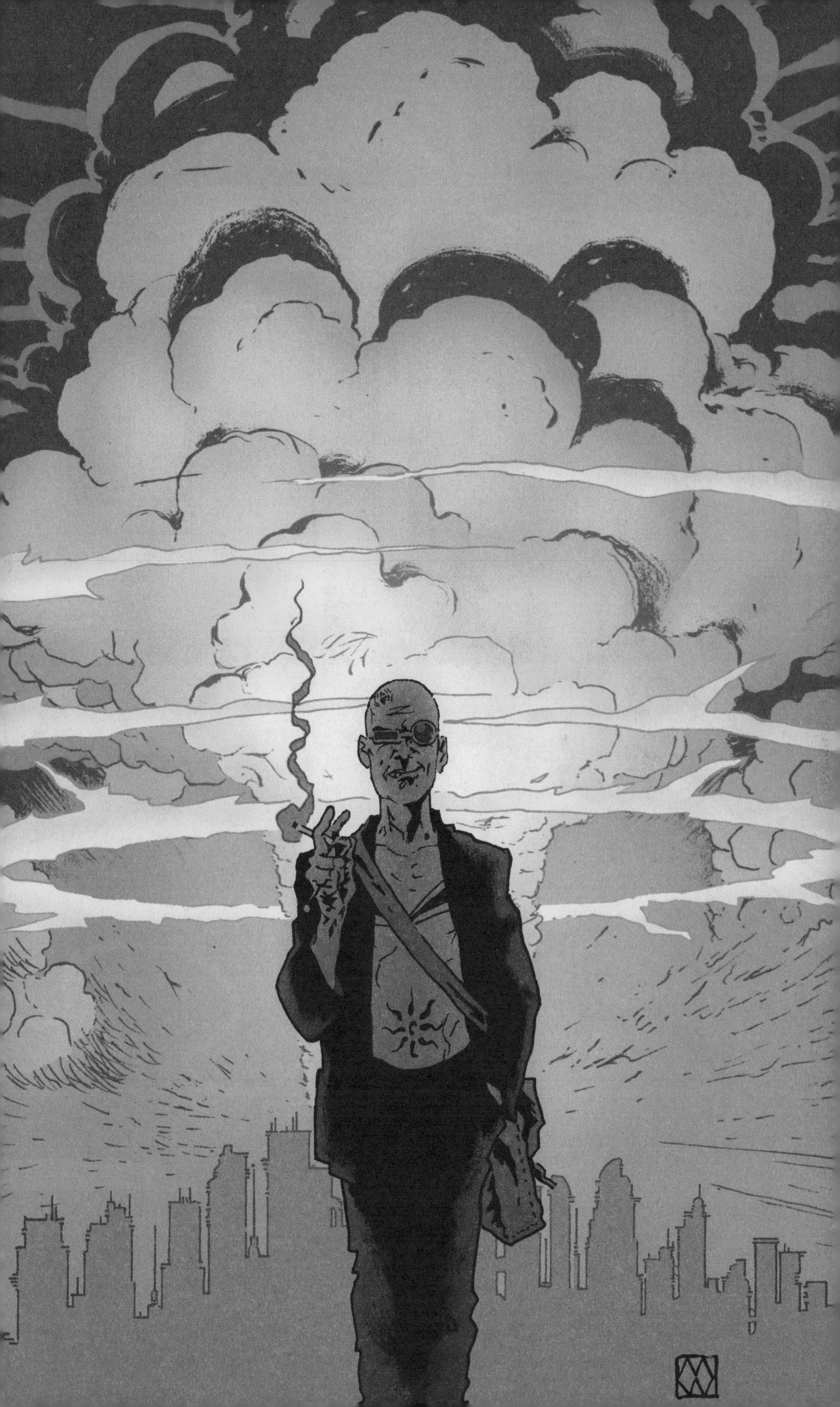

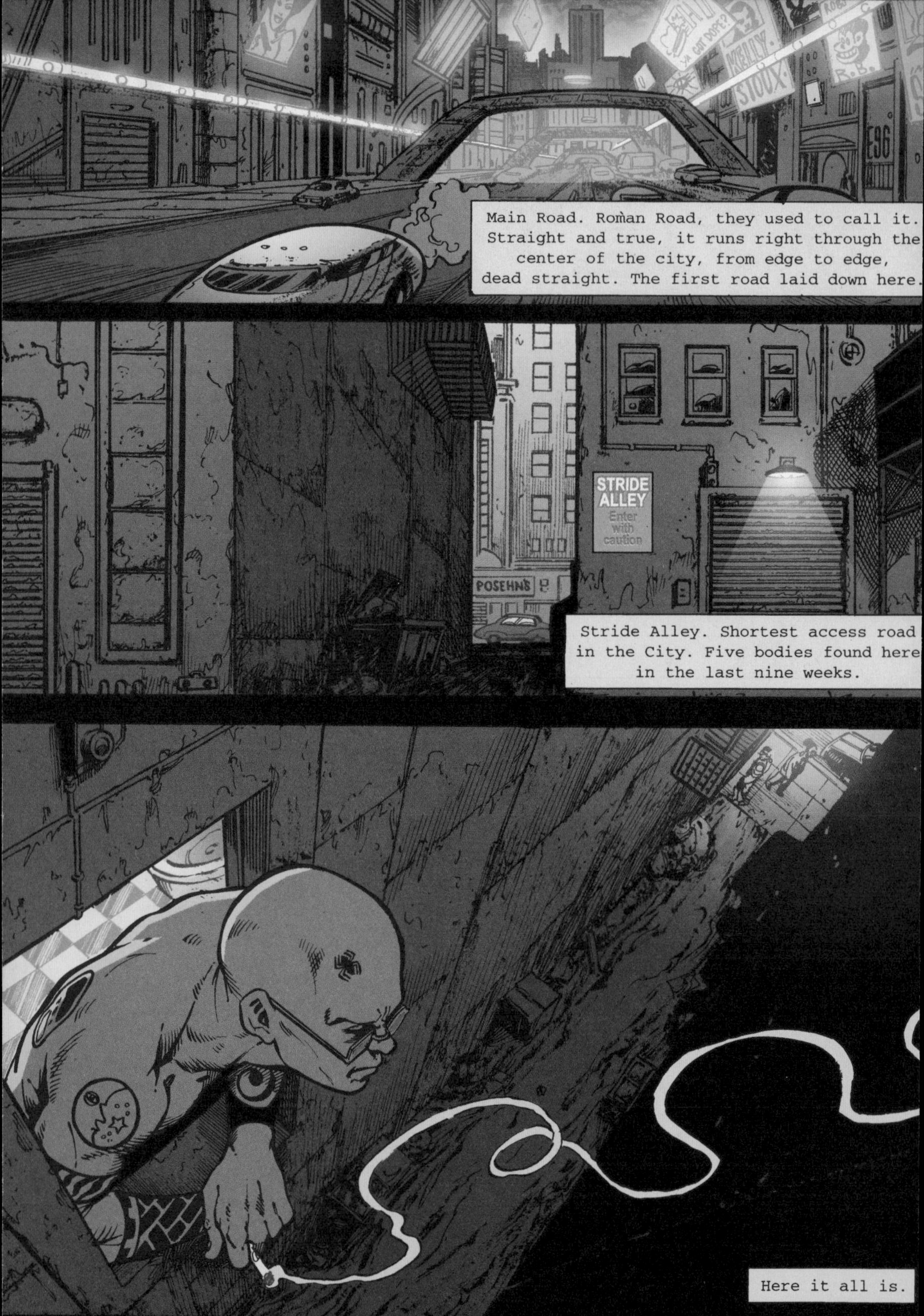

SIOUX
E96
Main Road. Roman Road, they used to call it. Straight and true, it runs right through the center of the city, from edge to edge, dead straight. The first road laid down here.
STRIDE ALLEY
Enter with caution
POSEHN'S
Stride Alley. Shortest access road in the City. Five bodies found here in the last nine weeks.
Here it all is.

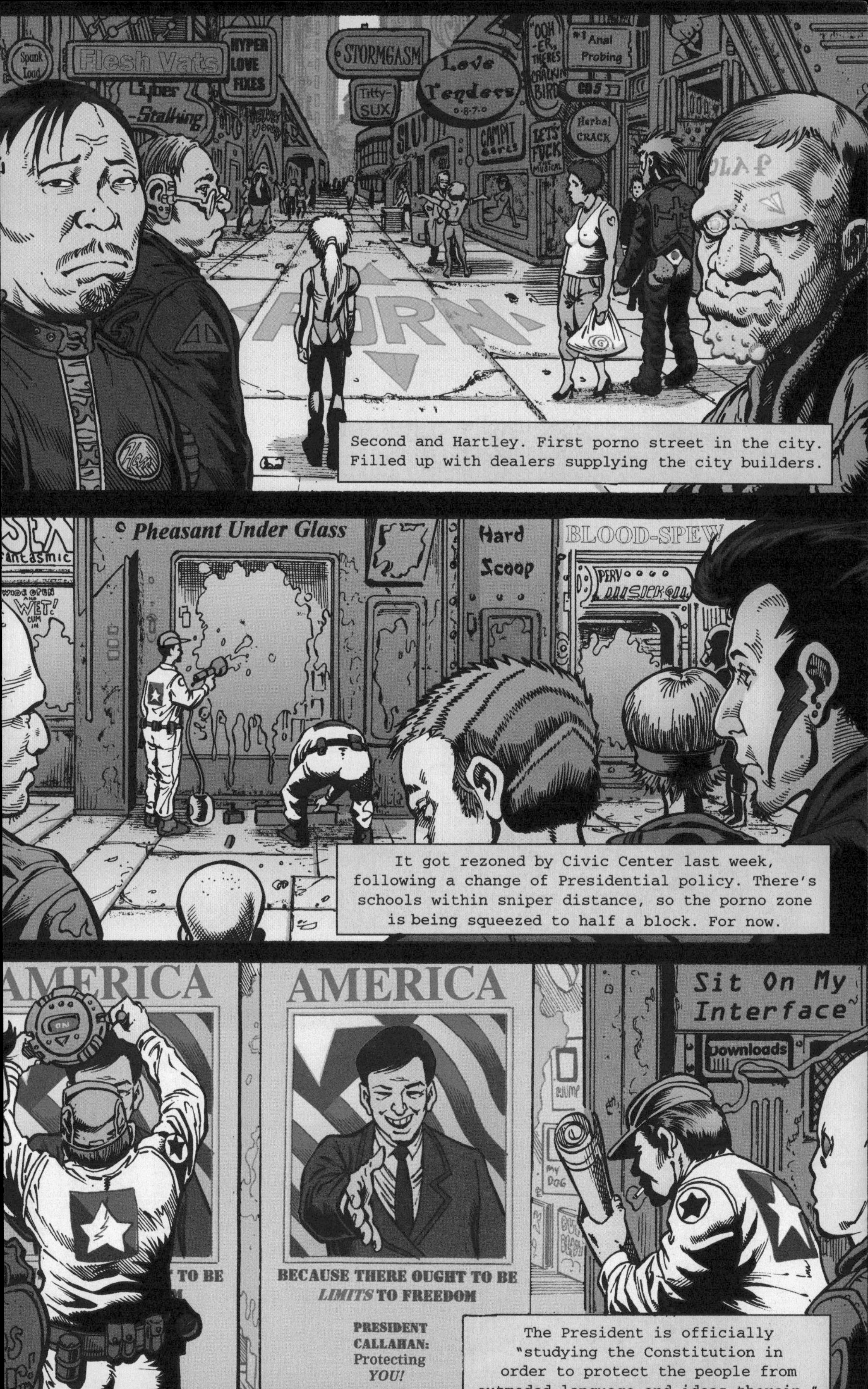

Spank Load
Flesh Vats
HYPER LOVE FIXES
Cyber -Stalking
STORMGASM
Titty-SUX
Love Tenders
"OOH -ER, THERE'S CRACKIN' BIRD"
#1 Anal Probing
CD5
Herbal CRACK
SLUT
CAMPIT GIRLS
LET'S FUCK THE MUSICAL
OLAF
PORN
Second and Hartley. First porno street in the city. Filled up with dealers supplying the city builders.
Pheasant Under Glass
SEX
fantasmic
WIDE OPEN AND WET! CUM IN
Hard Scoop
BLOOD-SPEW
PERV
It got rezoned by Civic Center last week, following a change of Presidential policy. There's schools within sniper distance, so the porno zone is being squeezed to half a block. For now.
AMERICA
TO BE
AMERICA
BECAUSE THERE OUGHT TO BE
LIMITS TO FREEDOM
PRESIDENT CALLAHAN: Protecting YOU!
Sit On My Interface
Downloads
ON
The President is officially "studying the Constitution in order to protect the people from outmoded language and ideas therein."

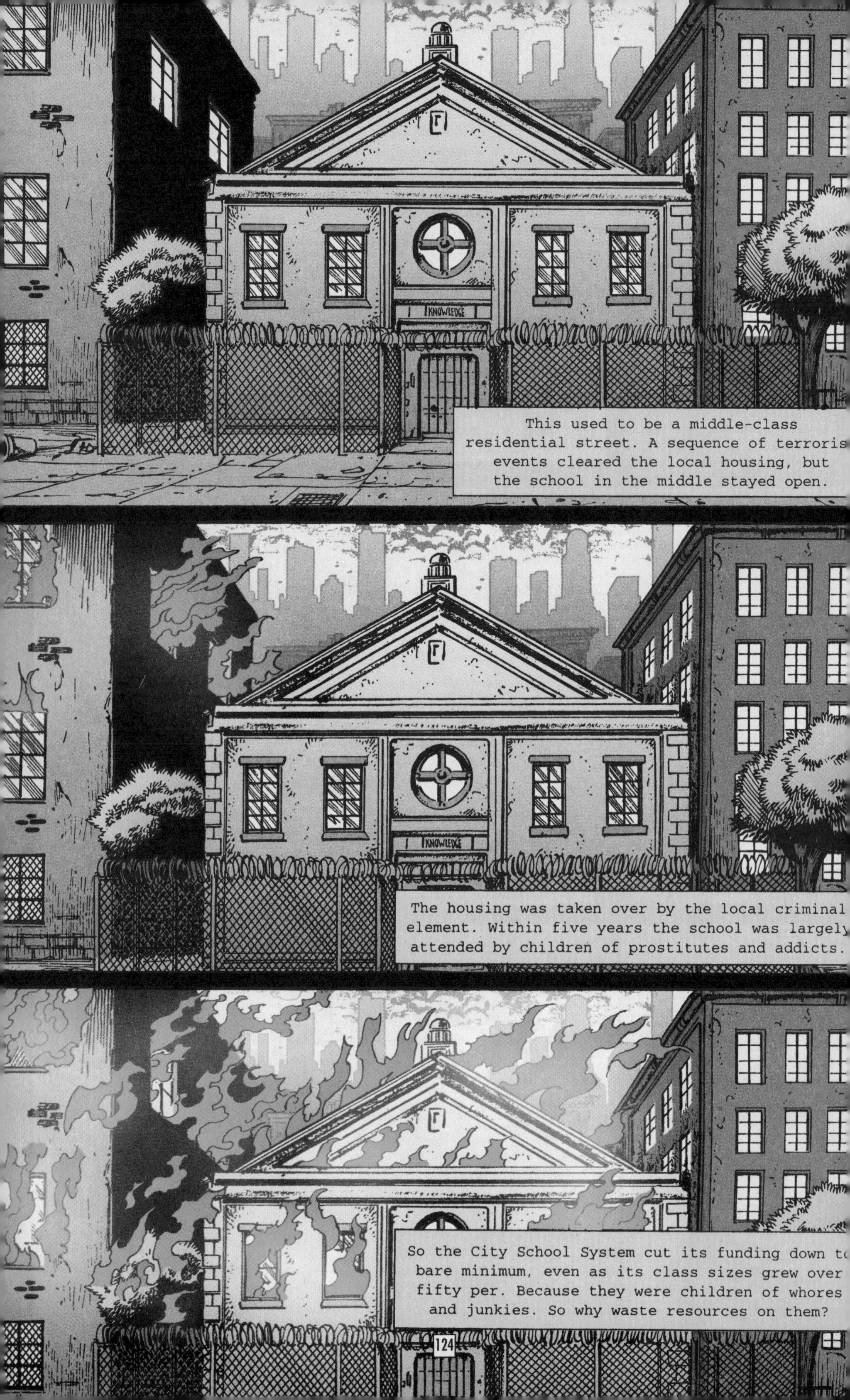
KNOWLEDGE
This used to be a middle-class residential street. A sequence of terroris events cleared the local housing, but the school in the middle stayed open.
KNOWLEDGE
The housing was taken over by the local criminal element. Within five years the school was largely attended by children of prostitutes and addicts.
So the City School System cut its funding down t bare minimum, even as its class sizes grew over fifty per. Because they were children of whores and junkies. So why waste resources on them?
124

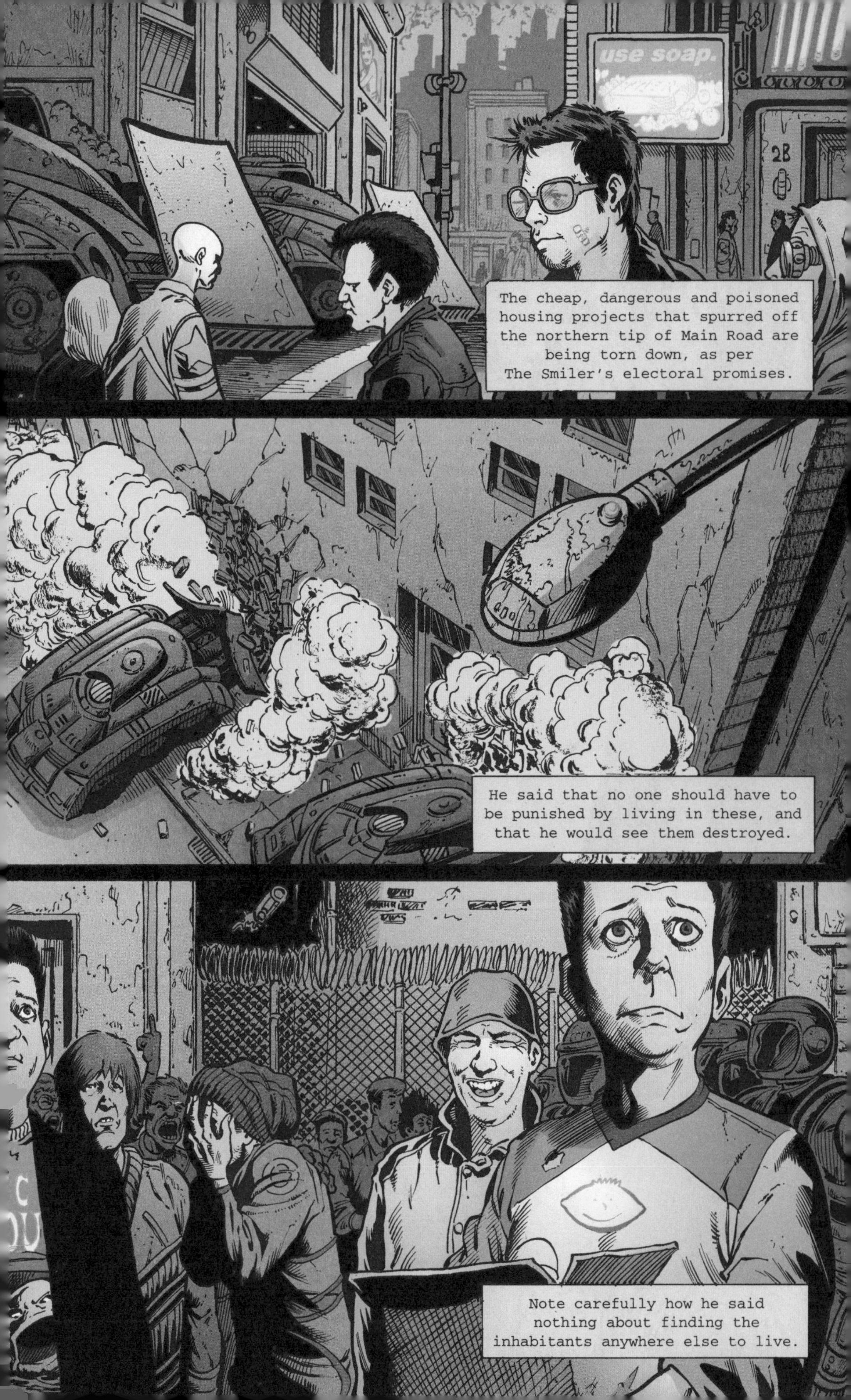
use soap.
2B
The cheap, dangerous and poisoned housing projects that spurred off the northern tip of Main Road are being torn down, as per The Smiler's electoral promises.
He said that no one should have to be punished by living in these, and that he would see them destroyed.
Note carefully how he said nothing about finding the inhabitants anywhere else to live.

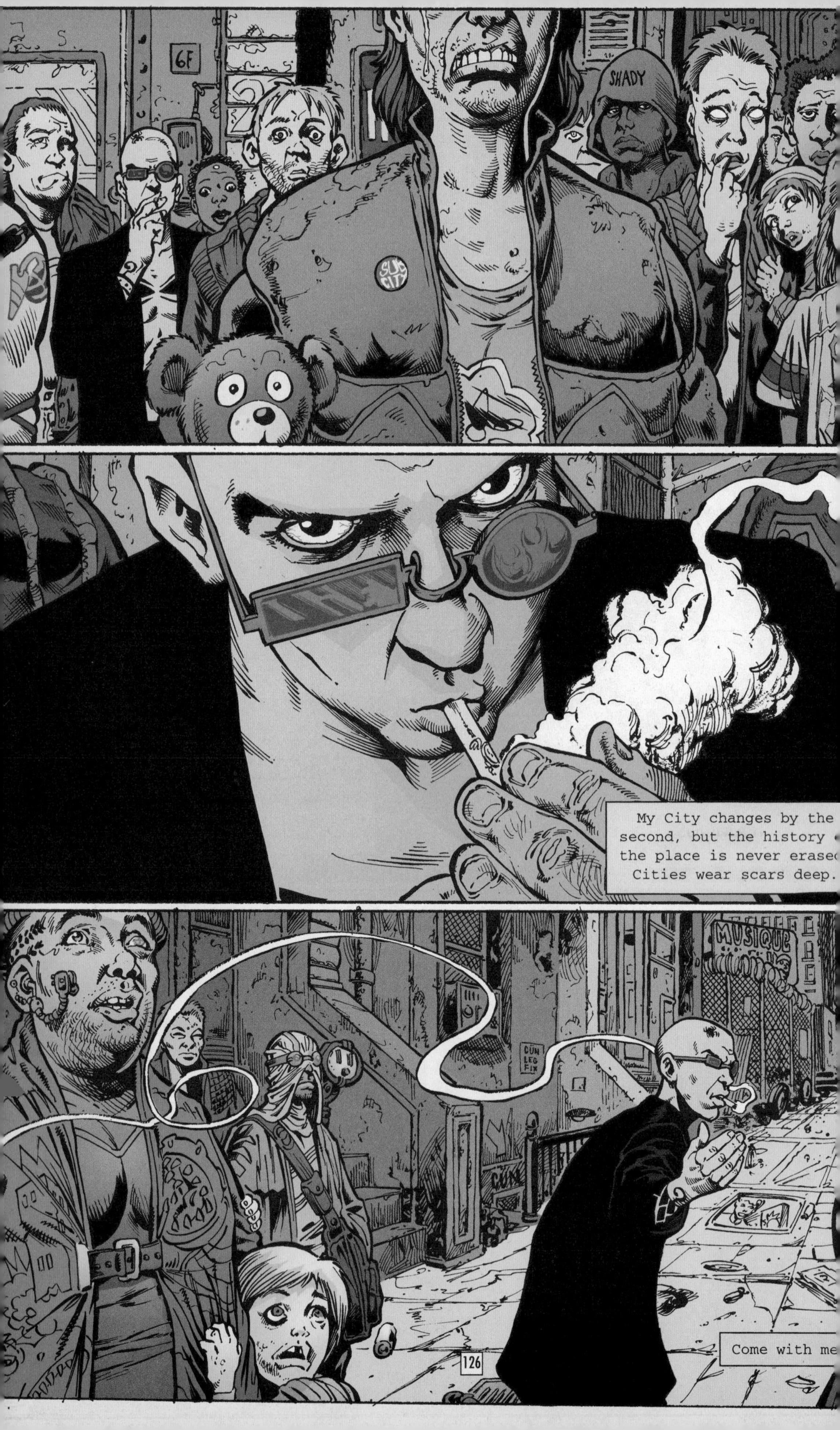
6F
SHADY
SUB CITY
My City changes by the
second, but the history
the place is never erase
Cities wear scars deep.
MUSIQUE
Come with me

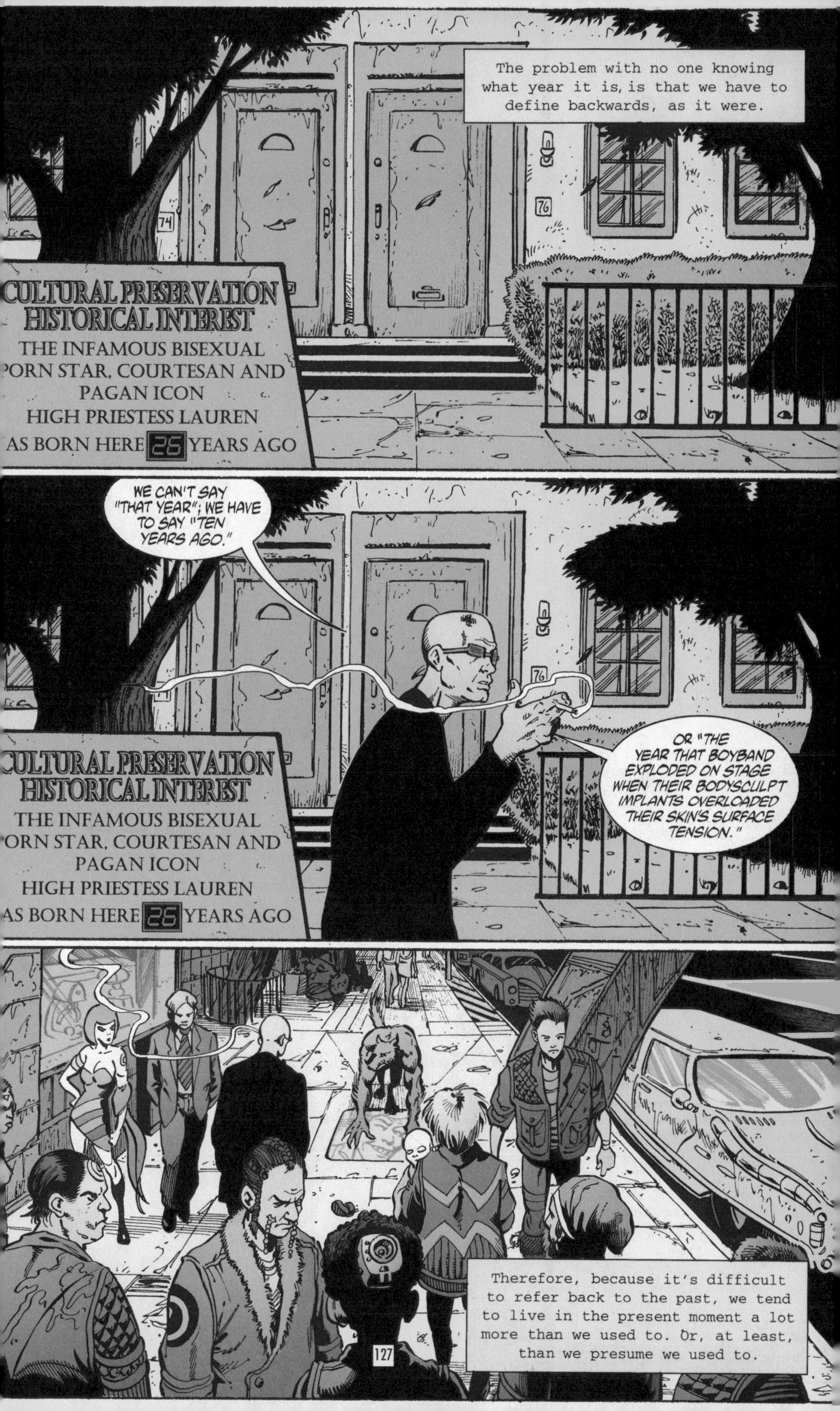

The problem with no one knowing what year it is, is that we have to define backwards, as it were.
CULTURAL PRESERVATION HISTORICAL INTEREST
THE INFAMOUS BISEXUAL
ORN STAR, COURTESAN AND
PAGAN ICON
HIGH PRIESTESS LAUREN
AS BORN HERE 26 YEARS AGO
WE CAN'T SAY "THAT YEAR"; WE HAVE TO SAY "TEN YEARS AGO."
OR "THE YEAR THAT BOYBAND EXPLODED ON STAGE WHEN THEIR BODYSCULPT IMPLANTS OVERLOADED THEIR SKIN'S SURFACE TENSION."
CULTURAL PRESERVATION HISTORICAL INTEREST
THE INFAMOUS BISEXUAL
ORN STAR, COURTESAN AND
PAGAN ICON
HIGH PRIESTESS LAUREN
AS BORN HERE 26 YEARS AGO
Therefore, because it's difficult to refer back to the past, we tend to live in the present moment a lot more than we used to. Or, at least, than we presume we used to.

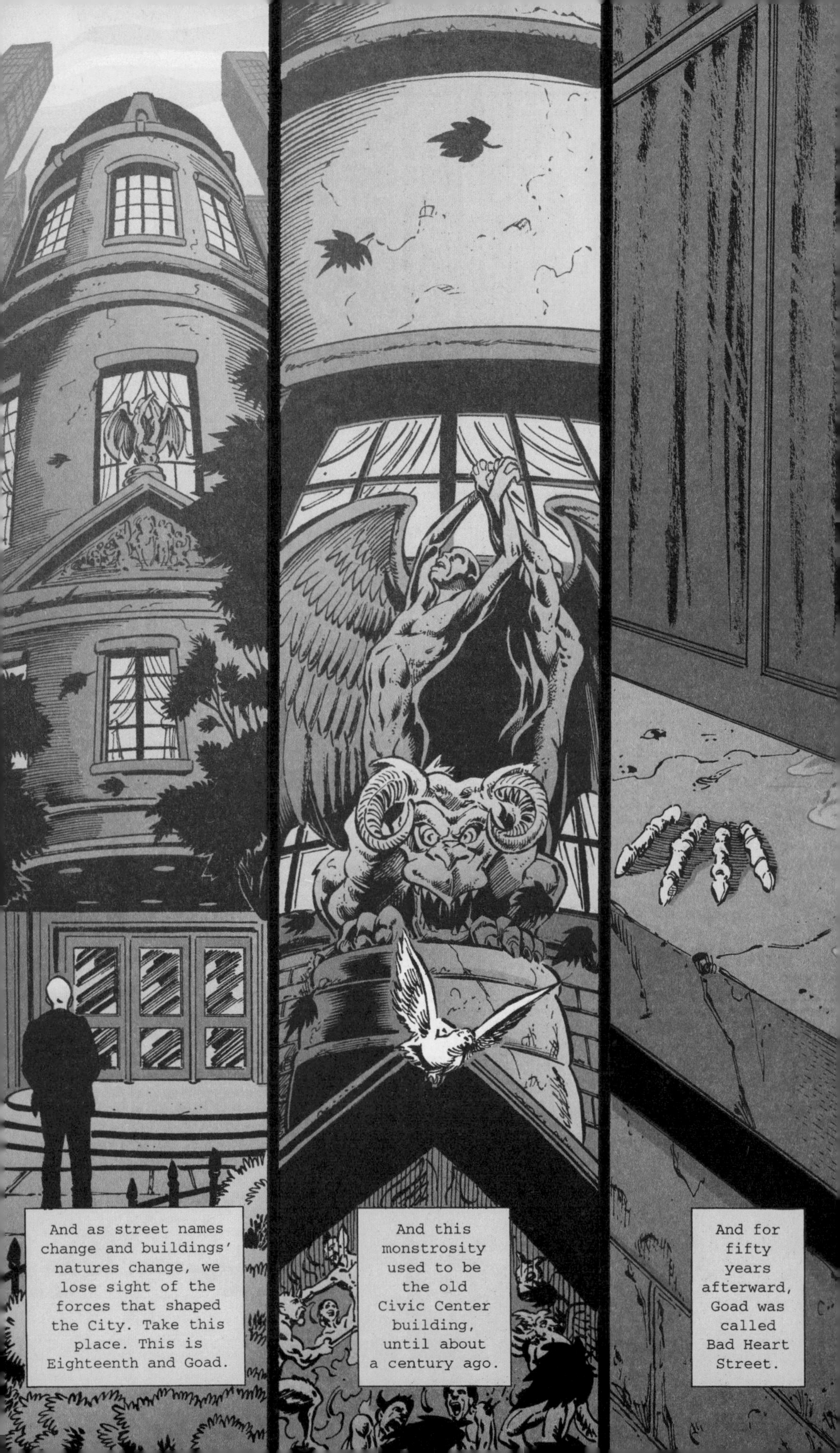
And as street names change and buildings' natures change, we lose sight of the forces that shaped the City. Take this place. This is Eighteenth and Goad.
And this monstrosity used to be the old Civic Center building, until about a century ago.
And for fifty years afterward, Goad was called Bad Heart Street.

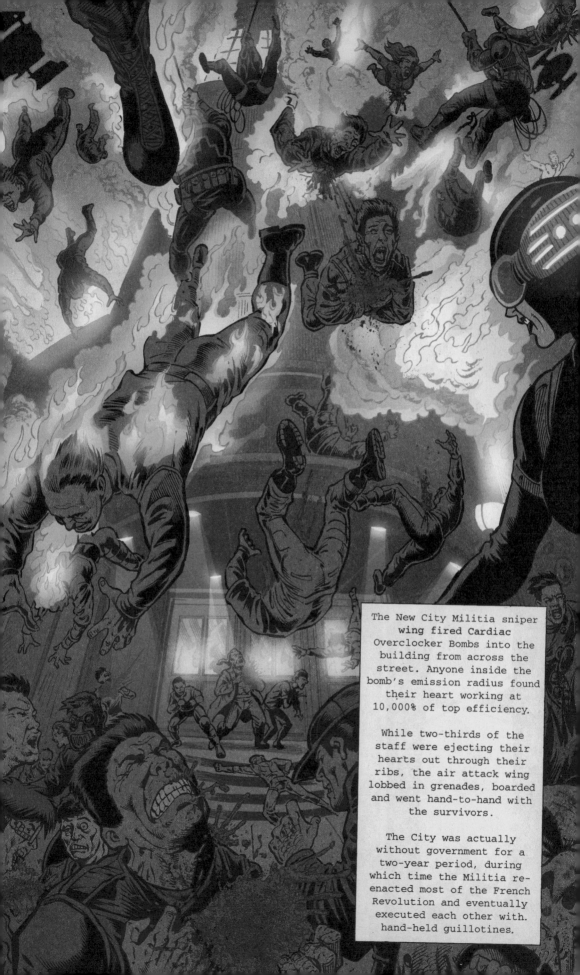

The New City Militia sniper wing fired Cardiac Overclocker Bombs into the building from across the street. Anyone inside the bomb's emission radius found their heart working at 10,000% of top efficiency.

While two-thirds of the staff were ejecting their hearts out through their ribs, the air attack wing lobbed in grenades, boarded and went hand-to-hand with the survivors.

The City was actually without government for a two-year period, during which time the Militia re-enacted most of the French Revolution and eventually executed each other with hand-held guillotines.

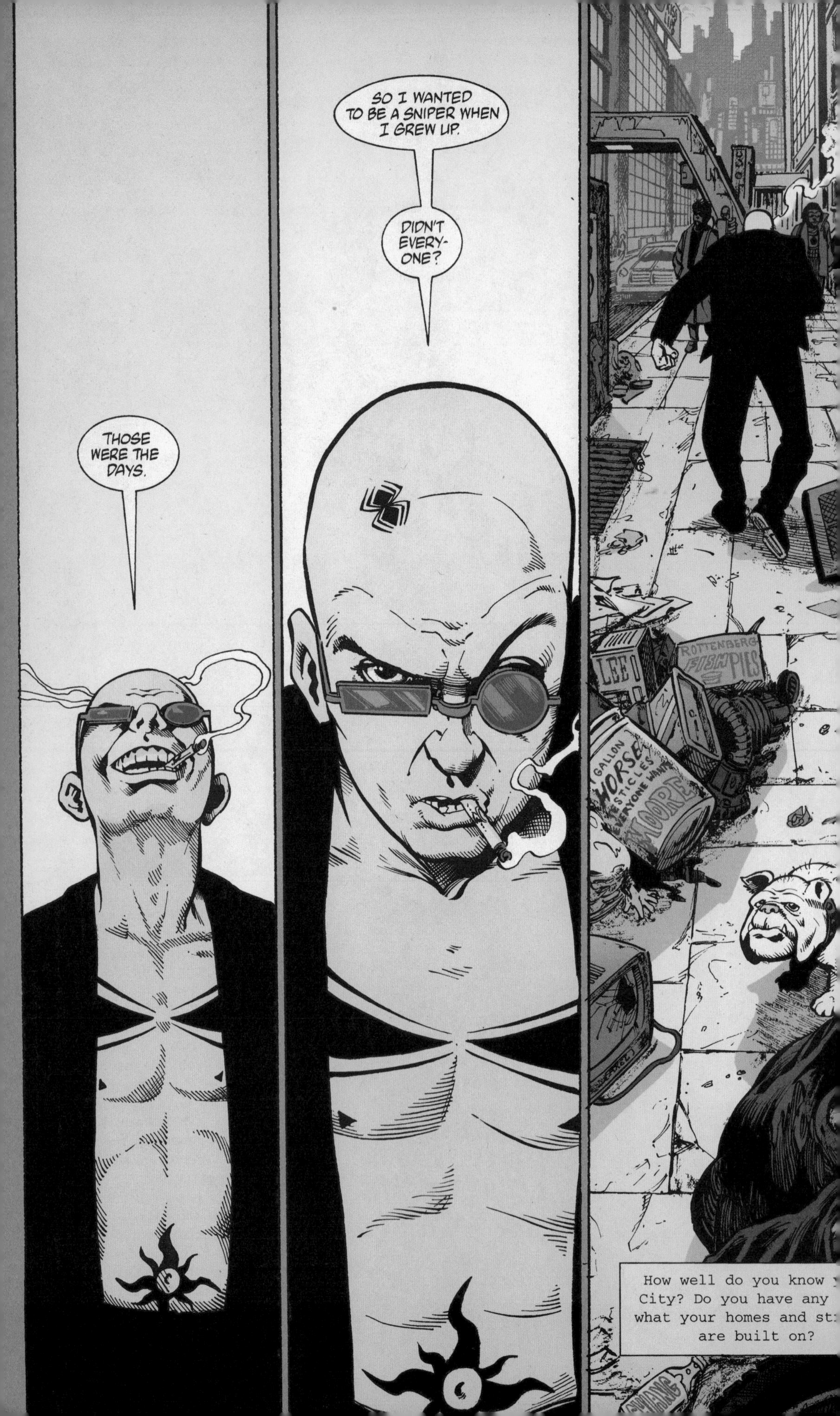
THOSE WERE THE DAYS.
SO I WANTED TO BE A SNIPER WHEN I GREW UP.
DIDN'T EVERY-ONE?
How well do you know
City? Do you have any
what your homes and st
are built on?

NEW AMERICA-- CLEANER, HARDER, STRONGER.

WE ARE A PIONEER NATION. LIFE HERE WAS NEVER SUPPOSED TO BE EASY--IT WAS SUPPOSED TO BE HARD.

IT WAS SUPPOSED TO BE GOOD.

president gary **callahan**

helping america take out the trash

president gary **callahan**

helping america take out the trash

president gary **callahan**

helping america take out the trash

weinhold's **books**
downloads • brainscans • traditional

PRESIDENT RY CALLAHAN

SIMPLE NEW TRUTH

IN STOCK NOW!
PRESIDENT GARY CALLAHAN'S
SIMPLE NEW TRUTH

ON SALE

A hundred years ago, this entire block burned down. Two thousand people burned alive in a flash blaze that consumed the whole place in under thirty minutes according to the authorities, and under five according to eyewitnesses.

The blaze was found to have emanated from an apartment building room in the center of the block. And that room alone was untouched by the fire. And that room was abandoned, freshly cooked food found cooling on the stove, a pencil dropped on the table in the very act of writing.

Writing what, no one's yet entirely sure. The place was covered in pages of arcane mathematical scrawl. They eventually found their way into the hands of a university, who studied them at CPD's behest.

The scrawl appeared to comprise three equations. The three equations seemed to represent a machine. A machine that was just three ideas in motion around each other. Solving the equations activated the machines.

It took a full ten years to evolve any workable theories as to what the creator — a half-educated seventy-year-old man who had worked as a janitor for fully fifty years of his life — was trying to do. He himself had had to invent his own mathematical language to do half the work.

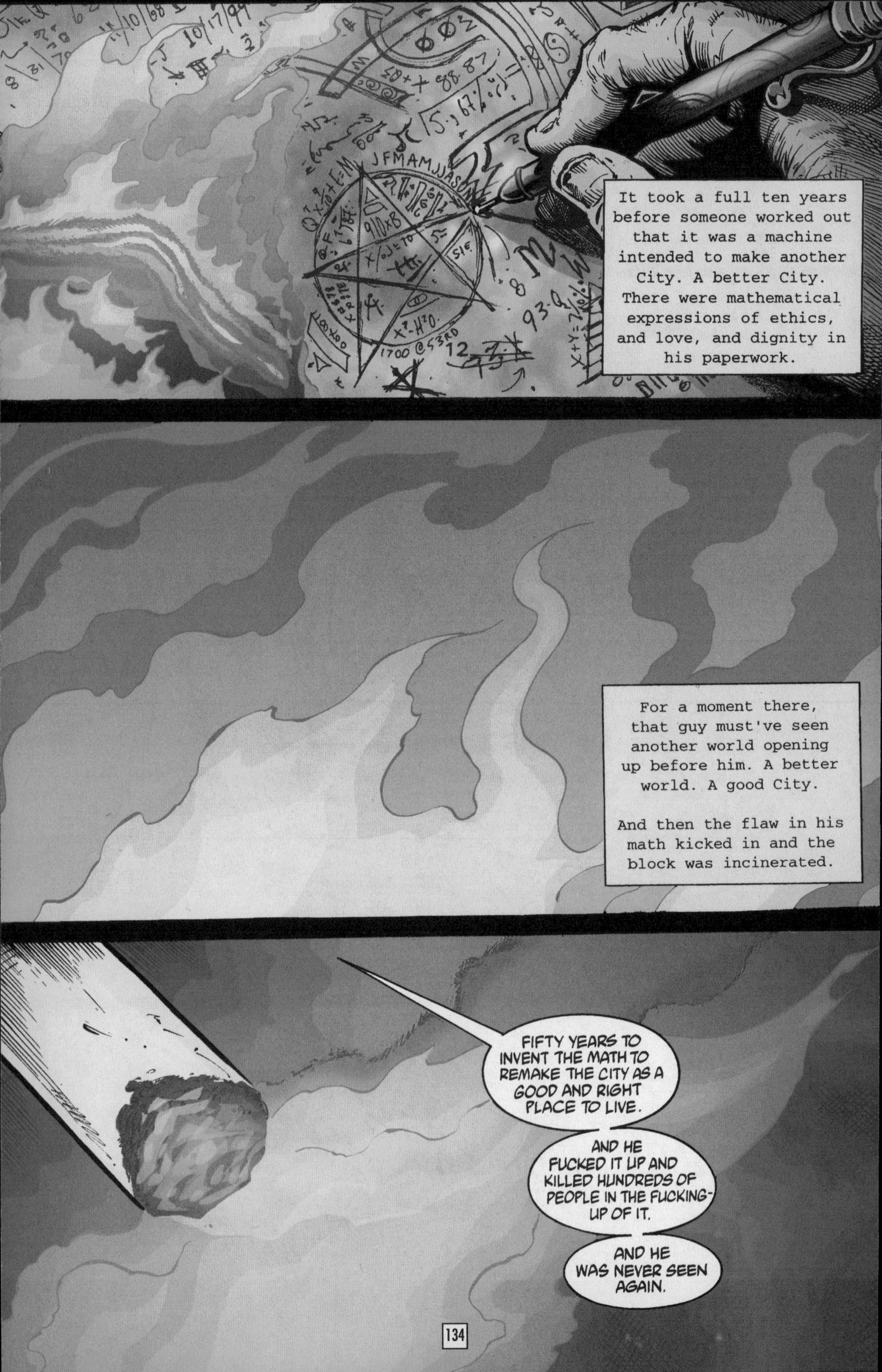
It took a full ten years before someone worked out that it was a machine intended to make another City. A better City. There were mathematical expressions of ethics, and love, and dignity in his paperwork.
For a moment there, that guy must've seen another world opening up before him. A better world. A good City.
And then the flaw in his math kicked in and the block was incinerated.
FIFTY YEARS TO INVENT THE MATH TO REMAKE THE CITY AS A GOOD AND RIGHT PLACE TO LIVE.
AND HE FUCKED IT UP AND KILLED HUNDREDS OF PEOPLE IN THE FUCKING-UP OF IT.
AND HE WAS NEVER SEEN AGAIN.

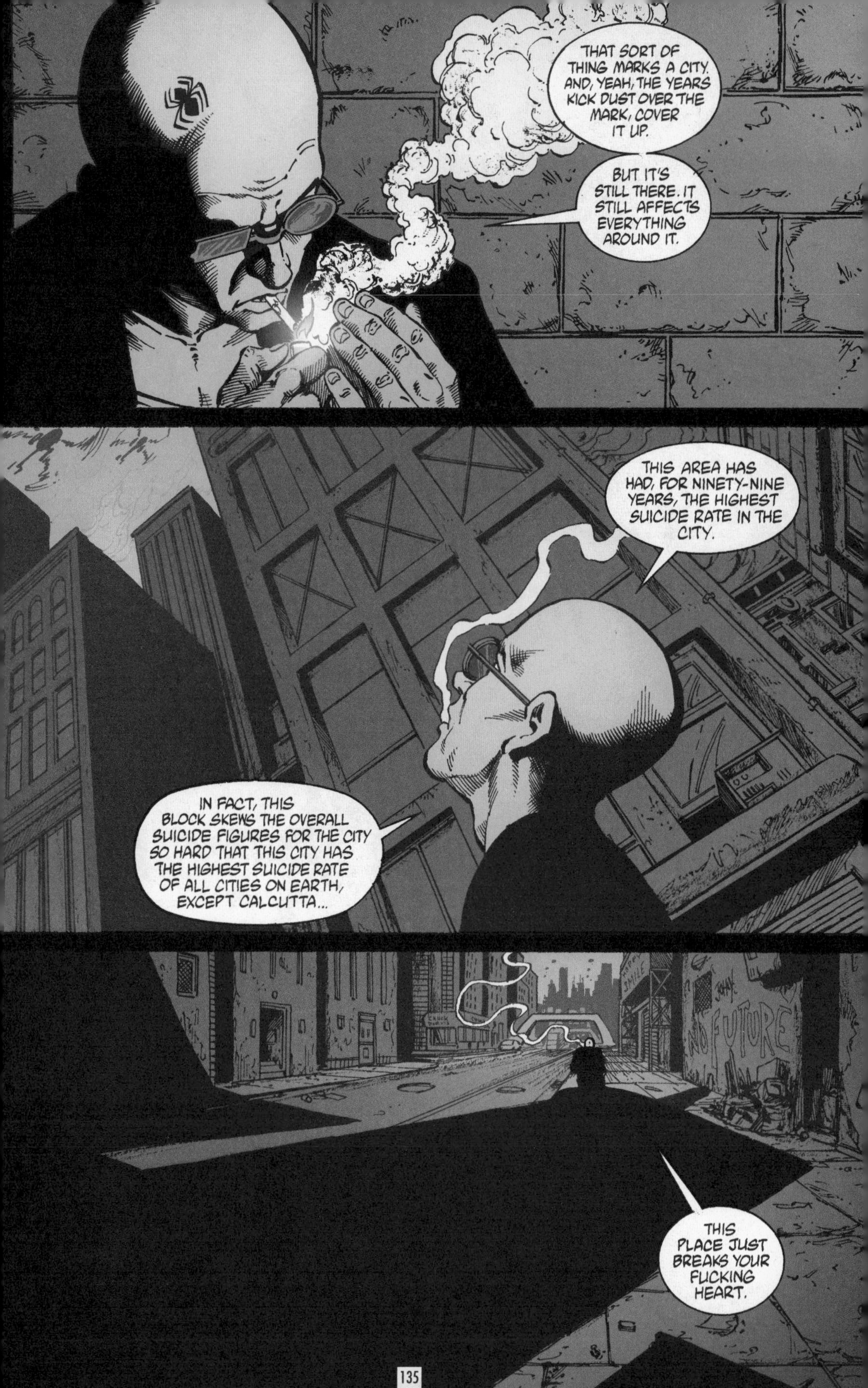
THAT SORT OF THING MARKS A CITY. AND, YEAH, THE YEARS KICK DUST OVER THE MARK, COVER IT UP.
BUT IT'S STILL THERE. IT STILL AFFECTS EVERYTHING AROUND IT.
THIS AREA HAS HAD, FOR NINETY-NINE YEARS, THE HIGHEST SUICIDE RATE IN THE CITY.
IN FACT, THIS BLOCK SKEWS THE OVERALL SUICIDE FIGURES FOR THE CITY SO HARD THAT THIS CITY HAS THE HIGHEST SUICIDE RATE OF ALL CITIES ON EARTH, EXCEPT CALCUTTA...
NO FUTURE
THIS PLACE JUST BREAKS YOUR FUCKING HEART.

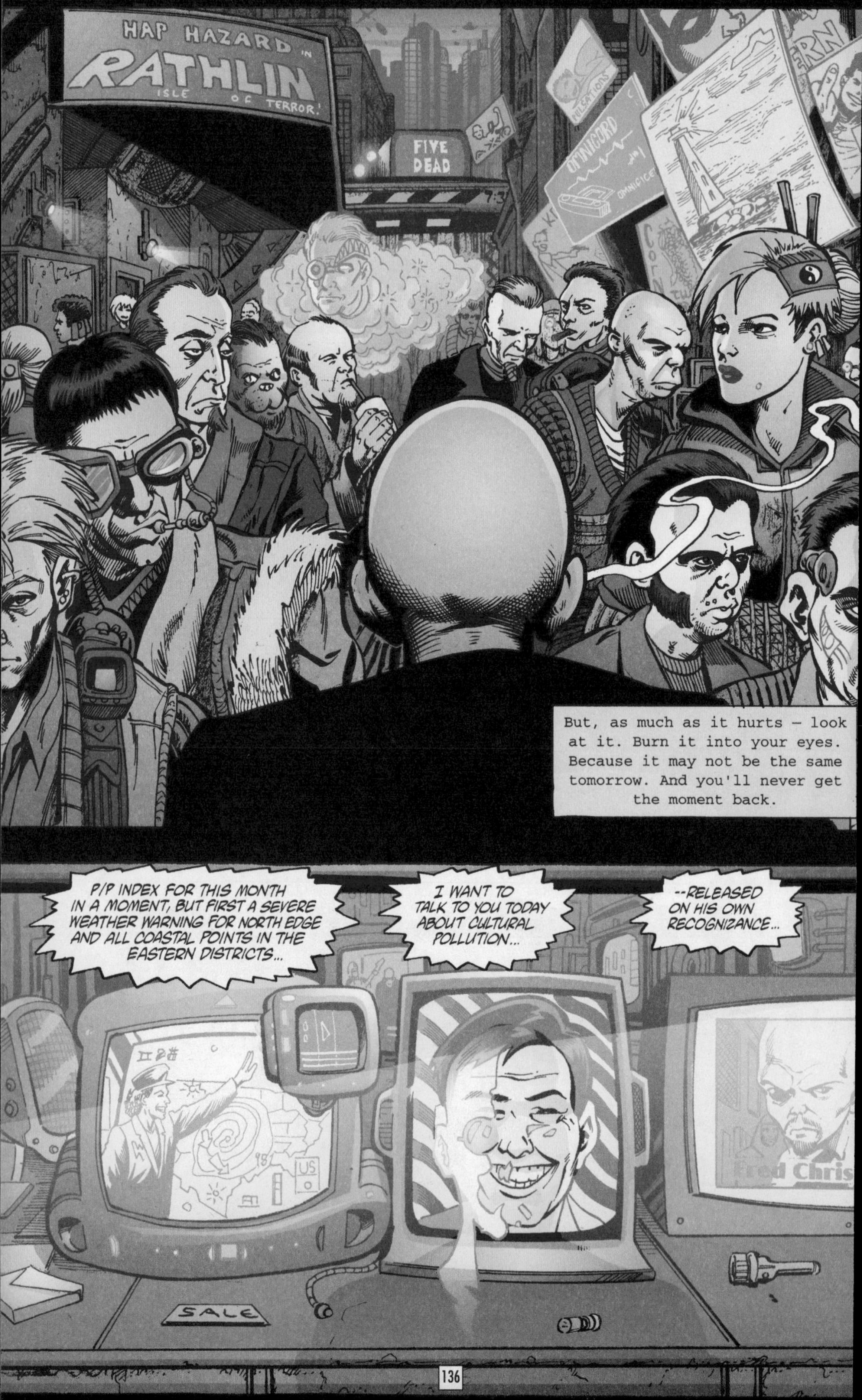
HAP HAZARD IN
RATHLIN
ISLE OF TERROR!
FIVE DEAD
OMNICORD
PULSATIONS
But, as much as it hurts – look at it. Burn it into your eyes. Because it may not be the same tomorrow. And you'll never get the moment back.
P/P INDEX FOR THIS MONTH IN A MOMENT, BUT FIRST A SEVERE WEATHER WARNING FOR NORTH EDGE AND ALL COASTAL POINTS IN THE EASTERN DISTRICTS...
I WANT TO TALK TO YOU TODAY ABOUT CULTURAL POLLUTION...
--RELEASED ON HIS OWN RECOGNIZANCE...
SALE

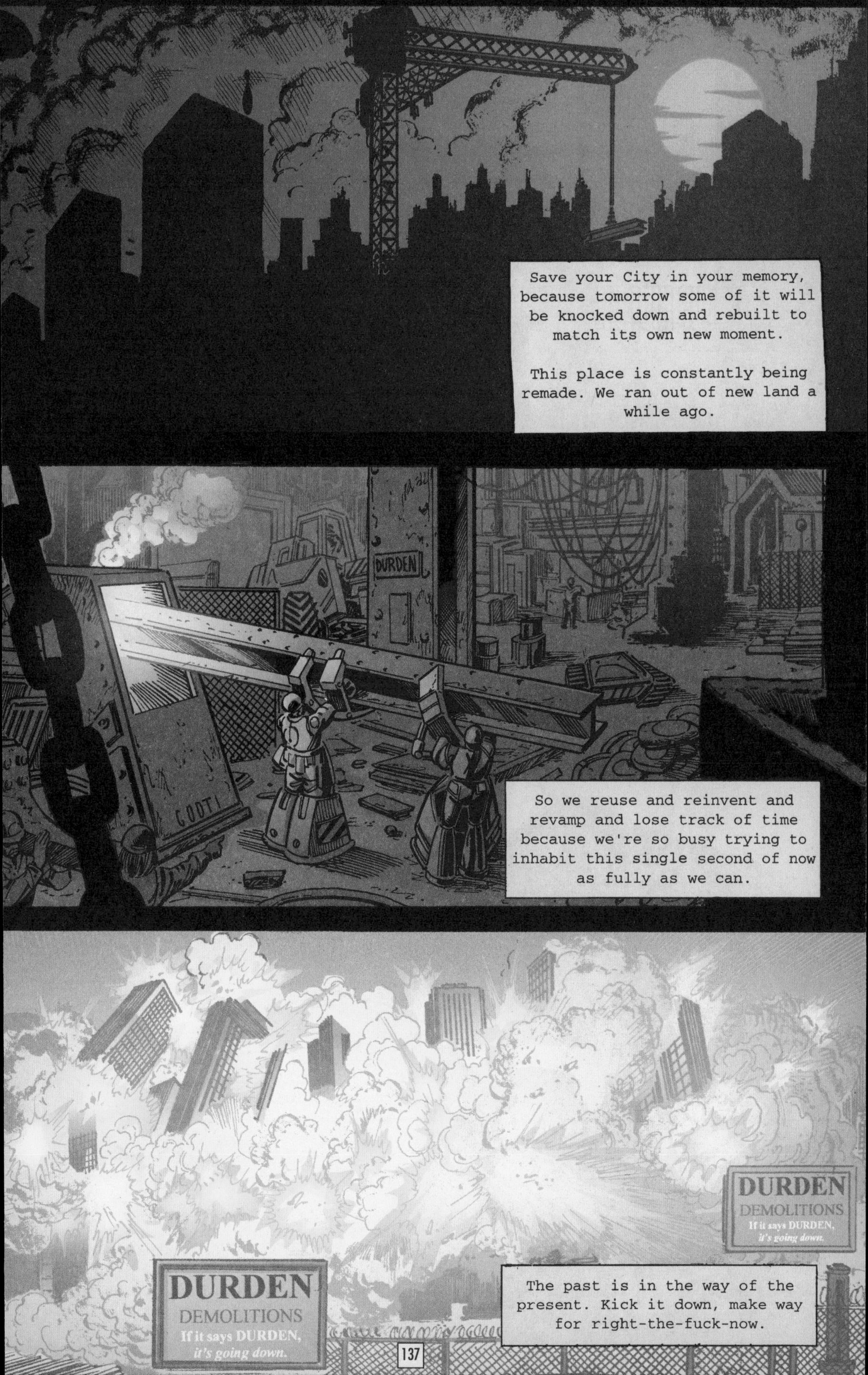
Save your City in your memory, because tomorrow some of it will be knocked down and rebuilt to match its own new moment.
This place is constantly being remade. We ran out of new land a while ago.
DURDEN
So we reuse and reinvent and revamp and lose track of time because we're so busy trying to inhabit this single second of now as fully as we can.
DURDEN DEMOLITIONS If it says DURDEN, it's going down.
DURDEN DEMOLITIONS If it says DURDEN, it's going down.
The past is in the way of the present. Kick it down, make way for right-the-fuck-now.

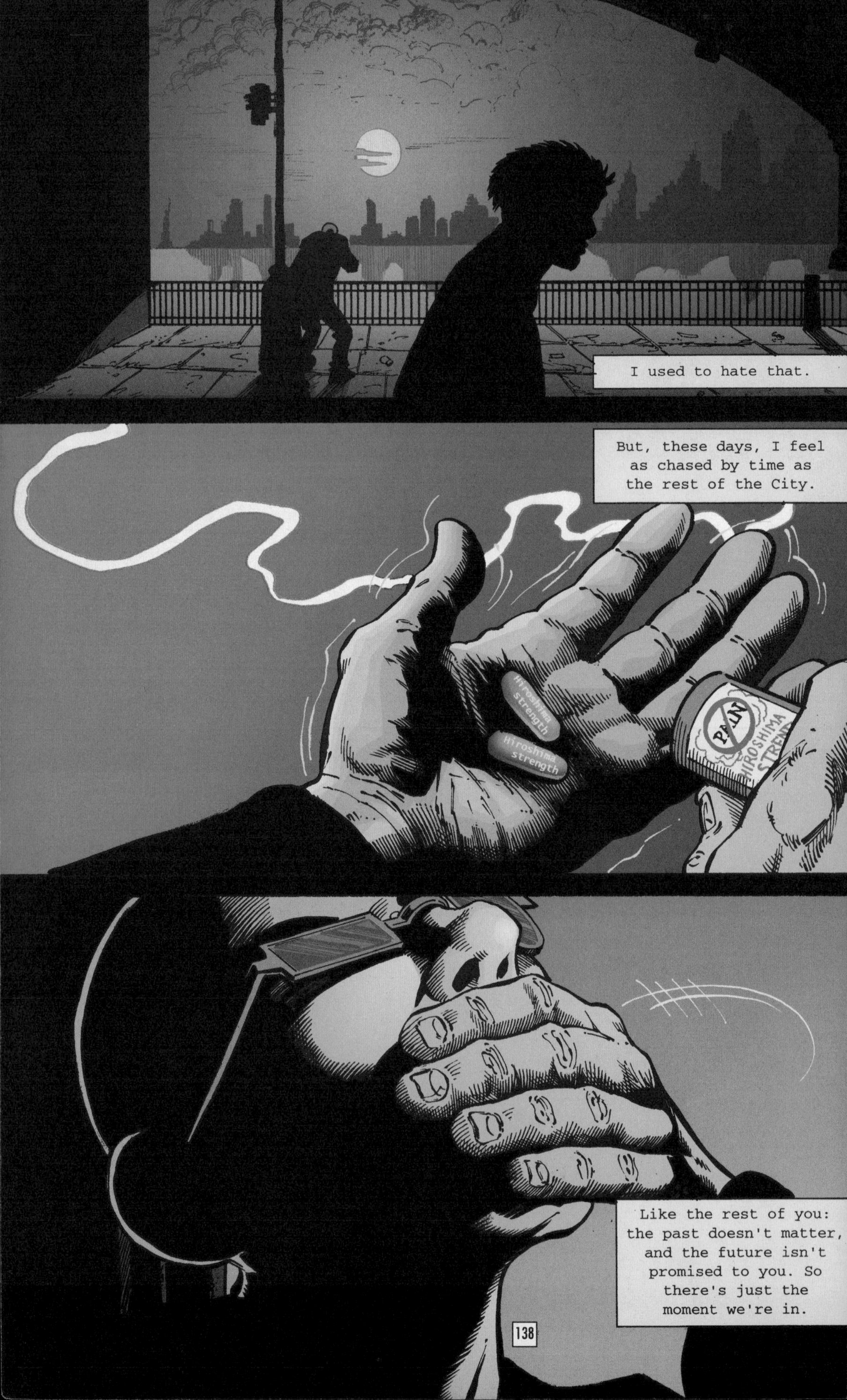
I used to hate that.
But, these days, I feel as chased by time as the rest of the City.
Hiroshima strength
Hiroshima strength
PAIN
HIROSHIMA STREN
Like the rest of you: the past doesn't matter, and the future isn't promised to you. So there's just the moment we're in.

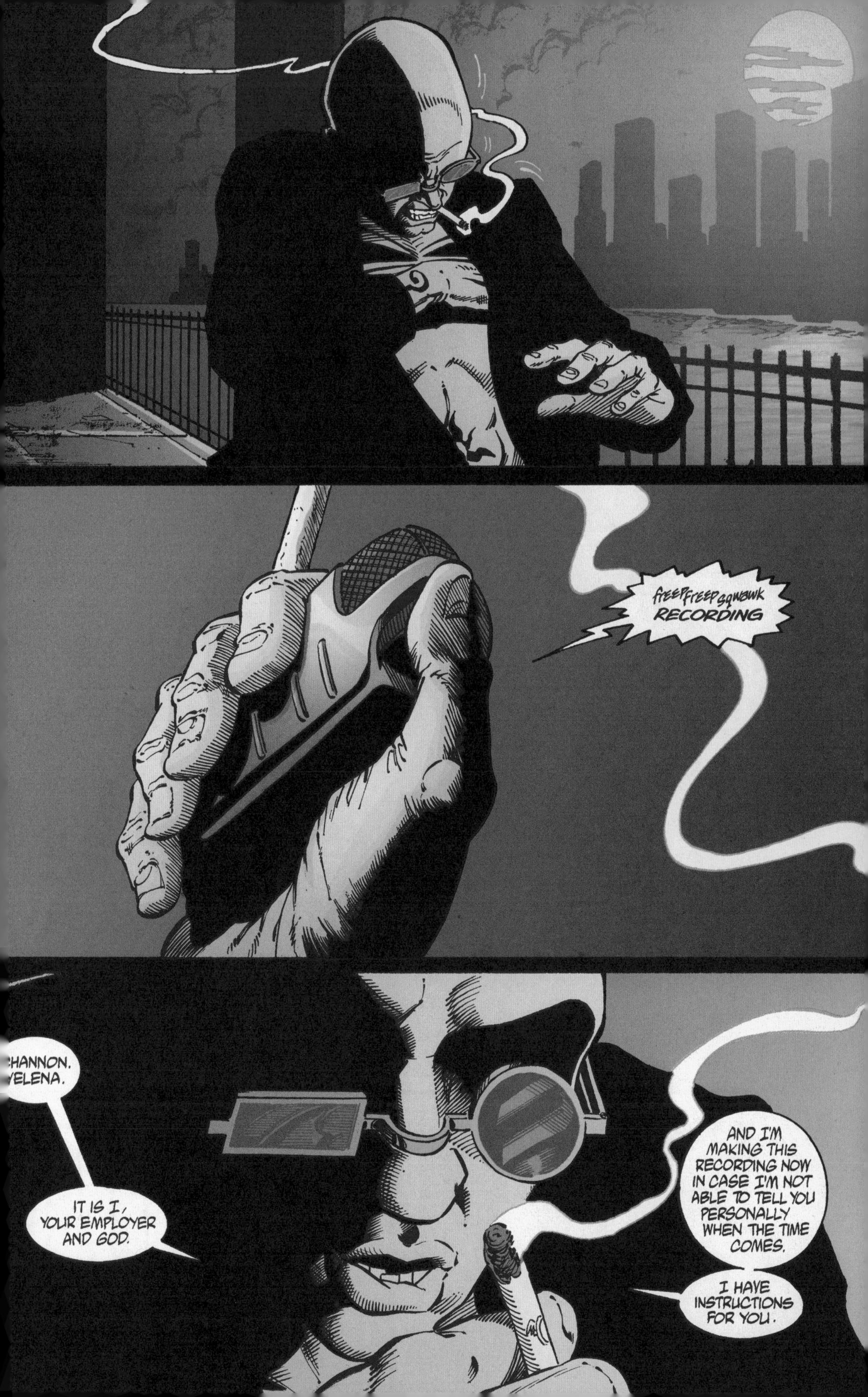

freepfreepsqwawk
RECORDING
CHANNON. YELENA.
IT IS I, YOUR EMPLOYER AND GOD.
AND I'M MAKING THIS RECORDING NOW IN CASE I'M NOT ABLE TO TELL YOU PERSONALLY WHEN THE TIME COMES.
I HAVE INSTRUCTIONS FOR YOU.

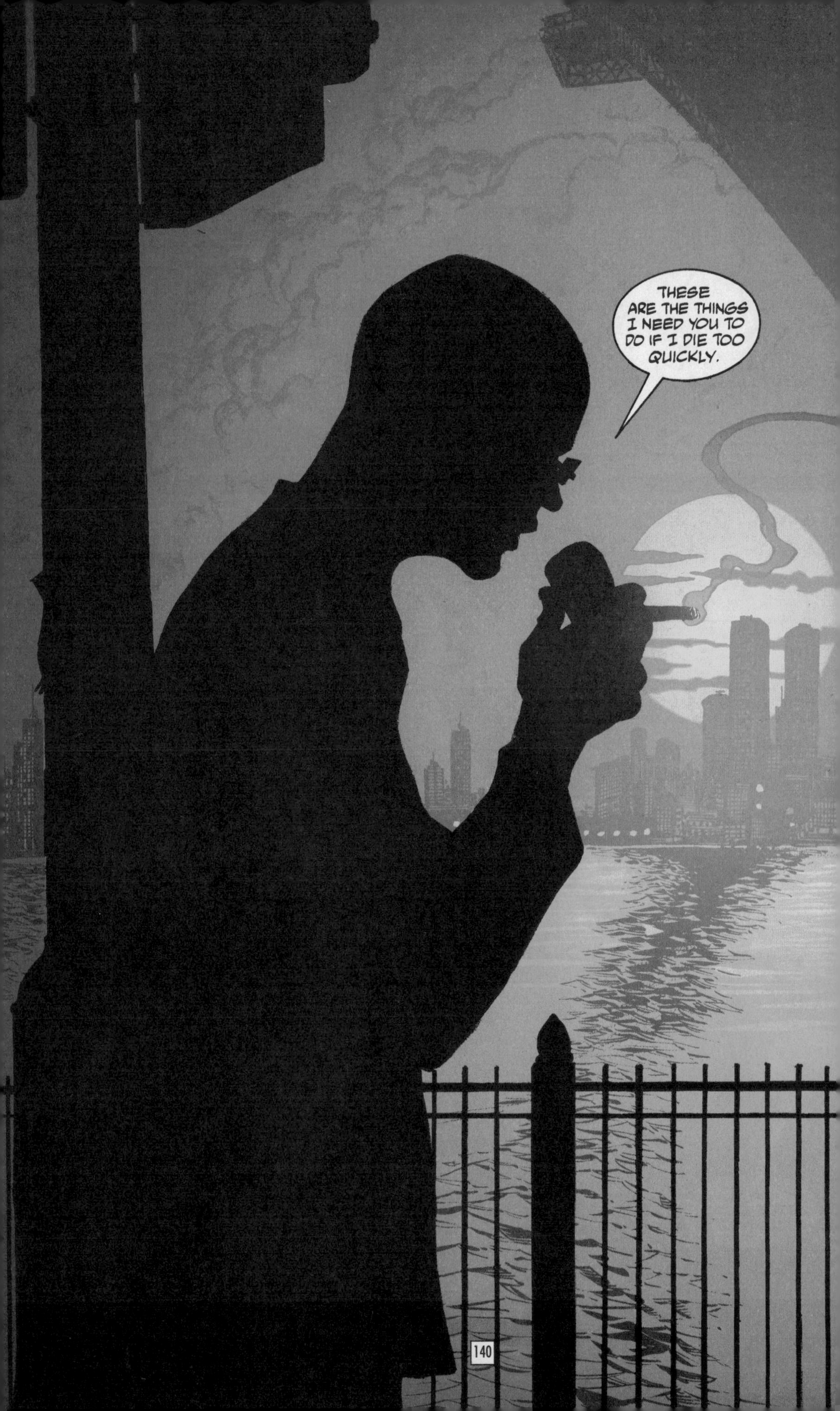
THESE ARE THE THINGS I NEED YOU TO DO IF I DIE TOO QUICKLY.

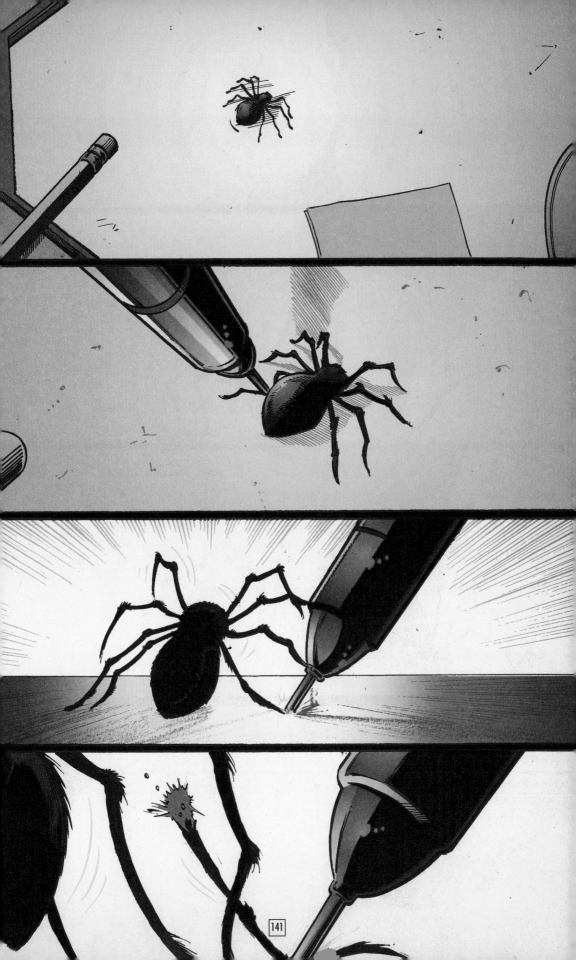

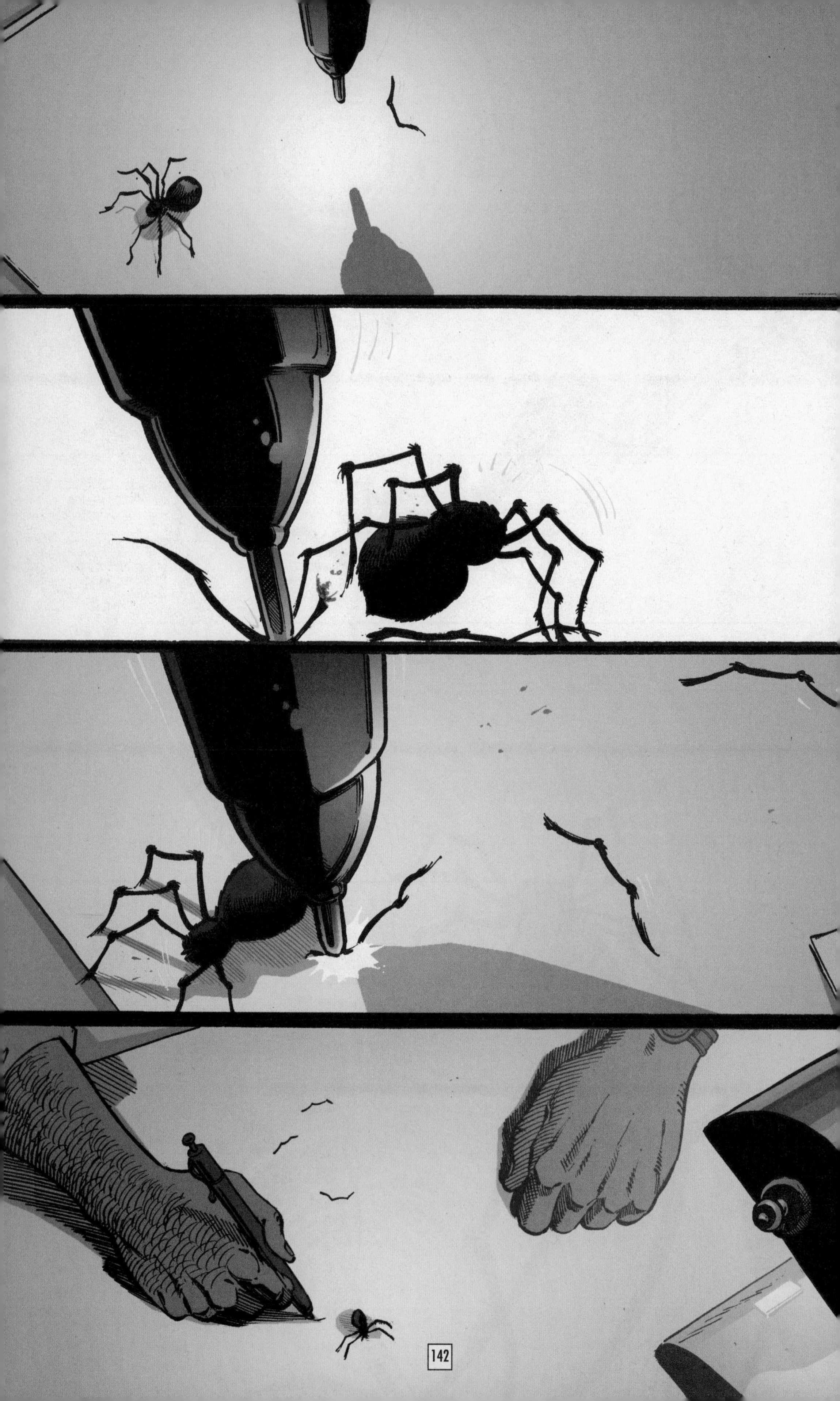

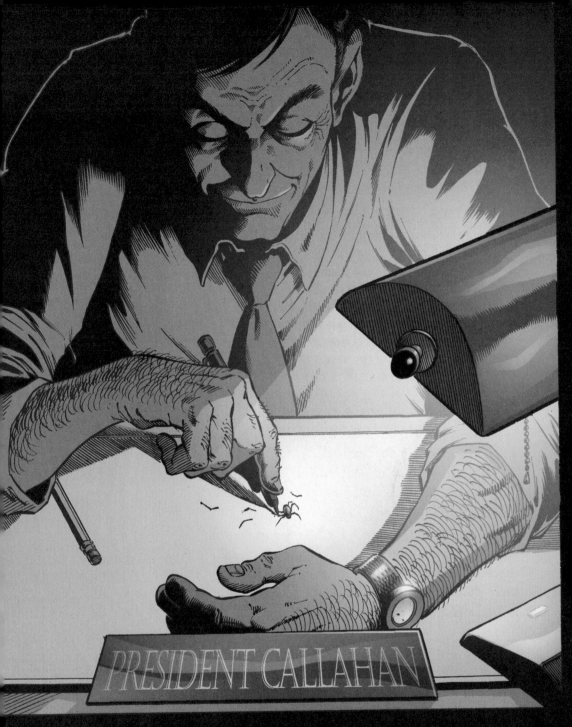

Warren Ellis writes & Darick Robertson draws

SPIDER'S THRASH

Rodney Ramos, inker

Clem Robins, letterer   Nathan Eyring, color and separations   Tony Bedard, editor
Cover by   Matt Wagner
TRANSMETROPOLITAN Warren Ellis and
created by   Darick Robertson